GABRIELE MARCOTTI
AND ALBERTO POLVEROSI

HAIL, CLAUDIO!

The Manager Behind the Miracle

YELLOW JERSEY PRESS
LONDON

1 3 5 7 9 10 8 6 4 2

Yellow Jersey Press
20 Vauxhall Bridge Road,
London SW1V 2SA

Yellow Jersey Press is part of the Penguin Random House group of companies
whose addresses can be found at global.penguinrandomhouse.com.

Penguin
Random House
UK

First published in hardback by Yellow Jersey Press in 2016
First published in paperback by Yellow Jersey Press in 2017

www.vintage-books.co.uk

A CIP catalogue record for this book is
available from the British Library

ISBN 9780224100687

Printed and bound by Clays Ltd, St Ives plc

Penguin Random House is committed to a sustainable future
for our business, our readers and our planet. This book is made
from Forest Stewardship Council® certified paper

MIX
Paper from
responsible sources
FSC® C018179
www.fsc.org

GABRIELE MARCOTTI AND
ALBERTO POLVEROSI

Italian journalists Gabriele Marcotti and Alberto
Polverosi have followed Claudio Ranieri's career for
many years. Gabriele first met him 16 years ago and
went on to work with him on his column for *The
Times*. Alberto's history goes even further back: one
of his very first assignments was to cover Catanzaro's
1981 pre-season training camp, where Ranieri was a
determined central defender.

Born in Italy and now living in London, **Gabriele
Marcotti** is a senior writer and analyst for ESPN,
World Football Correspondent for *The Times* and UK
correspondent for *Corriere dello Sport*. His previous
books include *The Italian Job: A Journey to the Heart
of Two Great Footballing Cultures*, shortlisted for the
William Hill Sports Book of the Year Award, and
Capello: Portrait of a Winner.

Alberto Polverosi was born in Montelupo Fiorentino,
Tuscany and has been writing for *Corriere dello Sport*
since 1977. He has covered eight World Cups and
seven European Championships. He lives in Florence.

014189209 6

To my parents, who blessed me with love and guidance at every turn.
– Gabriele

To my father, who took me on the journey to football.
– Alberto

Contents

Prologue

Gabriele Marcotti

It was a sweltering, humid July day in Bristol, Connecticut, when my phone vibrated into life. I had stopped to pick up a sandwich in a strip mall on the way to the ESPN campus, where I was due to tape the ESPNFC show, and was walking across the car park balancing my meal, car keys, wallet and phone.

I put the sandwich down on the bonnet of my rental car to take the call. A guy named Ian Stringer, a reporter for BBC Radio Leicester was on the other end.

We all find it hard to believe, he told me, but we have good information that Claudio Ranieri will be appointed tomorrow to fill the Leicester City vacancy. Would I come on the radio in a half hour to talk about what Ranieri had been up to since his departure from Chelsea, back in 2004?

I agreed. And for the next ten minutes I stood there, raiding my brain about Ranieri and what had happened in the fifteen years since I first met him. Deep in thought, I found myself staring out at the traffic on Route 10 rather than seeking the air-conditioned refuge of the car.

I remembered he had not been a popular choice when he replaced Gianluca Vialli as the Chelsea boss back in September 2000. Or, rather, he was a relative unknown appointed by an autocratic owner (Ken Bates), didn't speak the language and was taking over from a much-loved former player-manager who was charismatic and well-spoken.

That was not a good recipe. Especially not in 2000, when the Premier League was a very different place. Foreign managers – in fact, foreigners full-stop – were still somewhat exotic. They were viewed with suspicion, hired guns who saw football in an unfamiliar way, who brought alternative methods, tactics and mannerisms into England, accelerating the changes that had already been set in motion by the Bosman ruling in 1996 and the creation of the Premier League in 1992.

Ranieri's penchant for squad rotation and switching formations, even in the course of the same game, made him weird and different. Hence, that Tinkerman moniker which was actually kinder than some of the others directed at him in the press: 'Clownio' and 'Crazy Claudio' are two that come to mind.

He signed on to become a columnist for *The Times* and I was his ghostwriter. There was a certain formality in our relationship, something that I thought unusual for many years, indeed, until I began researching this book.

Ranieri is from Rome, yet he didn't speak or act like the Romans I knew. There was a quiet warmth to him, a ritual politeness. Years later, people would start talking about him as a 'gentleman' and now it's clear. That's what he is. His wife once jokingly complained that when he returned to manage

Roma, he had 'become Roman' again in the way he spoke and acted. And when he left the capital, he once again adopted the characteristics we know today: passion without volume, enthusiasm without bluster, cosiness without overbearance, kindness without familiarity. I was struck by the fact that never once did I hear him complain about the way he was often mocked in the media. Football managers need to be thick-skinned, sure, but it's one thing to criticise choices, another to make it personal.

The tide began to turn after Roman Abramovich bought Chelsea, something which would not have occurred without the team beating Liverpool on the final day of the 2002–03 season, a game that allowed the club to survive in the short-term and thrive in the long-term.

I was in Miami Beach that day. A close friend and Chelsea fan was getting married later on. We got up early to watch the match in a dark sports bar, a block from the Atlantic Ocean. When we emerged into the sunshine, I thought of Ranieri and how maybe next season he'd get some more respect.

Instead, he got sympathy, because it soon became clear that, despite protestations to the contrary, he was not going to be a part of Chelsea's long-term plans. Which was fine. He faced it all and stood tall. He cracked just once and, unfortunately for him, it was on the biggest stage of all: a Champions League semi-final against Monaco.

I followed his career from a distance, only speaking to him occasionally after he left Stamford Bridge. I noted how, time and again – at Parma, at Juventus, at Roma – he defied the odds. I knew how badly he wanted to return to England, how this country's football was, in many ways, his natural habitat.

I finished my Ranieri daydream when the phone vibrated

again for the BBC Radio Leicester interview. I was drenched in sweat by the midday sun. My sub sandwich (more specifically, a 'Grinder' as it's known in that part of the world) had effectively become a toasted panini on the hot bonnet of the car.

I don't exactly remember what I told BBC Radio Leicester that day about Ranieri's prospects with the Foxes. Probably something about him being a 'safe pair of hands' who tended to perform best in adverse conditions and was happy to work with what was available.

What I do know for certain is that I never imagined what would come next.

Nobody did.

Alberto Polverosi

I have a love-hate relationship with my favourite restaurant on the Croatian island of Hvar.

Pros: The seabass goes directly from sea to net to oven to plate to stomach in the space of a few hours. From dawn to late afternoon. There is nothing like it.

Cons: It has Wi-Fi. Which means that despite intentionally shutting off your data roaming because you're on holiday, you find that you can't resist checking back with the real world.

That's how I find out that Claudio Ranieri is the new Leicester City manager on 13 July 2015.

'Nice one,' I think to myself. 'He belongs in England, he's happiest working there. But . . . Leicester isn't London. What the heck is he doing *there*?'

The answer would come ten months later, of course. He's there to win the league.

I WhatsApp him, as I would do for most of the season: 'Claudio, try not to screw up Leicester too much.'

When I next log on to the Wi-Fi, I have his answer: 'Don't you worry about that.'

Two months later, he's proved right. No need to worry. Leicester start brightly.

I message him again: 'What the hell are you doing? Are you trying to win the Premier League?'

Minutes later, he pings me back: 'Hahahahahahaha.'

Maybe it's a generational thing, but he never uses emoticons.

It's now mid-December. Leicester are flying. Ranieri is in Rome and visits my paper, *Corriere dello Sport*. His face lights up. 'I have a guy in the middle of the park who gets to every ball, everywhere,' he announces, beaming. 'He's an octopus.'

That's his moniker for N'Golo Kanté. And it fits.

Fast-forward to April. The bandwagon is in full swing. The world is watching and crowding on board. They could win the title at Old Trafford.

I message him: 'United are unwatchable. But I don't think this is over.'

'It's not,' he replies. 'But we're not going to be moved. Not a centimetre. We're not letting this go.'

The rest is history, if not lore.

I've known him for thirty-five years and maybe what I admire most about him is how little he has changed – or been changed – by the passage of time. He's the same guy I met back in 1981 in the small hotel up in Ampezzo, in the north-east corner of Italy, when he was a grizzled veteran at Catanzaro's pre-season training camp.

He was bright, serious, conscientious, smiling. He was the

opposite of superficial, he dug deep, both in his work and in the way he related to others. We went our own ways and I encountered him again in 1993. He was manager of Fiorentina, I was the Fiorentina correspondent. We were both older and we grew close.

I could not help but become a fan of whichever team he coached. I admit, when the title slipped out of his grasp at Roma I felt sick to my stomach. But if that was the price to pay to win the Premier League with Leicester City six years later, it was a price worth paying.

I don't know if Claudio feels the same way. I don't know if he would have swapped Leicester's 2015–16 season with the Serie A title at Roma. After all, he's not just Roman and a former Roma player, he's a Romanista too.

But I don't care. That's how I feel. Leicester made everything worthwhile.

Apart from Tottenham supporters, we were all Leicester to some degree in that magical season. At first with a dose of *simpatico*, then with curiosity, satisfaction, passion, enthusiasm and, finally, trepidation.

Fans the world over cheered when Wes Morgan scored at Old Trafford. The same way Roma fans would for Francesco Totti, Juventus supporters for Paulo Dybala, Real Madrid fans for Cristiano Ronaldo, Bayern fans for Thomas Müller, Barca fans for Lionel Messi.

Ranieri helped turned Leicester into an archetypal tale, a story to which everyone could relate.

I also cheered him on because he deserved it. It bothered me that his own country did not appreciate him as much as he merited. They said he never won. Because all that matters is Serie A and the Champions League. That's the definition of success.

He won his first top-flight title at an age when he could appreciate it in the fullest, most true way. It doesn't give new meaning to his life in football. It's simply a chance to play Champions League football, to give fans – not just Leicester supporters either – the opportunity to experience new emotions, to live new dreams.

Ranieri never looks back. He doesn't remember the folks in Rome who called him 'minestraro' – a stupid pun on reheated soup – or those in Naples who wanted to fire him because he had the impertinence to think the club could win without Diego Maradona, or the Special One who said he was old and grey and past his sell-by date.

He's sixty-four years old and he never glances in the rear-view mirror.

In May 2016 I told him I felt like hugging him.

'And I'd like to hug every last person who believed in us,' he said.

That would be impossible. It would take too long. That's how many believers he converted to the cause last season.

1. Founding Myths

You may be familiar with the story of Romulus and Remus. Around 771 BCE, according to the Greek-born historian-turned-Roman-citizen Plutarch, a woman named Rhea Silvia is impregnated by Mars, the god of war. This is problematic on many levels.

Rhea Silvia is a descendant of the Greek hero Aeneas (of *Aeneid* fame), and her father, Numitor, was deposed by his evil brother Amulius. Numitor was king of Alba Longa, a settlement a day's walk from what is now Rome. To ensure that none of Numitor's children and grandchildren challenged him for the throne, Uncle Amulius killed all his male heirs and made the women become Vestal Virgins, which meant that they had to swear a sacred vow of chastity.

Vows are all very well, but Mars is an attractive and powerful fellow (plus, there's the whole god thing . . .), so Rhea Silvia is seduced and bears beautiful twins, Romulus and Remus. When Amulius finds out, he is – understandably – furious. He orders that the baby boys be killed, but the servant charged with doing it cannot bring himself to commit the deed. So he puts them in a basket and leaves it on the banks of the River

Tiber. When the river floods, as it periodically does, the two boys float away.

They are eventually found by a she-wolf, who suckles them, and a woodpecker, who does whatever woodpeckers do. This enables them to survive long enough to be found by a local shepherd, who takes them in and raises them as his own. They grow up, get into a beef with Amulius' shepherds and eventually go back to Alba Longa, kill Amulius and restore Numitor – their grandpa except they don't know it – to the throne.

Having done that, they wander down the Tiber and decide to found their own city. Except, as brothers often do, they squabble over where to build it. Romulus wants to construct it on what is now known as the Palatine Hill, whereas Remus is partial to the Aventine Hill. They pray to the gods and eventually – no surprise – each brother decides to build his own city.

And, being brothers, they mock and deride each other's cities mercilessly, and when Romulus starts to build a wall around his, Remus laughs at it. Romulus's feelings are hurt; he flies into a rage and kills Remus. He then finishes his city and names it after himself: Rome.

Thus – if you believe in foundation myths – was born the Eternal City. Not all Romans believe the story, but every single one knows it. Claudio Ranieri is no different. Growing up in the San Saba neighbourhood just south of the city centre, he was enveloped in Rome's creation myth and its history to come. A short downhill walk from San Saba are the Baths of Caracalla, built in the third century AD. Further up the Aventine Hill are some of the most breathtaking views of Rome, including a particular favourite of Ranieri's, a small opening in the city wall which offers a stunning panorama of Rome.

Down the opposite side of the hill, stretching out towards the Tiber, is Testaccio, one of Rome's most characteristic working-class neighbourhoods. It was here that Claudio's father, Mario, had his butcher's shop. This was to the Italian capital what the East End was to London. Like its English counterpart, these days it's been partly gentrified and yuppified, but local pride remains strong. For much of Rome's history Testaccio was the engine that drove the city. Rome sits inland, some twenty miles from the Mediterranean, and from Roman times rafts carrying goods and raw materials from around the world made their way upstream – initially pulled by oxen, later they relied on steam engines – into the capital. Testaccio was essentially Rome's harbour.

The name comes from the fact that in Roman times oil and other liquids were often transported in terracotta pots. When they arrived in Rome, the pots were emptied, and because they could not be re-used – they were often greasy or stained from the liquids and cleaning products weren't what they are today – they were smashed and the pieces dumped near the river, accumulating in giant mounds, which in time became the size of small hills. The largest of these grew to some 170 feet in height, became overgrown with grass and trees (nature always wins out in the end) and came to be known as Monte Testaccio after the Latin word for broken terracotta pottery, *testae*.

By the 1870s the railways had put the rafts out of business, and the district had gone into decline, so the city government razed it to the ground and covered it with public housing as Rome's population swelled after Italy's independence. Its grid of streets – so different from the ancient neighbourhoods that escaped redevelopment – became a byword for a certain typically Roman, fiercely proud, streetwise ethos. For the first twenty-odd years of his life this was Claudio Ranieri's world. Not Rome, really, just the triangle formed by the top of the Aventine, San Saba and Testaccio in the south-west of the city.

Mario had worked for the Giorgetti family, who ran the most important abattoirs, meat-packing and -supply companies in Rome. He then set up on his own and built his butcher's shop from scratch, establishing himself as the supplier of choice both for Rome's wealthy families, who would send their cooks to select and choose the meats, and also for the local population.

The family – Mario, his wife Renata, their daughter Paola and their three sons, Maurizio, Carlo and Claudio – lived up the hill from Testaccio in San Saba. This too was a planned community: until the early 1900s it was basically countryside, bar the seventh-century monastery of San Saba, which a thousand years earlier had been among the wealthiest in Europe.

San Saba had not been built for the working classes, but to house mostly mid-level white-collar workers: clerks, book-keepers and the growing ranks of bureaucrats who worked in Rome's newly established ministries after it became the capital of Italy. The area consisted of streets lined with low-rise villas, most with their own back garden or courtyard, huddled around Piazza Bernini, a square named for the seventeenth-century sculptor and architect. It was in that square that Ranieri first played football. San Saba was by no means a posh neighbourhood, but it was decidedly more genteel and aspirational than Testaccio.

Kids in 1960s Rome invariably spent their time outside school at either the *oratorio* – a church-affiliated club – or, if they were of a different political stripe, at its non-denominational left-wing equivalent. The *oratorio* had sports and games facilities, catered for arts and crafts, and, more generally, was a place to hang out. 'I was [at the *oratorio*] every day until eight o'clock at night,' Ranieri recalled in an interview with Italy's now defunct Gazzetta TV. 'You had to go to church, then they gave you some biscuits with jam and then you could go and play.'

San Saba's *oratorio* was close to the Ranieri house, but the one in Testaccio was bigger and had better facilities, including a five-a-side pitch with virtually continuous games. 'Five players per team – whoever got to three goals first would win and stay on,' Ranieri recalled. 'The loser would go off and a new team would come on.' Claudio was an athletic child who loved sport. He also played basketball up until the age of sixteen. A highlight of his career on the hardwood floor was when his basketball club picked him to be a reserve for the senior team in a third-division game. He didn't actually get on the court, but it was quite a thrill at a young age.

Football was a passion, but by no means the only one. He had a very close-knit circle of friends centred around the communities of San Saba and Testaccio. They didn't travel far, rarely venturing out of the area, but they weren't short on imagination and a sense of possibility. One of his closest friends from that era, Maurizio Berruti, recounts how the *oratorio* went out of its way to keep the boys off the streets, even getting them a printing press so they could publish their own magazine. It was called the *Triangle Club*, and Ranieri wrote a humour column. They were also allowed to take over one of the rooms at the church and turn it into a nightclub of sorts.

'Really, it was a bunch of communicating cellars,' recalls Berruti, 'but we decorated them properly, got a sound system, built a dance floor and had psychedelic lights.' Well, it was the late 1960s, after all. The Summer of Love was just around the corner and Rome was groovy too.

Ranieri was by now fourteen years old, and school was no longer a priority. He worked shifts at the butcher's shop, though nowhere near as many as the popular narrative suggests. 'I was the youngest. My brothers were there; I wasn't really needed that much,' he says. 'In fact, being the youngest in the family, I was given a lot of freedom.'

You wonder what Ranieri today would tell fourteen-year-old Ranieri back in 1965. One piece of advice – possibly – would be to persevere with his studies. His formal education was limited, though particularly as he grew into his late teens and later in life he became very much an auto-didact. He is naturally curious and an avid reader. And, perhaps, it's no coincidence that half a century later, in October 2016, when the University of Perugia – an institution founded way back in 1308 – awarded him an honorary degree, it marked a special moment for him. He looked genuinely moved as he stood there in traditional cap and gown throughout the ceremony, conducted entirely in Latin.

That moment would have felt very distant back in the mid-1960s when Claudio and his friends set up a football team – I Viola di San Saba (the San Saba Purples) – and enrolled in a local youth league. Ranieri was in goal. 'The problem with Claudio as keeper was that he could see the whole pitch and could not resist giving us all orders,' Berruti said. 'And when we inevitably ignored him, he'd get cross. Very cross.'

Before long he joined his first 'official' club – as opposed to the self-run San Saba Purples. It was called Dodicesimo Giallorosso – the Red and Yellow Twelfth Man. As the name implies, it was one of a galaxy of clubs loosely affiliated with AC Roma. In this team Ranieri was a centre forward, more for his athleticism, it must be said, than for his skill. His first coach was a man named Claudio Antonellini, his second another Claudio, Claudio Grippo. It was he who helped arrange a trial with Roma.

'It came towards the end of my second season,' Ranieri recalls. 'Helenio Herrera himself came to watch us, and I was playing up front. Everything went well that day, and I became a Roma player.'

Ranieri is somewhat blasé about Herrera, but it's difficult to exaggerate what such a visit must have meant to a dyed-in-the-wool Roma fan like the young Claudio. Herrera was a legend: he had won league titles in Spain in the 1950s – two with Atlético Madrid, two with Barcelona – before coming to Italy and winning another three with Inter Milan. He also led Inter to two consecutive European Cups and introduced the world to his version of *catenaccio* football. When the opposition had the ball, it was an uber-defensive, we-can-be-here-all-day system that frustrated opponents no end. But when his team won back possession, play turned into beautiful, free-flowing, choreographed counter-attacks. A bit like the ones Ranieri would conjure up forty-five years later at the King Power. Playing with Herrera watching in the stands was akin to a trial at Manchester United with Sir Alex Ferguson pitchside, saying nothing, but studying your every move.

His first coach at youth level at Roma was another legend: Guido Masetti. At the time in his mid-sixties, Masetti had been Roma's starting goalkeeper for thirteen seasons, right up until World War II caused the suspension of Serie A. He was also a member of the Italy squad that won the 1934 and 1938 World Cups. Ranieri's work rate was admired, but the club could not determine whether he had a future as a striker or even as a professional footballer at all. Still, his intensity and desire made it impossible to leave him out of the team.

The following season he moved up to the reserve team under Antonio Trebiciani. One of his teammates, Mauro Sandreani, would go on to become a successful Serie A coach and trusted adviser to Antonio Conte with the Italian national team. 'I remember Claudio very well as a young player,' he said. 'There was a lot of promise in the side, and he was one of the promising guys. He wasn't particularly creative or skilful, but he was hard, strong and never gave up.'

Strikers who don't score much at youth level tend not to get very far. Ranieri himself recalls the time as a period when he desperately wanted to make it, but every step of the way was tough. He had given up school entirely to focus on football, stepping up the shifts in his father's shop. He knew that would be his fallback if he did not make it and felt fortunate: not everybody has a family business to turn to if they don't fulfil their dreams.

'I played sometimes at centre forward, sometimes as an attacking midfielder, and I actually did score a few goals,' he says. 'But the truth is with every match things got tougher and tougher for me. I think maybe I was too emotional.'

'Good Claudio' is the smiling, gentlemanly joke-cracker we often see in the media. He's the patient fellow who demands effort and nothing more. He's the guy who understands that sport is a zero-sum game, that you have to accept defeat. Sometimes it will be your fault; sometimes the opponent will be better than you; sometimes it will just be sheer bad luck. Football, like life, is about balance and perspective, and you have to know how to lose with dignity.

And then there's bad Claudio. He's the one who can't cope, who never wants to be beaten, who can't accept that hard work sometimes is not enough. Knock him down ten times, he'll get back up ten times. 'That was crucial to me having a professional career for so long,' he said in a talk at the Italian consulate in London after the 2015–16 season. 'I never gave up, never accepted being beaten. If you wanted to get past me, you had to kill me.'

Gianfranco Zola has known Ranieri for some twenty-five years. 'I can see the dichotomy in him,' he says. 'Maybe all of us are like that a little bit – we have these two personalities – it's just that most are more at one end or the other. But if you want to make it, you need that other side, the nasty, determined one. I think I saw it in him at times. If you have it, you have to let it out.'

Ironically, it was bad Claudio who eventually prompted the decision that led to him changing his playing position and salvaging his career. If you subscribe to the notion that a butterfly flapping its wings at a certain time and place can cause a chain of events that leads to a tidal wave elsewhere on the globe, then if you follow the logic through, Leicester's 2015–16 date with history might never have happened if not for a fateful day late in the 1972–73 season. Ranieri might never have switched to defence, which means he would never have made it as a professional footballer, and, without a career in professional football, he would never have become a manager. Which in turn means that somebody else would have been in charge of Leicester City in 2015–16. And that Premier League title might never have arrived. On the flipside, Ranieri's success in his new position might have deprived the people of San Saba of a very fine butcher.

'The first team would scrimmage against us youngsters once a week, and typically Herrera would be the referee,' he recalls. 'As a centre forward, I'd end up getting marked by Aldo Bet and Sergio Santarini, two veteran hardmen who were our first-choice centre halves. They would kick lumps out of me, and of course Herrera would never call a foul on his guys, the first-team players. Nor could I retaliate, for obvious reasons.' With hindsight, it was something of a rite of passage – the old guys beating up the young guys just because, well, they could, and the manager saying nothing, believing perhaps that such experiences build character.

'So one day I decided I was going to play as a defender,' he says. 'I made my mind up all by myself; the coaches were sceptical. But I became the one giving out the punishment.'

Ranieri had the intelligence and vision to play up front, yet he lacked the technique to do so at the highest level. And his temperament – bad Claudio – wasn't doing him any favours. But he had the size and athleticism to play at centre back. And that was one area where players could be nasty, as forwards certainly did not get the protection they enjoy today.

Herrera admired the young man's confidence and noted that he could certainly do a job at the back. The coach didn't return the following season, but his replacement Manlio Scopigno nevertheless invited Ranieri to train regularly with the first team, and on 4 November 1973, at the age of twenty-two, he fulfilled the dream of many a Giallorossi fan, making his debut for Roma, away to Genoa. Roma lost 2–1, and the local paper *Corriere dello Sport* gave the following assessment:

'It was a bad day all round for the team and not the ideal circumstances in which to make your debut. That said, even allowing for the cynicism and trickery of the Genoa forwards, the number of fouls Ranieri was forced to commit was excessive.'

Ranieri himself, facing the cameras, said, 'I'm unhappy because we lost, and nobody wants to lose on his debut. Though I did get words of encouragement from the referee after the match.'

Paolo Conti was Roma's keeper at the time and watched Ranieri try to establish himself in a team which, truth be told, was probably above his level. 'He was a very serious kid and he was well liked,' he recalls. 'He wasn't particularly talented, but he didn't have obvious flaws either. He did the simple things; he was tough and he was reliable. He tried to improve every day and outwork everybody. But I think he knew his limits.'

Another teammate, Angelo Domenghini, a former Italian international, echoes this view: 'He was humble, sincere and determined. He continually wanted to improve. Nothing was going to stand in his way.'

If this was a fairy tale, nothing would have stood in his way. But this is reality. And the simple fact is that some people are simply born with more. You can buy into the 'ten thousand hours rule' of 'deliberate practice' described in *Outliers*, Malcolm Gladwell's study of success, if you like. And maybe that is how very gifted people ultimately fully exploit their talents. Yet in real life there is a ceiling. We are not all created equal. Ranieri had football intelligence, athleticism, a strong work ethic and a burning desire to succeed, but he simply did not have enough technical ability. At least not to build a career at a top Serie A side like Roma.

By the end of the 1973–74 season he was nearly twenty-three and had managed just six appearances for the side as a professional. He had to accept it was not going to work out at the club he had supported all his life. And so he moved on and moved down, to Catanzaro, in Serie B, Italy's second division.

2. Boys of '74

Catanzaro sits way down the Italian boot, near the toe, in the region of Calabria. For Ranieri, who had spent all his life in Rome – and perhaps the most insular part of Rome – it was like moving to a different country altogether. Calabria is one of Italy's poorest regions economically and one of the richer ones culturally. Steep, inhospitable mountains loom over the coastline. Outsiders are often viewed with suspicion, at least initially, though once you're accepted, you're in for life.

What many foreigners often forget is that while Italy has been a centre of world civilisation for thousands of years, it has only existed as a country since the latter half of the nineteenth century. After Italy was unified Massimo d'Azeglio, a leading thinker and politician at the time, famously said, 'We have made Italy. Now we need to make Italians.' Cultural differences abound and can be extreme. Scarcely a century had passed since Italian unification when Claudio Ranieri arrived in Catanzaro in the summer of 1974. Calabria and the south of Italy had been the domain of a branch of the Spanish Bourbon dynasty up to 1860, while Rome had been ruled by the Pope until ten years after that. Customs were different, from the food to working hours, which included a four-hour break in the middle of the day.

Two things were the same: his new club's colours, red and yellow like Roma; and the passion of its supporters. Catanzaro had been promoted to Serie A for the first time ever just a few years earlier in 1971. They had been relegated, but the fans and the club had real ambition. A few seasons before they had even been on tour to the United States, where they played Pelé's Santos in a friendly. What they lacked in money, they thought they'd make up for through ingenuity. They hired an ambitious young manager, Gianni Di Marzio, father of the journalist and transfer guru Gianluca Di Marzio, and told him he'd need to deliver on a shoestring budget.

Injury had cut Di Marzio's playing career short before he could even begin, and so he devoted himself to coaching youngsters, working obsessively and landing a job at Brindisi, in Serie B, where, at thirty-three, he was one of the youngest coaches ever in professional football. His appointment shocked many, but by mid-season they were top of the league and heading towards promotion. And then the story took a dramatic turn.

Pregnant with Gianluca and feeling unwell, his wife Concetta called and asked Di Marzio to take her to the doctor. 'We were on our way when we suffered a terrible accident,' he recalls. 'My face was completely destroyed – eye sockets, nose . . . It was a terrible blow. To add insult to injury, when I recovered in hospital I learned that Brindisi had sacked me.' Why? Because he did not notify the club that he was missing training to take his heavily pregnant wife to see a doctor.

Catanzaro immediately got in touch.

'The president, Nicola Ceravolo, was very clear with me,' Di Marzio says. 'He told me there was no money left; I'd need to build a team on the cheap. I accepted and, because I had several months before the end of the season, I spent them travelling around and watching reserve-team football.'

On his travels Di Marzio spotted Ranieri and his teammate Roberto Vichi. The former played fullback, the latter was a central defender. He felt they could help improve Catanzaro and, since Roma were ready to release them, he swung into action. 'I met his parents. I visited the butcher's shop. I remember being struck by the fact that Ranieri had made his debut in Serie A, playing in front of 80,000 people at the Stadio Olimpico, but still regularly helped out his dad, making deliveries on his day off. Convincing him to come to Catanzaro wasn't difficult, though he drove a very hard bargain in his contract negotiations.'

This wouldn't be the last time a club would comment on Ranieri's negotiating skills. Fortunately for him – and for his bank account – it's usually bad Claudio who shows up to talk contracts and wages.

Ranieri became an immediate starter and the linchpin of the stingiest defence in the division – Catanzaro conceded just eighteen goals in thirty-eight games. Di Marzio had overhauled the side, bringing in nine new faces, drawing upon reserves from Serie A and Serie B and players from the lower divisions. They finished joint third, which meant a one-game play-off on neutral ground with Verona to determine promotion to Serie A.

'The game was in Terni, in central Italy, equidistant from both clubs,' recalls Di Marzio. 'It was crazy. We took 30,000 supporters up from Calabria; they had a few hundred. We dominated. They crossed the halfway line once and scored. That's football.'

Still, that first season at Catanzaro revitalised Ranieri in more ways than one. Maybe it was the fact that so many newcomers had been catapulted into this strange place at the extreme end of Italy, but friendships were forged that endure to this day. Ranieri met perhaps his closest friend in football, Giorgio Pellizzaro. Like Ranieri, the goalkeeper was a foreigner of sorts in Calabria, hailing from Brescia in the north of Italy.

'We sort of sniffed around each other a bit, like dogs,' says Pellizzaro. It wasn't an instant friendship. The keeper might have been worried that the newcomers would let him down and make him look bad. But the two were on the same wavelength and have remained so to this day. They would spend five seasons as teammates and then a quarter-century coaching together. From Napoli in 1991, along every stop of Ranieri's career, Pellizzaro has been with him as a goalkeeping coach. That's twelve coaching stints, including Leicester, which, however, lasted only a few days.

'I went with him to Leicester, but I needed knee surgery and was told to take time off to recuperate,' Pellizzaro says, no doubt rueing the fact he missed out on the history-making campaign.

There were two non-footballing reasons that this close-knit group formed in Catanzaro. A developer had built a holiday complex of 'Californian-style' seaside villas in Copanello, a half-hour drive from Catanzaro. Seven different players, including Ranieri, took out mortgages and bought properties there. The villas would become their annual holiday homes for many years to come. And those who didn't buy were frequent visitors. 'I don't think anybody could have imagined that forty years later, now that most of them are grandfathers, they'd still be so close, still holidaying there,' says Di Marzio.

The other key was the players' wives, including Ranieri's new bride, Rosanna. She was the daughter of a football journalist and friendly with the girlfriend of one of his teammates, Adriano Banelli. 'When we started seeing each other, I was constantly getting ribbed by my teammates,' says Ranieri. 'We were all so close as a group. She was best friends with a teammate's girlfriend, who then became his wife . . . It was all very cosy.' The footballer's wife stereotype existed back then as well, but if there is one thing that defines Rosanna to this day, it's her independence. She has passions for cuisine, the arts and design, which she continues to cultivate. She owns a successful vintage and design boutique in Rome and is that rare individual who combines business nous with creativity.

'She is a great woman, one of the most creative people I have ever met,' says Concetta 'Tucci' Di Marzio. 'In the kitchen, she is unparalleled. And with paint and colour too. I own one of her paintings – it's in my living room – and she has also done fabulous work with porcelain.'

The fact that Rosanna and the other players' wives forged such a tight friendship in that season only served to cement the group that Catanzaro fans still remember as the 'boys of '74'.

'I don't think you'll find anywhere in football a relationship like the one we all had at Catanzaro – I mean a group of men and women who have remained so close-knit forty years later, despite the distance, despite the different paths our careers took,' says Fausto Silipo, another teammate. 'Scarcely a year goes by that we don't all get together and see each other.'

Disappointment at the play-off loss was quickly forgotten the following year. It would be remembered as one of the tightest, most dramatic seasons in history. Catanzaro, Foggia and Genoa finished joint top of Serie B, with Varese one point back and Brescia two points behind. It all came down to the final days of the season, and in Catanzaro's case things got even crazier. In the midst of the run-in the Italian FA decreed that a game earlier that season against Novara – which ended in a 1–1 draw – had to be replayed. Why? Because the referee's assistant had injured himself during the match. He was replaced by a pitchside photographer who also happened to be a qualified referee. The problem was that his licence had expired. When the FA found out, they insisted on a rematch, to be played three days before the last day of the season.

As it happened, things worked out even better for Catanzaro. This time they won, 3–0. And victory on the final day of the campaign, away to Reggiana, would seal their place in the top flight. It took a winner in the final minute. That final game of the season, with Catanzaro needing a win, was also another life lesson for Ranieri. Having been a regular all year, he was dropped, and did not take it well.

'I left him out and he was very upset,' Di Marzio says. 'But it was purely a footballing decision, a tactical choice. Claudio had been playing left back, and the player he'd be up against, Sileno Passalacqua, was a small, quick, tricky winger. It was going to be tough for Claudio to keep up with him. I had to think of the good of the team.'

Ranieri was hurt. And angry. But it taught him that being a

coach was about putting the team first and making painful choices. Perhaps every time he drops a regular, especially one he has grown close to, he thinks back to that afternoon against Reggiana. But when Catanzaro returned home for the victory celebrations, he was there too and all was forgotten. Expectations were high in Serie A, but the jump in quality was just too big. Ranieri, again, was a regular and coped well, but the side struggled to score and were relegated with two games to go.

When a team goes down, you expect heads to roll, perhaps to appease an angry fan base, and indeed Di Marzio left the club. Giorgio Sereni, a veteran lower-league boss known as a promotion specialist, returning after a two-year ban for attempted match-fixing, came in to replace him. But the supporters remained true. They were disappointed, sure, but their support for the club never wavered, and they felt connected to the side. They had bought in to what Di Marzio had created, this close-knit group of players – friends, really – who battled, entertained and thrilled.

Ranieri's intensity and warrior spirit was part of the thrill. Another came from a short, stocky, bushy-haired, mustachioed striker named Massimo Palanca. To this day, if you travel to Catanzaro you'll hear his name spoken of in hushed tones, the way local legends are spoken of at provincial clubs around the world. He would score eighteen goals to take Catanzaro straight back to Serie A in the 1977–78 season, including the winner on the final day of the campaign, in what amounted to a promotion play-off against Palermo.

While some of the boys of '74 had moved on from Catanzaro, the bonds remained. Other players arrived, and the group grew, though often after newcomers were put through a series of practical jokes. A favourite of Ranieri's was arranging with the club switchboard to put a call through to the dressing room to a new player. Ranieri or one of the other boys would pretend to be a journalist needing an interview with the newcomer. As the call went on, the questions would become increasingly absurd, and the rest of the team, listening in on another line, would howl with laughter. Nearly forty years later, Leicester's dressing room would also be the scene of pranks and practical jokes. Those who knew Ranieri in Catanzaro were not surprised.

'I think there's a good reason why Claudio repeatedly compared what we had in Catanzaro with what he built at Leicester,' says Alberto Arbitrio, one of the original boys of '74. 'We were winners; we worked hard, but we also had fun and we had a special group, a special sense of unity. We made sacrifices, but we did it with a smile.'

It wasn't all about fun. The friendships endured through hard times as well. Years later reserve goalkeeper Ubaldo Novembre's twenty-one-year-old daughter died suddenly and tragically. Ranieri, who in the meantime had become a successful and wealthy coach, showed up at his door one summer. 'He had sailed his boat to Brindisi, where I lived,' Novembre recalls. 'He simply said, "Come with us." And we did. We spent ten days sailing around the Aegean Sea. I was going through one of the darkest moments of my life and Claudio chose as his holiday to spend time with me, to do what he could to alleviate the pain. We are like brothers, all of us.'

During the summer of 1978 Sereni would be replaced by a man who – along with Di Marzio – would arguably be the biggest influence on Ranieri's career as a manager. Like Ranieri, Carletto Mazzone was from Rome and a Roma fan, yet in personality they were polar opposites. Mazzone was loud, brash, in-your-face, prone to temper tantrums but also a warm, patriarchal figure. Italians have a certain stereotype of Romans, and it is far closer to the Mazzone end of the spectrum. Indeed, in terms of character, Ranieri's politeness and jovial, respectful formality is much more in keeping with Calabrian ways. It may have been Rosanna's influence or it may have been the years – and summers – spent down there. Whatever the case, but for small inflections in his speech, most Italians who meet Ranieri probably would not guess he is from Rome.

Mazzone wore his origins on his sleeve. He was fiercely proud of his roots, famously telling Ranieri, years later, 'You can't call yourself a football manager unless you've managed Roma.' What he meant was that, for Romans like him and Ranieri, managing their hometown club was unlike any other experience in football: hugely draining and emotional and perhaps the toughest job there is. (It's hard enough for those who are not from Rome.) Mazzone would also go on to forge a rapport with, of all people, Pep Guardiola, who played for him some twenty years later at Brescia. It's difficult to imagine two more diametrically opposed figures than Mazzone and the future Barcelona and Manchester City manager. Yet while their ideas of football were so different, their human qualities and the way they related to people were strikingly similar, to the point that Guardiola credits Mazzone's influence to this day.

Mazzone had a reputation as a tough results-oriented manager, and his Catanzaro side certainly reflected that. From him Ranieri learned that while systems and tactics are important, the right frame of mind is critical. A team has to be a unit. There has to be both harmony and the correct degree of intensity.

Catanzaro were the surprise package in Serie A that season, flirting with the UEFA Cup places before finishing in ninth. One match stands out, the 3–1 away victory against Roma, which saw Palanca grab a hat-trick. He didn't just score goals; he had a particular speciality, one that happened to be extraordinarily difficult but looked easy as pie when he did it. He could score directly from corner kicks, which is how he scored his opener.

In South America, they call it an Olympic goal because the very first one was scored by an Argentine winger, Cesareo Onzari, against Uruguay, who had won gold at the 1924 Olympics a few months earlier. It's hugely rare, usually reserved for the greatest players. Ronaldinho, Roberto Baggio and Diego Maradona have all done it. So too have Thierry Henry and David Beckham. By contrast, despite a combined total of nearly a thousand goals, neither Cristiano Ronaldo nor Lionel Messi have pulled it off. Palanca would do it no fewer than thirteen times in his career.

He attributed his success to two factors. He had very small feet, which allowed him to strike a dead ball with extraordinary accuracy. To get a ball to go one way and then suddenly curve back the other way – which is the only way, given the angle, to score off a corner – requires hitting the ball at just the right spot, off centre. To then do it in such a way that the ball rises at the desired angle and with enough force that the keeper can't save it requires surgical precision.

Palanca's other secret? Ranieri. 'I don't think that I could do it quite so well without him,' Palanca says. 'He goes and stands next to the keeper. We work on the timing, but he makes sure that he jumps at just the right moment as my kick begins to swerve, thereby blocking the goalkeeper's line of sight, so that he doesn't actually see the ball until the last moment and after it has changed direction.' More than half his thirteen Olympic goals came that way. Opposing keepers hated it. They knew what was coming; they just didn't know how to stop it.

'We all were well aware of what Palanca could do, but there's not much you can do if you can't see the ball,' says Paolo Conti, the Roma keeper that season and a former teammate of Ranieri during his Roma days. 'His [Ranieri's] timing was perfect. He'd appear in front of you, and there was nothing you could do other than hope that Palanca mis-hit it, or try to guess where it was going to go.'

By this stage Ranieri was very much the leader of this Catanzaro team. He had moved from left back into central defence, playing as an old-school sweeper or libero. And even though he did not fit the footballing stereotype – too polite and well mannered off the pitch, some might say – his teammates looked up to him. If you were going to war, you wanted him on your side.

'Ranieri was our captain, and from the moment I arrived, I was struck by his calm and how he managed to remain cool no matter the situation,' says Piero Braglia, a midfielder who joined Catanzaro in 1978. 'I never saw him lose concentration, and his demeanour never changed. He had a natural sense of the team, the collective. He knew what to say to us and how to inspire. And, of course, on the pitch, he simply never gave up.'

He had also become a father, when Rosanna gave birth to their daughter Claudia. She may (almost) share a name with her father, but, taking after her mother, she became a strong, successful woman. She set up a communications consultancy which represents a number of Italian actors and entertainers. One of them, Alessandro Roja, became her husband and in time Ranieri became a grandfather. Roja became quite famous in Italy for his role in a historical mini-series set in Rome's 1970s underworld called *Romanzo Criminale*. But football, as ever, was not that far away. He was also cast to play the legendary Torino winger Gigi Meroni – dubbed by some the Italian George Best – in a docudrama.

The following season, 1979–80, would prove to be a turbulent one, not just for Ranieri and Catanzaro, but for Italian football as a whole. Mazzone was sacked with five games to go and the side teetering on the edge of relegation, and indeed the club did finish in the relegation zone. But the first major match-fixing scandal to hit Italian football would see both Lazio and Milan punished with automatic relegation. Catanzaro, who had finished fourteenth out of sixteen – with the bottom three going down – were thus bumped up to twelfth and avoided the drop. That year would also see the debut of a gifted homegrown Catanzaro player, Massimo Mauro, who would become famous for being the only player to play alongside Zico, Maradona and Michel Platini, and would write a book about it. Ranieri would later coach him at Napoli and Mauro would unwittingly contribute to his departure from the club.

Meanwhile Catanzaro turned to Bruno Pace, an up-and-coming young manager who had won the title in the Italian fourth division in his very first job two years earlier. It would turn out to be an inspired choice. Catanzaro would finish the 1980–81 season in seventh place, their best-ever finish in Serie A. For a town of barely 100,000 people, it was like winning the European Cup. Mauro was hailed as one of the most promising young wingers in the league, while Palanca scored a few more Olympic goals and would end the campaign as the second-top goalscorer in the league.

Many expected Catanzaro to fall off in 1981–82; instead, they defied everyone and again finished in seventh place. But the campaign was less enjoyable for Ranieri. A regular starter in the first half of the season, he fell out with the manager and did not play in the latter half of the campaign. The decision to leave was not easy. Catanzaro was home – his daughter Claudia had been born there – but he was now in his thirties and he wanted to make every day he had left as a footballer count.

3. Forged Down South

So Ranieri made the short trip across the Strait of Messina to Sicily. Just as he had done nine years earlier when he left Roma, he dropped down a division – and was reunited with his old friend Gianni Di Marzio, who was in charge of Calcio Catania. 'We had a strong team and we were gunning for promotion,' says Di Marzio, 'but I needed somebody who was an experienced leader, who I could trust and who understood my system.' It would prove to be the right decision. He was named captain and, for the third time in his career, won promotion to Serie A. It wasn't as straightforward as some had hoped. Catania finished level on points with Como and Cremonese for the third and final promotion spot.

A mini round-robin play-off would determine the winner. This being Italy in the early 1980s, each game turned out to be an epic battle. There were two scoreless draws and the third game, between Catania and Como, finished 1–0 to Di Marzio's crew. Curiously – perhaps cruelly – the Como match saw Ranieri pitted against Palanca, his old teammate and partner in the Olympic goals routine. This time Palanca could not muster the old magic to score direct from the corner kick. Perhaps Ranieri knew him too well.

For Ranieri it was a bitter return to Serie A. Catania began with two draws but then slid down the table. Di Marzio was sacked, and Ranieri did not take it well. 'He marched right into the office of our president, Angelo Massimino, and told him he had made a grave mistake,' Di Marzio recalls. 'And then he went even further. He faced the TV cameras and repeated the exact same things he said to Massimino. That sacking me was a serious, foolish mistake. Claudio acted like a real man,' he adds. 'He could easily have hidden, kept his head down. Instead, he went out there and put himself on the line for me. How can I ever forget a gesture like that?'

There's an Italian expression – *schiena dritta* – straight back – used to describe those who speak their mind without fear and don't bow before the powerful. That was Ranieri. Catania's president was an autocratic self-made millionaire, someone used to being revered. The shock of having somebody stand up to him and say to his face that he had made a mistake was bad enough; to then have that same insubordinate person go and do it in public, where fans and media alike could then weigh in, was beyond the pale. Many predicted that this would be the end of Ranieri in a Catania shirt. But something odd happened. President Massimino instructed the new manager, Giovan Battista Fabbri, to make his team and tactics selection as if nothing had happened. Ranieri had been insubordinate, yes. And, in some ways, he had humiliated his president by criticising him in public. But he had also shown plenty of guts. Or, as the Italians say, *palle* – balls.

Massimino did not like what Ranieri had done, but he respected it. Maybe Catania were heading down, and maybe he had in fact made a mistake in sacking Di Marzio. But if they were going to be relegated, it was not going to be without a fight. And if they were going to fight, he wanted Ranieri to be on the pitch to lead the battle. Sometimes bad Claudio came in handy. And with his career ticking down, the last thing Ranieri himself needed was good Claudio meekly accepting a perceived injustice or even just a mistake that hurt the team.

He had another year's contract with Catania, but it was clear to everyone that he would not be staying. Massimino may have respected his outspokenness the year before, but after relegation there were going to be cuts. And he did not need a thirty-three-year-old veteran scrutinising his decisions again. Ranieri, too, was ready to move. What nobody expected was that he'd join Palermo, Catania's perennial rival for Sicilian footballing supremacy, or that he'd drop down two divisions, to Italy's Serie C1, to do it.

The two cities have been rivals for much of Sicilian history. They even squabbled for a long time over St Agatha of Sicily. Historians remain unsure as to whether she originally came from Palermo or Catania, but what we do know is she was martyred for refusing to renounce her faith some time around the year AD 250 and is buried in Catania. She is one of the four protectors of Palermo, but is also the patron saint of Catania. Such was the acrimony that the Catholic Church, to calm things down, encouraged Palermo to adopt St Rosalie. She lived some 900 years after Saint Agatha – she died in 1170 – but at least in her case we are fairly certain that she was born and died in Palermo.

Today the Festa di Santa Rosalia is a massive event in Palermo and with good reason. Back in 1623 Palermo was in the grip of the plague. Bodies were piling up in the streets and, despite prayers and offerings to Saint Agatha, thousands continued to die. A young seamstress, Girolama La Gattuta, was on her deathbed when, the story goes, St Rosalie visited her and wiped her brow. She was soon better, and St Rosalie appeared to other people around the city. By 1625 the plague was gone. Palermo had a new heroine and, though not an official patron, she became the most revered saint in town. As for St Agatha, many remain devoted to her in both cities.

Palermo is roughly twice as big and is the capital of the island, but Catania, situated on the east coast of Sicily, is closer to the mainland and the rest of Italy. Palermo is historically a bigger club and for much of their history the two teams were in different divisions, but the fact that they did not face each other that often only intensified a rivalry dating back to 1910 for something called the Lipton Challenge Cup. It was named for Sir Thomas Lipton, of Lipton Tea fame, and, until World War I, was a competition bringing together teams from southern Italy. Sir Thomas had a habit of commissioning the manufacture of trophies – all of them named after him – and donating them to sporting competitions. He sponsored the Thomas Lipton Trophy, an embryonic world football championship back in 1909, involving teams from Switzerland, Germany, Italy and England. He donated the Copa Lipton in 1905, a trophy fiercely contested by Argentina and Uruguay ever since. Another Lipton Cup went to the winners of an annual rowing competition in Canada, but he was perhaps best known – tea empire aside – for leading the European challenge in the America's Cup via the Royal Ulster Yacht club, which he bankrolled. He was perpetually unsuccessful in that endeavour right up until his death in 1931, though perhaps would take solace in the fact that the United States would continue to defend the trophy right up until 1983, when they were finally defeated.

Back to football. Ranieri became a mainstay for a Palermo side that had spent big to ensure immediate promotion.

'He had a great relationship with our manager, Tom Rosati,' recalls Gianni De Biasi, a teammate and close friend of Ranieri, who would later go on to manage Albania. 'Rosati wanted him on board and handed him the keys to the defence. By that point he was solely a sweeper. Not the kind that steps up into midfield and builds play – he did not have the technique for it perhaps – but his clearances out of the back were always timely. He had a knack for saying the right thing at the right time in the dressing room, whether lowering the tension when necessary or, the opposite, ratcheting up the intensity when required,' De Biasi adds. It was a skill that would serve him well in his next career.

Palermo raced through the first half of the season and were comfortably on their way to promotion. There was a real team spirit and a wonderful vibe around the club, so much so that the players all decided to spend New Year's Eve together, throwing a big party in a small town just outside the city.

'It turned into quite the celebration,' recalls the journalist Salvatore Geraci. A former Palermo correspondent for *Corriere dello Sport*, he was master of ceremonies that evening. 'Everyone got a bit carried away. Ranieri was the life of the party, singing on stage with gusto and then, as a prank, pouring a bucketful of water on my head. It looked as if the night would go on until the small hours. Instead, just past midnight, he left. He wanted to be ready for training the next morning. That was Ranieri. Ever the professional.'

They eventually finished second in the league to secure

promotion to Serie B. But despite success on the pitch, a few months later things took a tragic turn, and it would be a traumatic and painful year for all involved.

The club president was a man named Roberto Parisi, a Turin-born entrepreneur who had moved to Palermo and set up a successful business providing lighting and municipal services to a number of local administrations, including the city of Palermo. He was a hugely committed man, a workaholic who had experienced personal catastrophe just three years earlier, when he lost his wife and daughter in the Ustica tragedy.

Ustica remains one of the many mysteries which tormented Italy in the 1970s and 1980s. On 27 June 1980 Parisi's wife and daughter and seventy-nine others were on a plane travelling from Bologna to Palermo when something caused the hull suddenly to break apart. The plane fell into the sea near the island of Ponza. There were no survivors. To this day the exact cause has never been determined, with various theories ranging from a bomb on board to the plane being mistakenly shot down in the midst of an aerial firefight between NATO and Libyan forces. There were allegations of a cover-up, missing hours of radar; dozens of military and government officials would later be found guilty of attempting to pervert the course of justice and providing false testimony. But to this day the truth has never been established.

One morning nearly five years later Parisi was being driven to work when two cars pulled up alongside his vehicle and as many as five men opened fire, killing him and his driver. It later emerged that the Mafia – sadly an ever-present force in Palermo over the past century – had been attempting to blackmail him. Some twelve years later, a turncoat named Emanuele Di Filippo cut a deal with prosecutors and took responsibility for the murder. As a result of cooperating, he was sentenced to just fifteen years in prison.

Gianni De Biasi revealed just how shaken-up everyone was at the news. We were on the road before an away game when we found out,' he recalls. 'It was terrible, and it hit us very hard. Parisi was an incredible man, with the courage to refuse to bow down to organised crime.' This wasn't the only tragedy to hit the club. Earlier that season, Rosati had been diagnosed with terminal cancer. 'We all knew, but he never talked about it and we respected that,' says De Biasi. 'He was a paternal figure. He didn't want our pity and he did not want to worry us. We were his boys, his men. He shielded us as much as he could.'

A warm man with a particular fondness for Ranieri, Rosati passed away the following summer, less than two months after winning promotion back to Serie B. Antonio Valentin Angelillo, a former Argentine international who once held the Serie A scoring record with thirty-three goals in thirty-two games, took charge of the side, but without Rosati it wasn't the same, and with Parisi gone, there was no further investment in the team.

'I didn't have a great relationship, either with Angelillo or, after his sacking, with his replacement, Fernando Veneranda,' recalls Ranieri. 'Everything was coming to an end.' That year he was in and out of the side. He was a veteran who was easy to blame and who made an insecure coach uncomfortable. Palermo somehow avoided relegation, but the worst was yet to come. The club was involved in a corruption scandal which would see them automatically relegated. Not that it mattered anyway. After Parisi's death investors pulled out, and the club was declared bankrupt the following summer.

Ranieri was on the move again, but what opportunities were there for a thirty-five-year-old?

'I wanted to keep playing and I believed I could still do it, at least for a year or two,' Ranieri says. He returned to Rome and trained with Roma's youth team, taking only a brief holiday that summer, at the house down in Calabria. Again it was Di Marzio who would help determine his next step. Via a mutual friend, he had met the president of a team called Vigor Lamezia. The president had big plans for his club, which at the time were in non-league football. And he needed a manager.

Di Marzio sold him on Ranieri. It was perfect. Lamezia was no more than a forty-minute drive from Copanello. Ranieri would not even have to move. Di Marzio drove to see him and shared the news. Ranieri was far from enthusiastic at first. While the prospect of coaching was appealing, he wasn't quite ready to hang up his boots. Dropping all the way down to the dusty regional leagues outside the Italian professional football pyramid wasn't appealing either. But Di Marzio was, among other things, a wonderful salesman. He told Ranieri it would be the perfect chance to learn about being a coach.

'I thought about it overnight,' Ranieri recalls. 'The next morning I had made my decision. Let's try this coaching thing and see how it goes.' Of course Ranieri was still Ranieri. One step ahead. He insisted that he did not just want to be manager, but player-manager. And so he became one of the first Italians in the modern era to sign a contract as a player-manager. In his mind he thought he could still play. A few months earlier he had been starting in Serie B. Surely he could cope against guys three tiers below that?

The club told him that nothing less than immediate promotion was acceptable. That was fine with Ranieri; he didn't mind the challenge. And he still wasn't sure about this coaching thing. If it didn't work out, he would at least have gained valuable experience, he told himself. However, Ranieri found himself sucked into management to a degree he could not imagine. Despite his history-making player-manager contract, he never actually stepped on the pitch; he was fully immersed in his new role.

At that level of the game, especially back in the 1980s in the south of Italy, there were no physiotherapists or fitness coaches, so Ranieri pretty much did everything on his own. He read as much as he could and introduced a range of innovations. He insisted on punctuality and organisation and, even though the players weren't professional, expected them to behave as such, right down to wearing the official club outfit every time they were out representing Lamezia.

'He made us feel important, better than we were,' says Antonio Gatto. At the time Gatto was a sixteen-year-old midfielder who Ranieri had plucked out of the youth team. This in itself was a statement of intent. At that level players tended to be veterans; the idea that a sixteen-year-old, however talented – and Gatto was a good player, but not one who anyone expected to go on to have a professional career, even in the lower leagues – would get on the pitch seemed crazy. 'Ranieri didn't care about hierarchy,' says Gatto. 'He treated the youngsters like veterans. And he treated us all like professionals, with respect.' His human side also shone through. When Fabio Fraschetti, the club captain, injured his knee, Ranieri called in some favours and took him to see the medical staff at Catanzaro, where he was still treated like royalty. And when Fraschetti got depressed, he opened his home to him. 'I had only known him for a few weeks, but he went out of his way to help me, even inviting me to his house to have dinner with his family,' Fraschetti says. 'He wanted us to be like a family.'

Ranieri introduced concepts to Lamezia that at the time were simply foreign to the Italian game at that level. Most Italian clubs followed the old paradigm of man-marking, with two men picking up the opposition's two strikers and a sweeper behind. But in other parts of Europe teams were marking zonally. This was anathema to the traditional Italian mindset, which was safety-first, but it was making inroads. A man named Arrigo Sacchi had won the third division the year before with little Parma, and had done it by playing a pure zonal-marking system that was initially dismissed as suicidal by other managers. Sacchi would go on to manage AC Milan, twice making them European champions with a legendary zonal defence that included the likes of Franco Baresi and Paolo Maldini.

Ranieri decided to import zonal marking into Calabria. 'Defending zonally was a massive change for many of the players,' recalls Gatto. 'But not the only one. His training sessions were actually fun, mainly because the ball was at the centre of everything, in contrast to what we were used to: long sessions of endless, repeated sprints and runs.'

Results followed. Lamezia were dominating the league and were unbeaten through twenty matches. But then the Vigor Lamezia president told Ranieri they wanted to make changes and bring in some new personnel. Ranieri felt such a mid-season upheaval was unnecessary and was not comfortable working with the individuals the club wished to bring in. One individual familiar with the situation called it an 'ugly story' of the sort which, sadly, was not unfamiliar to non-league football in the deep south of Italy. Despite the team flying in the league, he resigned just before Christmas. They would go on to win promotion.

'I don't know the details of what happened; I just know we were all sorry that he left,' Gatto says. Fraschetti too claims to be in the dark, other than to say there were 'non-footballing reasons' for Ranieri's departure.

Ranieri was sad to leave, but he had caught the management bug. He had realised that, if he was going to stay in football, it would be as a manager, and the foundations of what was to come next were laid.

4. Climbing the Pyramid

Leaving Vigor Lamezia halfway through the season meant that Ranieri had time not just to think about what sort of manager he wanted to be – the innovations he brought in Lamezia were meaningful but extemporaneous, given that he had so little time to prepare for the job and still thought of himself as a player – but also how he would climb the ladder. Football folk everywhere are an incestuous bunch and, while Lamezia were a tiny club way down the pyramid, his achievements there did not go unnoticed. An old friend, Giorgio Perinetti, a former low-level club official during his time at Roma, who was hugely well connected in the game, set up a meeting with Luciano Tarantino, director of football at Campania Puteolana, a fourth-division club from Naples.

They met for lunch at Il Sarago, a famous Neapolitan restaurant, and within three hours Tarantino was fully convinced. Or, better yet, seduced: Ranieri was their man. The old adage goes, 'You never get a second chance to make a first impression.' First impressions are Ranieri's forte, particularly when it comes to prospective employers. Time and again throughout his career, those who hired him talked about how they were bowled over at the very first meeting, whether it was a casual chat or a formal interview.

Ranieri was enthusiastic, motivated, prepared (he had swotted up on the club) and, most of all, full of ideas. He wanted this opportunity and was going to seize it with both hands. An ambitious young coach desperate to manage will take any job, and Campania Puteolana was hardly a plum assignment. For a start they were very much the 'other team' in Naples. The top dogs, as you'd expect, were Napoli, captained by a certain Diego Armando Maradona. They had done the Serie A–Coppa Italia double the previous season.

The city itself was football-mad, sure, but the madness was all for Napoli. Campania Puteolana was the result of a merger of several clubs, most of which had spent much of their history in semi-professional and amateur football. The only reason they were even in the fourth division to begin with was that a decade earlier some local investors (Romantics? Fools? Who knows?!) had poured money into a new club called Campania, named for the region which is home to Naples. The team had scaled the pyramid all the way to the third division, but in the summer of 1986, laden with debt, the owners merged the club with Puteolana, an outfit from neighbouring Pozzuoli (technically not Naples proper, but part of its metropolitan area). Or, rather, they didn't merge with Puteolana, because the club had gone bankrupt a few months earlier, but instead with the entity set up to replace it, which was due to start over from the lowest rung of amateur football.

The whole thing was a bit of a dog's breakfast. Puteolana were bankrupt, and a businessman named Giocondo Mauriello, one of the first in Europe to trade with Communist China, wanted to own a club called Puteolana, but not if it meant starting over from the very bottom of the pyramid. Nor was he willing to invest to save Puteolana in its current state. So he got the bankruptcy tribunal to hand him the rights to the club instead, bought Campania – whose owners were tired of losing money – and merged the two. That way he could take over Campania's slot in the professional football pyramid but own a club called Puteolana instead.

Confused?

These sorts of things happened in the Italian game, especially in the 1980s. Clubs went bust; judges were left to sort out the mess, and purporting to represent the interests of the fans allowed clubs to reform with new ownership, with the old club seeing its debts written off.

The main problem was the new club – Campania Puteolana – was always going to have trouble being a viable operation. Football fans in Naples could choose: do you pick a fourth-division side from Pozzuoli playing on a shoestring or do you support your local title-winning team and watch the likes of Maradona and Careca every weekend? Ranieri's earnings reflected this. He earned 30 million lire after tax, which may sound a lot, but adjusted for inflation works out at around £30,000 a year gross in today's money. Not a terrible salary, but not what he was used to as a footballer by any stretch. Still, he was now a manager. And taking this job at those wages was first and foremost an investment in himself and in his career.

'He had revolutionary ideas for a club our size,' says Tarantino. 'He insisted that we go away for a preseason training camp somewhere in Umbria and that we go on team retreats the night before matches. There was virtually no budget to speak of, but Ranieri insisted these expenses were worth it and he spent much of his time finding the cheapest way to make them happen. And sometimes he opened his own wallet to do it.'

'On one occasion the entire team kit went missing,' says Tarantino. 'We tried to order new kit, but we were too much in debt. The supplier demanded cash up front and we simply did not have it. So Ranieri went and paid to kit out the whole team himself.'

Ranieri had a decent career as a professional footballer, but we're still talking about a guy in his mid-thirties who had spent only six seasons in the top flight, five of them at relatively small clubs like Catanzaro, and one at a bigger club, Roma, albeit on a youth team player's wages. And back then footballers were nowhere near as wealthy as they are today.

Ranieri got creative. He noticed that the team's pitch in Pozzuoli was extremely narrow – in fact today it would probably not receive a licence. He tried to turn this into an advantage by working on set-pieces, particularly throw-ins, designing specific training routines to improve the distance and force of throws. He wanted a big strong target-man but, given the club's lack of money, struggled to find one and instead played the reserve goalkeeper up front on several occasions, although eventually he did sign a giant of a centre forward, Carlo Torregrossa – whose surname appropriately means big tower.

The side was direct, no-frills and practical. If Vigor Lamezia had played some pretty football, this team was all about aggression and route one. Given his resources and the conditions – Puteolana played on a dirt pitch, which meant that when it rained it turned into mud, and when it was dry it was dusty and hard, the ball taking huge unpredictable bounces – he felt it was the only way they'd have a prayer of staying up.

The club's supporters got into it though. It was the polar opposite of what Maradona and co. were serving up a few miles away, but it was fun, even if the team spent the first half of the season in and around the relegation zone. At that level every game was a battle, with rowdy, unforgiving fans. After an away win against Nocerina, for example, the home supporters ran amok and laid siege to the visiting dressing room. Ranieri and his players stayed locked inside until enough police arrived to clear the stadium, a full eight hours after the final whistle.

Rather than blaming Ranieri for the inconsistent results, the fans' anger was directed at the club owner and the players. Tarantino remembers a January game away to Francavilla. 'We lost 1–0, and on the way back our supporters ambushed us in the countryside. They stopped our bus and demanded that the players file out so they could face the fans' wrath. We were all terrified. But Ranieri took charge. He was the only one who got off the bus to talk to the supporters. He said he – and not the supporters – would be the one addressing the players. And if they had something to say, they should say it to him. It calmed them down, and we were able to go home.'

The owner saw things differently. After the Francavilla defeat Ranieri was replaced, despite Tarantino's objections. The new manager was soon sacked and a third arrived, but results continued to deteriorate. Then the club president stepped down. With him gone, Ranieri was recalled for the final four games of the season. They finished second-bottom and were relegated.

Two full seasons had passed since Ranieri had made his managerial debut and he had scarcely lasted – albeit for vastly different reasons – more than half a year in each job. Happily for him there were folks who do not simply judge a manager on where his team finishes in the table. People who asked around found out the context of each job and listened to the views of others who were better informed. Ranieri was beginning to build a reputation as somebody who was different, who was willing to work hard with limited resources, who understood the game and could relay his ideas to his players.

But, ultimately, seeing is believing. Today a club seeking a manager only needs a smartphone and a subscription to a service like Wyscout to call up and watch just about any professional game anywhere in the world. And they can do it in seconds. In the late 1980s, other than the very top games, you had to be there in person if you wanted to know what a manager's brand of football was like.

In that sense Ranieri was hugely fortunate. His next employer had seen his work up close the previous year and walked away impressed. Carmine Longo was the director of football at Cagliari, the biggest team on the Mediterranean island of Sardinia, and while scouting a player he had watched Ranieri's Vigor Lamezia side. He was right by the pitch and eavesdropped on Ranieri during the warm-up and throughout the match. He made a mental note: *That guy who used to play for Catanzaro . . . Looks like he can coach a bit too.*

As luck would have it, the following season Cagliari would be in the same division as Ranieri's Campania Puteolana. Cagliari had just been relegated from Serie B despite going all the way to the Coppa Italia semi-final the year before. In the fixture against Puteolana, Cagliari had been firm favourites but were comprehensively outplayed and lost. Longo's impression from a year earlier had been vindicated: this guy knew what he was doing. Longo's boss, Cagliari president Tonino Orru, was at that match too.

They beat us and played very well, of course, but I was struck by something he said before the match. There was a portion of their pitch that was cordoned off, grass had just been laid and I guess the groundskeeper wanted the players to stay off it until kick-off. Our guys went out for the warm-up and paid no attention to it. They started to kick the ball around wherever they pleased. Puteolana's players got angry; they saw it as a sign of disrespect.

I'll never forget what Ranieri said to his men: 'Go ahead and let them do as they please . . . they obviously don't realise where they are and think they're still in Serie B. Let's let them think that and hope they don't wake up.'

It was a way to at once defuse the situation and fire up his men even further. The fact that Longo and Orru independently reached the same conclusion was a sign: Ranieri was their man. From Ranieri's perspective, Cagliari was a huge leap forward and a massive opportunity. Yes, it was still the third division, but lower leagues often include teams punching above their weight (way above their weight in the case of Puteolana) as well as fallen giants.

Cagliari had spent most of its post-war history in Serie B, with spells in Serie A as recently as seven years previously, in 1982–83. And, almost twenty years earlier, they had actually won the Serie A title, the Scudetto, in a feat which in some ways mirrors that of Leicester many years later. It's not a perfect parallel: Cagliari were a provincial club, but the team had finished in the top six three times in the previous five seasons and had been runners-up the season before. And up front they had the legendary Gigi Riva, who to this day is the all-time leading goalscorer in the history of the Italian national team.

Leicester's feat is in a league of its own, but Riva's Cagliari were also a small provincial team sticking it to the big guns who won year after year. And on the island many spoke of the triumph as if it had occurred only the previous season, rather than eighteen years earlier. The underdog spirit lived on, even in the third division.

Of all the clubs where Ranieri worked, Cagliari represented perhaps his smoothest start. It was an instant fit, straight from preseason training. Everything felt right. One day his wife Rosanna rang him up to ask how things were going. 'I think they've given me a Ferrari,' Ranieri told her. 'Honestly, if I don't mess this up, we're going straight back to Serie B.'

Cagliari held their preseason training camp in Roccaporena, a remote mountain village in Umbria, known as the birthplace of St Rita of Cascia. Though maybe 'village' is a generous term: its permanent population is seventy-one. There was a hotel, a restaurant, some houses hanging on to the mountaintop and not much else for miles around. Ranieri was instantly smitten. It was the perfect place to work and train and prepare for the new season. Religion also played a part. In the Roman Catholic faith people sometimes devote themselves to a particular saint, usually someone whose life inspires them or who is associated with causes close to their heart. St Rita struck a chord with Ranieri, and he became devoted to her. Given events in Leicester twenty-seven years later, it may not be a surprise to learn that she also happens to be patron saint of the impossible. From that summer on, whenever he could, Ranieri would bring whichever team he was managing to Roccaporena. His connection to the place was strong, and he felt he could do his best work there.

Shortly after joining Cagliari, Ranieri would meet a man

named Angelo Antenucci, who in many ways would prove just as crucial to his career. Antenucci had played football to amateur level before becoming a scout. Scouting meant long hours and even longer road trips, but it did not deter him; he was in love with the game. He worked as an advance scout for Cagliari, which meant travelling around Italy to study the team's next opponents. Again, today you can bring up any side on Wyscout, and in any case plenty of matches are televised. Back then though, advance scouts were essential. There were no dedicated sports channels on television and, had they existed, they certainly would not have been showing third-division games. At best you got a few minutes of highlights a week, and that was about all.

Antenucci was good at what he did and made no secret of the fact that he harboured managerial ambitions, but Longo had stopped him in his tracks. 'Look, you're never going to be a manager, so forget about it,' he told him. 'But who knows? Maybe one day you can help a manager do their job.'

Ranieri had taken the Cagliari job without people of his own and was tasked with assembling a staff. Part of this meant evaluating those who were already at the club, and so he asked for some scouting reports to see how perceptive the scouts were. Longo gave him one that Antenucci had prepared on Ranieri's own Campania Puteolana the previous season.

My goodness, thought Ranieri after reading Antenucci's report. *This guy knows more about Puteolana than I do . . . and I managed the team!* Antenucci became Ranieri's assistant, and it would be a relationship that would last seventeen years.

'I had never met him before; I spoke to him for the very first time at Roccaporena,' Antenucci says.

The first week alongside Ranieri was somewhat bumpy.

'I helped out in training, but Claudio had been used to working on his own. Before every session he would always speak to the players on his own for a good ten minutes. None of the assistants were a part of that; it was just him and the squad. I respected that, obviously. It was his right.

'One day, after about a week of preseason, he asked me what I thought of the team and the work we had been doing. I told him that we'd be back in Serie A in three seasons. Ranieri smiled. And from that day on I was alongside him for every pre-training talk. We were on exactly the same wavelength.'

Cagliari were a team on a tight budget. The coaching staff was really just Ranieri and Antenucci, plus a man named Sergio Bertola. He was the goalkeeping coach, but he also had a day job, working as a licensed optician. Ranieri devoured all the literature he could on every aspect of the game. Since there was no fitness coach, strength coach or nutritionist, he felt he had to learn as much as possible about all the specialisms.

'We both loved the process of learning and experimenting,' says Antenucci. 'The big thing at the time was combining fitness with tactics in the same session, so we tried to invent new routines that would do that. We also made some mistakes that would frankly horrify any self-respecting fitness coach, like making the players do a bunch of uphill shuttle runs and then sending them on a long, slow run. But the environment was just right. The players believed in Claudio and in everything he asked them to do.'

Cagliari played attractive, sophisticated football. Ranieri would often change systems during the course of a game to keep the opposition off balance and above all valued the speed and efficiency of transitions. Halfway through the campaign there was little doubt that they would get promoted. They seemed to be getting better week on week.

'I remember asking him at the midpoint of the season whether, if we won promotion, he'd have me back,' Antenucci says. 'Claudio looked at me as if it was a silly question. "Of course you're coming back," he said.' The club won the league easily to return to Serie B, and they also won the Serie C Coppa Italia, a competition reserved for teams from below the second flight, akin to the Football League Trophy in England.

Before the 1989–90 season even began, Ranieri faced something of a coming-out party in the Coppa Italia. Cagliari took on the mighty Juventus in the first round, and for many of the club's players – and Ranieri – it was the first time they had taken on opposition of that calibre. 'For us this game means we've reached the finish line,' he told the squad before the match. 'Now go out there and play with joy.'

A more macho manager might have pounded his chest and talked about how this was only the beginning and they could soon expect to face the likes of Juventus every week, but had Ranieri said that, he might have lost credibility. The players knew what he meant: it was incredible that they had got this far. They were fully prepared for the game and shouldn't feel any pressure. All they had to do was go out and execute what they had learned. And do it with a smile. Nobody was going to judge them on this result.

In fact, Ranieri put Dino Zoff's Juve to the sword. Cagliari were first to most balls; they broke down the Juventus attacks; they were always ready, always working for each other. Only a late, late goal from Alexander Zavarov gave Juventus the victory deep into extra time, with penalties just a few minutes away. 'We deserved more out of that game,' Ranieri would say afterwards. Most agreed. But more important than the result, Ranieri showed he could compete with the best.

Fans and local media expected a transition season in Serie B, maybe settling in the top half of the table, with the real assault on Serie A coming the following season. Instead, after a bumpy start – one point from three games – Cagliari cruised through the rest of the campaign and eventually finished third, sealing promotion with three games to spare. Promotion in successive seasons is not a bad record for any manager, but it was clear to Ranieri that if they were to avoid immediate relegation the squad needed to be strengthened. After all, the bulk of the side was made up of players who had won the third-division title two years earlier. And at the time Serie A was the best league in the world.

A massive boost came with the signing of Gianfranco Matteoli from Inter Milan. Two seasons earlier he had been the midfield playmaker for Giovanni Trapattoni's Inter side, which had not only won the Scudetto but had dominated the league thanks to a star-studded side that included the likes of Walter Zenga, Beppe Bergomi, Andy Brehme, Lothar Matthäus, Ramón Diaz and the league's top goalscorer, Aldo Serena. Matteoli was a native Sardinian – albeit from Nuoro at the other end of the island – and like many had emigrated to the mainland (what Sardinians call the continent) to further his career. He jumped at the chance to return home.

Promotion meant that Cagliari would now be allowed to sign foreign players, up to three in total. It was important to the club that at least one of them was younger with the potential to improve and be sold on at a profit. They had been tracking a Uruguayan centre forward, Daniel Fonseca, for some time. He was still only twenty and had made just fourteen appearances for Montevideo's Nacional, showing lots of potential but also a certain rawness. Nevertheless, he was included in the Uruguay squad for the 1990 World Cup.

Ranieri had seen video of him and loved what he saw. Antenucci was dispatched to Stuttgart, where Uruguay had set up their training camp ahead of the tournament. He was impressed with Fonseca's blend of speed and power, but the centre forward wasn't the only Uruguayan to stand out. A hard-nosed defensive midfielder, José Herrera, also caught his eye. A few days later Longo, Ranieri and Antenucci went to Brescia, where Uruguay were playing a friendly. Their impressions of Herrera and Fonseca were only reinforced by what they saw but Ranieri and his colleagues knew they needed to make an impression themselves. While Serie A was a wealthy top league they were, after all, Cagliari. Not exactly a glamour club.

They went to the Uruguay team hotel and blagged their way into the room where the players were eating dinner. Off to one side was a man named Paco Casal, one of the most powerful agents in the world, a man who had a virtual monopoly on Uruguayan footballers in particular. They chatted about Fonseca and Herrera, about how the former could be the cover boy of Ranieri's new Cagliari and the latter its beating heart. Casal, like all good agents, insisted that he was overwhelmed with requests for his players, that there were plenty of clubs ahead of them in the queue.

Then a tall, svelte, almost regal-looking figure approached the table. The Cagliari contingent recognised him immediately and fell silent. This was Enzo Francescoli, arguably the greatest Uruguayan footballer since the 1950s, a man who would be included in both *World Soccer*'s list of the 100 Greatest Players of all time and Pelé's equivalent FIFA 100. At the time he was playing his football at Olympique Marseille, and among those who idolised him and sought to emulate him was a very young Zinedine Zidane.

Francescoli put his hand on Casal's shoulder and said, 'Paco, just to remind you, I want to play in Italy.'

Before Casal could answer, Ranieri blurted out, 'Great! Come and play for us!'

Francescoli smiled. He clearly had no idea who they were. If he had, he might have chuckled politely and then gone into another room to guffaw. He was the man they called El Principe – the Prince. He was at a wealthy, ambitious French club. Sure, he wanted to come to Italy, but he was thinking more Juventus or Milan or Inter. Cagliari? Where was that?

Nevertheless he nodded and said, 'OK.'

Obviously there was a lot left to do on the deal. Casal was a wily negotiator, but Longo was no mug either. Cagliari pushed for all three in one go, figuring they'd help each other settle in Italy and, crucially, hoping a package deal would give them more leverage with Casal. In other words, it was all or nothing. With hindsight, this was stunningly shrewd.

Herrera was an unheralded guy who, despite being a Uruguayan international, played his football at Figueres in the Spanish second division. Given that most countries had limits on the number of foreigners and nobody had shown much interest in him, Casal knew that if he wanted to place him in Serie A and get himself the commission that went with it, Cagliari was really his only option. But to do that he had to deliver the other two. Fonseca was just a kid. There had been interest from other clubs, sure, but he would go anywhere Casal told him to. To a twenty-year-old from Uruguay back then, unless you were talking Juventus or Milan, all the other Serie A clubs were much of a muchness. What would influence him was what Francescoli did, because he was eight years older and an idol to a whole generation of Uruguayan players.

So El Principe was the key. Casal had the incentive to deliver him in the form of Herrera and, if he could, Fonseca would easily follow. Francescoli would turn twenty-nine later that year. He had won silverware in Argentina and France, where he had just been voted the best foreigner in the league, but after four seasons in Ligue 1, he wasn't averse to moving on. Cagliari may not have been an ideal destination, but it was by the sea, the weather was good and he'd be playing in the best league in the world.

Casal delivered his package deal, and Ranieri had his three Uruguayans. The media laughed, joking that to get Francescoli, Cagliari had had to agree to take two other no-names. 'Buy one, get two free!' They were proved wrong . . . eventually.

Cagliari had a very rough start to the season. They won away to Napoli in the second week and then did not record another victory until 30 December. Of the three, only Herrera, whose football was simpler, settled quickly on the pitch, mainly because his job was to run and tackle and not much more. Francescoli struggled with the defensive intensity and the tactical nous of Serie A football. Every time he got the ball, there were two defenders on him, ready to either dispossess or foul him. Fonseca was homesick. Word got around that he loved to sleep and that he'd spend twelve, fourteen hours a day in bed.

One day Francescoli sat down with Ranieri and said, 'Look, I know I'm performing at maybe 20 per cent of my potential right now. And not just me, but Fonseca too. If you want to drop me, go ahead and do it. Right now I don't merit a place in the line-up.'

Ranieri got up in his face and said, 'As long as I'm the manager of Cagliari, you'll be my number ten.' He had a similar conversation with Fonseca.

'I consider Ranieri to be my second father, my footballing father,' Fonseca says. 'I just wasn't used to the ways of Italian football, the tactics, the marking. At one point I went sixteen games without scoring. And he kept faith with me, telling me time and again that I would be the difference-maker that year, that I would score the goals that kept us up. And that's what happened. I owe it all to him.'

Ranieri, despite the early poor results, built his side's attack around the two Uruguayans: Fonseca the finisher and Francescoli the creator. It was lightning-quick transitions, it was hard, fast, aggressive running. 'You could say I was the Jamie Vardy of Cagliari,' Fonseca says. Which would make Francescoli its Riyad Mahrez.

Results began to change at the turn of the year, and everything began to click. Cagliari lost just twice in the second half of the season, and Fonseca scored eight goals, all from open play – not bad for a raw twenty-one-year-old. And Francescoli began delivering the magic and assists his pedigree had suggested he would. For Ranieri it was both triumph and vindication. Had Cagliari's first half of the season matched their second in terms of points, they would have ended the season in fifth place. Instead, they were fourteenth, still comfortably safe from relegation.

The Italian game was changing. Ranieri was part of a new breed of emerging managers. And the big clubs had taken notice.

5. Moving on from Maradona

Ranieri had kept in contact with his old pal from his Roma days, Giorgio Perinetti. They were the same age, born in 1951. The difference was that while Ranieri played football, Perinetti consumed everything around it.

'I was actually at university at the time and I managed to blag a job at Roma, basically doing all the little things that needed to be done around the youth teams and the reserve teams,' he recalls. 'Whether it was accompanying the team on away trips, booking travel, helping the kit man out. I just wanted to be around football.'

Perinetti had built a huge network of contacts, which he'd eventually parlay into a scouting job at Napoli. It was he who had connected Ranieri with Campania Puteolana after his stint at Vigor Lamezia. Just as Ranieri's career had taken off, so too had Perinetti's. At just forty years of age he had become director of football at Napoli.

As if the job wasn't daunting enough, there were two massive tasks ahead. He needed to find a new manager to replace Alberto Bigon, the man who had delivered the club's second league title in 1989–90, just twelve months earlier. The president, Corrado Ferlaino, a colourful and often uneven character, blamed Bigon for the club's subsequent eighth-place finish. But replacing Bigon paled in comparison with the other massive hole Perinetti had to plug. Diego Armando Maradona, at the time widely considered to be the greatest player who had ever lived (alongside Pelé) was gone. He had tested positive for cocaine the previous March, and FIFA had imposed a fifteen-month ban.

Maradona wasn't just far and away the best player in the world at the time; he had guided Napoli to their only two Italian championships, turning the long-established hegemony of the northern clubs – Inter, AC Milan and Juventus – on its head. His status among some Neapolitans bordered on that of a deity. There were murals and shrines dedicated to him in the alleyways and backstreets of the inner city. It's hard to overstate the influence he wielded and the depression into which Naples was plunged when he fell from grace.

Ferlaino needed to re-energise the city. He said he was ready to spend to prove that Napoli was great and would continue to be great even without Maradona, so he told Perinetti to get him the best number ten playing outside Italy at the time, whoever that might be. An enquiry was made for Dejan Savićević of the Red Star Belgrade team that had won the European Cup a month earlier. Napoli were rebuffed. Perinetti later learned that Milan had already been in contact with Red Star; Savićević would join them a year later for a fee of £4 million.

'We were getting nowhere, so I focused on getting the right manager instead,' Perinetti says.

Arrigo Sacchi had just left Milan after winning two European Cups and playing some outstanding football. 'We made a huge offer or, more aptly, a stratospheric offer,' says

Perinetti. 'But he said the only side other than Milan he could imagine coaching at this stage of his career was Italy. Which, of course, he eventually did. So eventually I convinced Ferlaino: if we can't get the number one, let's not go for the number two or number three . . . let's go instead for the young manager who can one day become the number one. Let's go for Claudio Ranieri.'

Ferlaino wasn't convinced but nevertheless agreed to meet Ranieri. And Ranieri pulled off one of his interview masterclasses. He was fully prepared on Napoli's situation (Perinetti may have had something to do with that) and sold Ferlaino on his basic argument: Maradona is the greatest and cannot be replaced, so don't even try. 'Any big star that comes in will suffer compared to Maradona,' he told Ferlaino, according to Perinetti, 'so let's instead rebrand. Let's push youth. You have a very talented young player with similar characteristics, this Gianfranco Zola boy. Push him instead.'

The plan was brilliant. By backing Zola, Ferlaino would gain kudos through giving youth a chance. What's more, the Napoli fans had come to adore the little Sardinian striker and were bound to be patient with him. Far more so than with another pricey superstar, who would be compared to Maradona and come up short from day one.

If it worked, Ferlaino would look like a genius; if it didn't, they could always push the boat out for a superstar later. Or, since Maradona would be back from suspension in September 1992, when he'd still be only thirty-two, they could wait for him and spin a tale of the fatherly club offering the wayward son a second chance.

Either way, Ferlaino would be saving himself a whole load of money.

The Napoli president said yes to both the plan and Ranieri, and his new manager set to work alongside Antenucci. This time Ranieri was able to bring in his own goalkeeping coach and turned to his old teammate and close friend Giorgio Pellizzaro.

Zola only found out later that he had been unwittingly instrumental in getting Ranieri the Napoli job. Just as he would be key, years later, during his time at Chelsea. 'I guess I was a first-team player, but I was still young,' he says. 'I can see the logic, but it was a tremendous leap of faith in my ability. I can only be grateful for the trust shown in me.'

Preseason wasn't great. After a defeat in a friendly at Pescara, Ranieri's mobile rang. It was one of those first-generation cell phones, the size of a brick and weighing about as much. Ferlaino was on the other end, and he read Ranieri the riot act. He wanted to know exactly what had gone wrong and how Ranieri was going to fix it. And he also had plenty of advice.

'Mr President, listen to me,' Ranieri said, slipping into bad Claudio mode. 'You have two options here. You can either be quiet and let me work. Or you can sack me.' With that he switched off his phone, probably wishing he had never got it or at least had not given Ferlaino the number. But results soon picked up.

Zola was no Maradona but that season he formed a very impressive partnership with Antonio Careca, the Brazilian superstar, and won his first caps for Italy. In midfield another Brazilian, Alemão, teamed up with Fernando De Napoli, an Italian international. At the back Ciro Ferrara played alongside a key new signing, Laurent Blanc. 'He wasn't really a defender; he only played at the back,' says Zola. 'Blanc was a midfielder masquerading as a defender. He could pass the ball with millimetric precision, put it anywhere on the pitch. As a forward, I only needed to run into space, and I knew he'd find me without me needing to break stride.'

Blanc was an atypical player. Tall and strong, he was exceptional in the air and so naturally played in central defence, but his range of passing, especially over longer distances, was sublime. His only flaw was a maddening lack of pace. Still, Ranieri saw him as the perfect man to lead the transition, or counter-attack. And he was proved right. Zola explains:

> The main difference between the football we played under Ranieri and that under his predecessor, Bigon, is that before we were all about balance. And by that I mean not conceding, and giving our superstars, Maradona and Careca, the freedom to create and invent as they pleased. With Claudio, it was much more orchestrated: we were much more a team, everyone had to contribute, everyone knew their job. And we had more variety too, now that we had a weapon like Blanc at the back. We looked to impose our game on the opponent, rather than reacting to them and exploiting their weaknesses.

Defensively there were changes too. Ranieri was the first Napoli manager to play zonal defence, though as Ferrara explains, the system was more of a hybrid. 'Let's call it a mixed zone,' he says. 'But it was definitely different and we had to adapt. We had only ever played man to man. Suddenly we had to adapt and to do it with a sweeper like Blanc. Who of course was an outstanding player but also someone radically different from the sweepers we were used to. He didn't sweep; he passed the ball out of the back.'

Ferrara, who Ranieri had named club captain in Maradona's absence, was one of those who found it most difficult to adjust. So much so that at the end of the season he asked to talk to Ranieri. 'I would like to apologise because this season I did not play as well as I could have,' Ferrara said. Ranieri was moved; not many players would have had the humility to do this. Yet in many ways this was Ranieri's doing. He had continued to trust Ferrara throughout his poor performances, confident that he would turn it around. And it got to the point that the player himself began to feel guilty that he could not live up to his manager's trust.

Napoli would finish the season in fourth place and earn plaudits for their style of play. This was a team on the rise, especially if Ferrara regained his form again. Ranieri was proud of the job his men had done, but he was also increasingly annoyed by Ferlaino, who had given up trying to influence Ranieri's team selection but had taken to lecturing him about the importance of putting pressure on the referee. According to the Napoli president, this was a job that started a few days before the match with public remarks of the 'Let's hope so-and-so has a good game, because we often end up with decisions that go against us when he's officiating' variety. It was meant to continue pre-match, with some friendly banter and persuasive chat before kick-off, to culminate, during the game itself, with some choice words from pitchside.

Ranieri had no time for this. Worrying about referees was not his style. It never was and never would be. Indeed, throughout his career he very rarely criticised the officiating post-match. 'Mr President, if you think talking about the referee and talking to the referee is so important, it's probably something you should do in person rather than sending me,' he said. 'I'm sure it would have a lot more authority and influence if it came straight from you.'

The relationship was uneasy, but, as long as Napoli did well, Ferlaino was manageable. He did insist on selling Blanc that summer, arguing that he was 'too modern'. In fact, Ranieri felt that he had been an important part of Napoli's success, but Blanc had been pilloried for some of his defensive lapses by the media, and the club felt they had to cut him loose. Years later, Ranieri would confess that if he had to do it again, he would have fought tooth and nail to keep Blanc. But as a forty-one-year-old manager with just two years of top-flight experience, he did not have the clout to do that. 'Blanc scored seven goals for us. He was so important every time we won the ball back in our own half,' recalls Zola. 'Sure, you lost something defensively when he was on the pitch, because of his lack of mobility. But it got to the point where that's all anyone talked about, rather than appreciating his other qualities.'

With Alemão also departing, Jonas Thern arrived from Benfica. The club insisted that the final signing should be a big-name striker. This meant going back to a front three, with the newcomer joining Zola and Careca.

George Weah was Perinetti's choice, but for a number of reasons Ranieri was never able to watch him live. And so he switched his attention to Dennis Bergkamp, then at Ajax, and Napoli actually agreed personal terms as well as a fee with the Dutch club. The future Arsenal legend however asked for a few days to think about it. He had just turned twenty-three and wasn't sure he was ready for the jump from a club like Ajax to the cauldron that is Naples. And so the club veered towards a man Ranieri knew well, Daniel Fonseca, who had done so well for him at Cagliari.

The idea was that we'd be even more attacking, with myself, Careca and Fonseca. Unfortunately it didn't quite work out that way,' recalls Zola. 'It affected us and our balance, and we lost something.' Early on though Fonseca looked like the most inspired of choices. Napoli travelled to face Valencia in the UEFA Cup and beat them 5–1, with the Uruguayan scoring all five goals.

'It was about as perfect a game as we had at Napoli under Claudio,' recalls Antenucci. 'He went to the next level. The speed of our attacks was breathtaking – we'd win the ball in midfield and with two or three touches Fonseca was clear to shoot on goal at the other end.' But results in Serie A were poor, in part because of a tough early schedule. Napoli lost at home to Inter and Juventus, before being defeated 5–1 at home by AC Milan.

'I remember that game all too well,' says Zola. 'Marco van Basten scored four goals. I still don't know what went wrong. I'd love to talk about it with Ranieri one day. Because we, the players, believed in what we were doing. At least, that's the perception I had. I was only twenty-four, but I had been there a while and I think I had a good sense of my teammates and their mindset.'

The irony is that Ranieri may well have been sacked even if they had beaten Milan. And it was all over something extraordinarily stupid: the players' post-match menu. Napoli had drawn 0–0 away to Paris Saint-Germain and were knocked out of the UEFA Cup, having lost at home, 2–0, in the first leg. The squad were dining together when word got to them that Ferlaino was not happy with what the players were being served. He said they were being spoiled. (Maybe he thought gruel with maggots would have been an appropriate menu.) The team did not take it well, especially Massimo Mauro, Ranieri's former teammate from his Catanzaro days and a bit of a hothead. In fact, he became very angry and answered Ferlaino in kind.

A few hours later Ranieri received a call from Ferlaino. 'If Mauro gets on the pitch on Sunday against Milan, you'll be fired the very next day,' he warned.

'Mr President, I am the manager of Napoli and I pick the starting eleven based on the available squad,' Ranieri replied. 'If a player is in my squad, he's eligible to be picked. And I decide who gets picked. If he's not in the squad, I won't pick him.' This was a clear challenge to Ferlaino. If he wanted to exact revenge on Mauro, he'd have to do it himself by suspending him. Ranieri was not going to be doing his dirty work for him.

Sure enough, Sunday rolled around and Mauro was in the starting line-up. After the game Ranieri was duly sacked. They had taken just six of a possible eighteen points from nine games in Serie A and were out of the UEFA Cup.

'It was a poor start, but we were all sorry to see him go,' says Zola. 'I think over time we would have improved.' Ranieri was disappointed, but he was especially hurt by the rumours circulated by certain individuals that he had been disloyal to Napoli and had been plotting a move to Roma.

Bad Claudio soon showed up.

'These are lies and they really hurt me,' he said. 'I don't have any sort of deal to join Roma. Nor did I ever have one. I knew Napoli would be a difficult club to manage, with many challenges, but I was convinced that, working together, we would overcome them. It's normal, given our poor results, that the blame would fall on the manager. But the Napoli fans always stood by me. I can't ask for any more than that.'

And then Good Claudio returned.

'You expect me to criticise the club, but I'm not going to do that either,' he added. 'I can understand why they did what they did. It's customary in football. Things go poorly and you try to shock the system by replacing the manager. I'm not the first manager to be sacked and I won't be the last. This experience helped me grow. I made some mistakes, but they were my mistakes; I can't be blaming anyone else, least of all the players.'

He took time off, travelled around Europe watching football, and returned to the seaside house in Copanello. He wasn't out of work for long, his next appointment was as much down to chance as anything else.

6. 35,000 Strong at 3 a.m.

Until the 1993–94 season, when Serie A began playing one game on Sunday night as part of a new pay-TV deal, there was no live league football on Italian TV. So some of those in and around football – managers, agents, club officials – would go to the offices of RAI, Italian state television, to watch the live feeds of the matches. The coverage would later be cut and edited together for *Novantesimo Minuto*, Italy's long-time football highlights show. 'On more than one occasion I'd bumped into Mario Cecchi Gori, the president of Fiorentina,' recalls Ranieri. 'He'd insist on watching the games with me and we got along well.'

Cecchi Gori was a film producer and distributor and a rabid Fiorentina fan. He had poured money into the club and had made it his mission to restore them to greatness before he died, yet 1992–93 had been a horrible year for the Florence club. Despite the presence of the hard-nosed German international Stefan Effenberg, gifted Dane Brian Laudrup, fresh from victory at Euro 92, and the legendary Gabriel Batistuta up front, they were relegated to Serie B for the first time in fifty-five years.

'It wasn't just about restoring Fiorentina to Serie A,' says Oreste Cinquini, the club's director of football at the time. 'It was about restoring the image of the club and building for the future. You needed somebody with a special sensitivity as well as a sense of culture and history. That man was Ranieri.'

Ranieri was eager to get back to work. He took the club to Roccaporena – where else? – for preseason training. The first challenge was persuading some of the players under contract to stick around despite the drop. 'I went to see them after a week of preseason and I was shocked,' says Cinquini. 'There were players who would have cut off their arms to get out of Florence and avoid Serie B just a few days earlier. Now they were all committed and on board with Ranieri. He won them over with three simple words: humility, respect and work.'

It seems like a corny message, but as with anything of this sort it's all in the delivery. Ranieri made it believable. 'He excelled at making everything clear and explaining things directly,' says Stefano Pioli, a defender in the team who would go on to become a successful manager. 'Before every session he'd pin the day's training plan to the dressing-room wall. It clearly explained all the objectives and what we were trying to achieve with each exercise. He opened our minds. And he was exceptional at creating a team, at man-management, at giving players confidence. He told us that we would win Serie B. And we believed him.'

The fans, though not unhappy with Ranieri, were still furious about relegation and were very transparent in blaming the players. During training camp a group of supporters broke into the team hotel and demanded to speak to Effenberg, whom they blamed for not working hard enough to avoid the drop. They did not get their wish, and Ranieri's response was to give Effenberg the captain's armband ahead of Batistuta, who was the moral leader in the dressing room. Ranieri thought it would help make the German – immensely talented but also often undisciplined – take responsibility, make him feel more a part of the team. He also had a soft spot for his ability. Years later he would compare Frank Lampard to Effenberg, his face lighting up as he described in detail the qualities of the two players.

Effenberg did appear to respond, at least in terms of attitude and work ethic. The problem was that his performances were still lacklustre. And he had the habit of going away with his national team and returning late. After the second time it happened Ranieri did not want to hear excuses. Effenberg was stripped of the captaincy.

'Ranieri is not afraid of conflict; he just deals with it differently,' says Cinquini. 'He engages calmly but firmly and directly, without raising his voice or disrespecting anyone.'

That season was an easy romp through the division, with the club finishing top and gaining promotion with several matches to spare. The fans were jubilant; Ranieri was far more matter of fact. 'What's there to celebrate?' he said. 'The fact that we did our duty and achieved our minimum objective, taking this club back to where it belongs?' He meant it too. He knew the real challenge lay ahead.

Mario Cecchi Gori had passed away the previous November, before he could see his beloved Fiorentina back in Serie A. He was replaced by his son, Vittorio, an entirely different character, who years later would be found guilty of fraud in the bankruptcy of Fiorentina, effectively destroying the club his father loved so much. He was also arrested in 2001 on suspicion of money laundering. When police searched his home, they found large quantities of cocaine, which he said was saffron. But in 1994 the younger Cecchi Gori was happy to invest in the club, and Ranieri brought in one of the most naturally gifted players to ever grace Serie A, Manuel Rui Costa.

The Portuguese midfielder arrived from Benfica with a reputation as a hugely skilled and creative passer. On paper he was the perfect complement for Batistuta, the ultimate provider for the ultimate finisher, but to jump to Serie A, especially in those days, was tough. Qualitatively, it was several notches above the Portuguese league. Just as important, Italian teams were far more tactical and better prepared, which meant Rui Costa had less space and time. On top of that, Ranieri favoured speed of execution, especially in transition, and that meant fewer touches for the midfield maestro.

Rui Costa had such confidence in his ability to shield the ball if necessary that he felt he could easily take multiple touches, even in a congested midfield. Ranieri felt otherwise, not least because, given the way Serie A sides counter-attacked then, losing the ball meant giving the opposition a free run at Francesco Toldo's goal. He did not want Rui Costa to hold the ball for more than two seconds; the risks were far too great and they certainly did not outweigh the benefits. There was a far greater chance that the opponent would adjust and cut down the passing lanes than there was that the extra touch would help Rui Costa provide a better assist.

As a result, Rui Costa was substituted on a regular basis during that first season in Florence. This was hard to take for someone who saw himself as a leader and who was willing to take on responsibility. One day in Vicenza he came off with twenty minutes to go, went straight to the dressing room and lost it. He overturned tables, threw kit on to the floor, smashed whatever was smashable.

Both he and Ranieri were stubborn. Antenucci mediated. 'I had to play good cop. I was the guy pre-emptively talking to him after each substitution, to help avoid what happened in Vicenza,' he says. 'Eventually, Rui Costa came round. Claudio was never going to give up on him anyway.' Indeed, Rui Costa, who became Benfica's director of football, and Ranieri are now close. With the boss–employee relationship in the past, both say that, despite the age difference, they are genuine friends.

Ranieri also took on none other than his top goalscorer, Batistuta. Here it wasn't so much a case of Batigol – as he was known – not doing what was asked of him on the pitch. He was adored by the fans, he scored plenty of goals, he was selfless and reliable. The issue was another one. 'Claudio was very direct with him, maybe even a bit hard,' says Antenucci. 'He told him that he had to stop coming and simply doing his job as if he were a factory worker clocking in and out of work. He needed to do more: he needed to take the team by the scruff of the neck and make his voice heard, be a more vocal leader rather than someone who led by example.'

Ranieri believed Batistuta had the personality to do it but sometimes was too respectful of his teammates, especially new ones. He wanted Batistuta to roar, not just to be the first into battle. He had been there longer than most. He wasn't just a player, he was an icon.

Both men responded to Ranieri in the way he wanted. Batistuta went on to score twenty-six goals, becoming Serie A's top goalscorer and equalling the Swede Kurt Hamrin's club record. Rui Costa would provide countless assists. Fiorentina finished tenth, which was a respectable outcome for what was, after all, a newly promoted side.

The team was evolving and showing promise. They were the second-highest scorers in Serie A, but were exceptionally leaky at the back, with the third-worst defence. The media pointed the finger at the new centre back, Márcio Santos, fresh from winning the World Cup with Brazil but also slow to adapt to the Italian game, but Ranieri knew it was more of a collective issue. He also knew this was an issue that needed addressing: good as Fiorentina were going forward, no team could concede nearly two goals a game in Serie A and stick around for long.

In the summer of 1995 Márcio Santos left and Fiorentina got themselves a brand new centre-back partnership: Lorenzo Amoruso, who arrived from Bari, and Foggia's Pasquale Padalino. They were twenty-three and twenty-two respectively, and they weren't the second coming of Franco Baresi, but they were committed, hungry and, crucially, coachable. The club also raided Arsenal to bring in Stefan Schwarz. The Swede was tough, clever and could run all day. In some ways, he was the N'Golo Kanté of that side.

The new additions shored up the team defensively, as did the growth of goalkeeper Francesco Toldo. This would be his third season as Fiorentina's number one, and he had just won the European under-21 championships with Italy. Hand-picked by Pellizzaro and brought to Florence the year the club were in Serie B, he would go on to become one of the best keepers in the world.

Fiorentina finished third that year, level on points with Lazio and behind Juventus and AC Milan. The gap between the two giants and the rest was big, but the Viola were dreaming. Serie A's substantial television deal had benefited what came to be known as the seven sisters – Juventus, Milan, Inter, Roma, Lazio, Parma and Fiorentina – who were among the biggest-spending clubs in the world. It's all relative of course, and of the seven Fiorentina were definitely the baby of the family. And that's why the other great feat of 1995–96 stands out so much. Fiorentina reached the Coppa Italia final, where they took on Atalanta. Their opponents were a mid-table side, and when the Viola only won the first leg 1–0 at home, there were plenty fretting about the return leg. But two second-half goals gave them a 3–0 aggregate win and Ranieri his first top-flight trophy.

It was the club's first piece of silverware in a quarter of a century. They flew back with the trophy that same night, and when they touched down just before three o'clock and switched on their mobiles the same message came through to everyone: 'You need to come to the Franchi. Immediately.'

The Stadio Artemio Franchi was Fiorentina's stadium. Some of the supporters – roughly 10,000 – who could not make the trip had watched the game there on a giant screen set up by a local broadcaster. But the majority of Fiorentina fans had watched on television or in bars and restaurants, pouring out on to the streets at the final whistle. Many, taken by the enthusiasm, had spontaneously started to make their way towards the Stadio Franchi, even though nothing was planned. The police thought maybe a few thousand might show up, joining those who had watched on the mega-screen. They'd let them get their jollies running around the stands and then usher them off home.

There was no question what the team had to do: they had to come straight from the airport, with the trophy, and salute their supporters. So they did. The scene was chaotic. The team walked around, lapping up the cheers but not quite knowing what more to do. After all, nothing was planned, this was entirely spontaneous. Eventually they attempted to have a kickabout, but there were far too many people. Fans streamed on the pitch, and it all ended in a gigantic group hug.

Health and safety officers would not have approved. The forces of law and order weren't thrilled either. But there was no need for concern. Those who were present got to witness an incredible display of civic pride and the genuine bond between a football club and its supporters. It lasted until dawn. But in some ways it lasted for ever.

Expectations were sky-high for the following season, especially after Fiorentina defeated Milan in the Italian Super Cup, the equivalent of the Charity Shield. But that summer also marked the first application of the Bosman Ruling, which lifted all limits on the number of foreign players clubs could employ as long as they were European Union nationals. Other clubs used it as an opportunity to go on spending sprees. Fiorentina largely stayed with what they had, adding the Brazil-born Belgian Luís Oliveira and few others. As it turned out, the squad could – and probably should – have been refreshed further.

Part of the problem was that the Florentine public was so in love with this group of players that they had unrealistic expectations. Batistuta may have been the best centre forward in the world and Rui Costa one of the most gifted playmakers around. But that did not mean that the rest of the players were equally great. And yet such was the supporters' infatuation that many seemed to view them that way. So when Ranieri failed to deliver wins week after week, many came to the conclusion that it must be his fault.

One of the biggest culprits was also the one whose opinion mattered the most: Vittorio Cecchi Gori. He was not a patch on his father – a true gentleman – and his many civil and criminal prosecutions (plus the minor fact that he bankrupted the club to keep his other, failing, interests afloat) are evidence of his flaws. Cecchi Gori Junior was obsessed with a forward named Anselmo Robbiati. Nicknamed Spadino – the little sword – he was indeed a gifted player, but he was also thin and frail, and Ranieri correctly felt that he was not somebody who could regularly play ninety minutes. Certainly not with the work rate he demanded anyway.

To make matters worse, Cecchi Gori's knowledge of the game – unlike his dad's – was limited. Or, more correctly, it was akin to a child's. Maybe it was his show-business background, but he was convinced that the more attacking players you crammed on to the pitch, the better you attacked and the more games you'd win. Robbiati was an attacking player – and one Cecchi Gori was convinced was one of the best around – and therefore Ranieri was a fool not to play him. Actually Robbiati appeared in plenty of games, but Ranieri used him most often as a super-sub/game-changer. Cinquini, Fiorentina's director of football, says:

I used to sit near Cecchi Gori during games. I'd spend half the time watching the games and half the time watching him. Whenever he got up, I'd need to bolt out of my seat too and run to the concourse to intercept him. Because, invariably, he'd be on his way down to the bench to yell at Ranieri for some reason or another, whether it was Robbiati or somebody else. I'd need to stop him on the stairs and try to calm him down or distract him and eventually talk him out of getting involved. This happened game after game. Sometimes I was successful, sometimes I wasn't. And when I wasn't quick enough or persuasive enough or when he was just too angry, it would end up with the manager getting an earful.

At other times Cecchi Gori turned into some kind of demented superfan during matches. At the Stadio Franchi there's a marble balustrade in front of the directors' box. He would often climb on to this so that everyone in the ground could see him and play to the crowd, more often than not giving the players stick or expressing anger or desperation. It got to the point that the home fans in the Curva Fiesole stand would chant, 'Vittorio! To the balustrade!' and not stop until he did just that, at which point he'd get an ovation. It was childish, it was silly, it was helpful to no one and it was maddening that Cecchi Gori never quite realised the supporters weren't laughing *with* him; they were laughing *at* him.

Ranieri has a knack for dealing with authority and strong-willed owners who like to offer 'advice'. From Cecchi Gori to the Sensi family in Rome, from Ferlaino at Napoli to Jesús Gil at Atlético Madrid, from Dmitry Rybolovlev in Monaco to Roman Abramovich at Chelsea, he has a way with billionaires – and those who act like them – but Vittorio Cecchi Gori was wearying and annoying.

That said, Ranieri made a crucial mistake that season in his handling of the media, an area where since then he's been strong. Managers in Serie A are often put through the wringer at press conferences, expected to answer very specific – and sometimes pedantic – tactical questions in great detail. It's a weekly ritual they go through even when they're winning.

Ranieri of course went along with the ritual, but one day the questioning got to him. He was taken to task because his side weren't 'entertaining' enough. This is classic media bait, since for many there is nothing more entertaining than a good result.

'If you want entertainment, go to the theatre,' Ranieri said. 'You'll get plenty of it. In fact, the price of admission virtually guarantees it. But here at Fiorentina we think first and foremost about results.'

This gave his critics ammunition and convinced Cecchi Gori that Ranieri was purely a defensively-minded coach. And it fed into the narrative peddled by a minority – albeit a vocal, visible one – that this was a team of superstars held back by the manager's conservatism. Criticism generally washes off Ranieri's back, but at Fiorentina some of it really hurt. None more than when a banner appeared at the Stadio Franchi's Curva Fiesole which read, RANIERI, HOW ABOUT ONE MORE MAGIC TRICK? DISAPPEAR. This was a play on words – in Italy a top manager is occasionally referred to as a *mago* – magician.

All of this was playing out less than a year after the 35,000-strong 3 a.m. rendezvous in the Stadio Franchi, and while Fiorentina were embarking on their second-greatest European season since winning the Cup Winners' Cup in 1961.

Fiorentina had advanced to the semi-final of the 1996–97 Cup Winners' Cup, overcoming among others Benfica in the quarter-final, with the home leg featuring another epic Cecchi Gori strop at the fact that Robbiati only played the final half hour. Their next opponents were Bobby Robson's Barcelona in the semi-final. Assisting the legendary Geordie manager was an ambitious young Portuguese coach, who would cross Ranieri's path time and again, José Mourinho.

Barca's front three were Luís Figo, Hristo Stoichkov and the original Ronaldo, evidence that, twenty years before MSN (Messi, Suarez, Neymar), the Catalans weren't short on high-end attacking trios. The Fiorentina press pack wondered how Ranieri would deal with them, in particular Figo, who was in the form of his career. Many imagined some kind of uber-complicated defensive arrangement. After the press conference the day before the match, a particularly dogged and obsessive correspondent named Alessandro Rialti decided to follow Ranieri back through the hotel complex and cornered him at the side of the pool.

'OK, come on. Tell me how you're going to stop Figo,' Rialti said. 'Who's going to mark him?'

Ranieri, shocked at Rialti's impertinence, replied, 'No, I'm not telling you.'

'Oh, yes you will!' said Rialti, getting right into Ranieri's face.

'No!'

Rialti, a large, strong man, grabbed Ranieri by the neck and growled, 'Tell me!'

Ranieri did not know whether to punch him in the face or start laughing. The scene was surreal. The journalist, who Ranieri had nicknamed the Walrus, was nearly lifting him off the ground, huffing angrily. There was a very real chance that both men would end up, fully clothed, in the swimming pool. That's when the absurdity of the situation hit Ranieri. He had a lot of respect for Rialti, and the pair remained good friends for many years, but it suddenly struck him just how the pressure of the job and the occasion – a European semi-final against Barcelona at the Camp Nou – had clearly got to him.

All Ranieri could do was laugh and blurt out, 'Pusceddu!'

'*Pusceddu!?* You're crazy! Crazy!' Rialti let go of Ranieri, stunned. Pusceddu was a workmanlike left back who had been in and out of the team all year. This was Fiorentina's biggest game in years and all Ranieri could say was *Pusceddu*?

Ranieri, who had been giggling uncontrollably, gave Rialti a hug. The big journalist seemed genuinely upset.

'Just wait and see . . .' Ranieri whispered to him, before racing off with a twinkle in his eye.

The incident may have had little to do with events the next day, but it did relieve the tension and gave Ranieri a much-needed laugh. And his choice of Pusceddu proved a masterstroke. The unfancied defender played the game of his life as Figo hardly touched the ball. Fiorentina drew 1–1 but deserved more. Robbiati was through on goal, one-on-one with Barca keeper Vítor Baía when the referee, Germany's Bernd Heynemann, took the unusual decision of blowing for full time just before the Fiorentina striker could shoot. He also gave a highly questionable booking to Batistuta, which meant the Argentine striker would miss the return leg.

Without their skipper, Fiorentina could do nothing to stop Barcelona in the return leg. First-half goals from Fernando Couto and Pep Guardiola sealed the win for the Catalans, who would go on to win the competition.

Ranieri doesn't like to dwell on what might have been, but plenty of Fiorentina fans to this day will tell you that if the referee's whistle had not stopped Robbiati's run and if Batistuta had not been given that harsh booking, they would have won the Cup Winners' Cup. And had that occurred, Ranieri's career might have taken an entirely different turn, not least because it would have been very difficult for Cecchi Gori to get rid of him.

By this stage Ranieri knew that the Cup Winners' Cup was

probably his last lifeline, and now it too was gone. Fiorentina were heading for a ninth-place finish but, more than that, the relationship with Cecchi Gori had become unsustainable. At once preachy and self-centred, the Fiorentina president would needle Ranieri, always stopping short of giving him ultimatums. It was death by a thousand cuts. Or a thousand verbal barbs.

At the end of the season Cecchi Gori invited Ranieri and Antenucci to dinner at his palatial villa in Rome. They knew what was coming. It was an odd choice of venue. When you sack somebody, you normally choose a public place, like an office. You don't do it over dinner at your house, unless you're specifically trying to make the night as agonising and awkward as possible. Antenucci recalls Cecchi Gori appearing grumpy and unpleasant from the moment they walked through the door. Small talk was awkward. After the starters he launched into a diatribe about Fiorentina's problems that season and everything Ranieri and his staff had done wrong. His voice was especially harsh that evening and the monologue seemed endless.

'I just stared at my plate in silence; I could not look at him or Claudio,' Antenucci says. It was as if this lecture was part of their punishment.

Ranieri looked his boss in the eye and said, 'Look, I can do everything you want, but I don't agree with a single word that you have said tonight. And so I won't.'

One can only wonder if the evening reached new levels of discomfort for all three men, or perhaps Ranieri's words had the opposite effect. Perhaps they actually released the tension. At any rate, Ranieri would never have to listen to Cecchi Gori ever again.

7. Señor Rinaldi Conquers Valencia

It was the autumn of 1997 and Francisco 'Paco' Roig, the president of Valencia, had a problem. The club viewed themselves as third – behind Real Madrid and Barcelona – in terms of stature in Spain but they had not won any silverware since the late 1970s. Many of their supporters held the team in even higher regard, and that was part of the problem too. And yet they had invested heavily in both managers and players in the 1990s. They had hired European Cup winners (Guus Hiddink) and World Cup winners (Carlos Alberto Parreira), hugely experienced wise men (Luis Aragonés) and romantic young upstarts (Jorge Valdano). On the pitch they had spent big to acquire the likes of Romário, Ariel Ortega, Andoni Zubizarreta and Valeri Karpin.

All to no avail. Valdano had been hired the previous November and talked a great game. The media loved him and his romantic notions of free-flowing attacking football, the game being a metaphor for life and the struggle between the individual and society. Alas, he delivered more in terms of Valencia being pretty to watch than results; he had begun the

1997–98 season with consecutive defeats. In the third match Valencia faced Racing Santander away at El Sardinero stadium.

Roig figured he might have to sack Valdano soon if results did not improve, but he knew it was going to be difficult. Intelligent and articulate, the supporters, despite results, loved him too. Or at least they heeded his calls for patience and his reassurances that 'beautiful football' would eventually yield results. Because good – ultimately – triumphs over evil and beauty over ugliness. (OK, Valdano didn't actually say that last bit, but it's the sort of thing you could hear him saying.)

At the time, post-Bosman, there was no limit to the number of foreign players from the European Union you could have on the pitch, but when it came to non-EU foreigners, the maximum was four. With Valencia 2–1 down twenty minutes into the second half, he ordered the Brazilian striker Marcelinho Carioca on for Fernando Cáceres, a Spanish defender. Nothing unusual there – you're losing and you send on a forward for a defender – except Valencia already had four players who were considered foreign on the pitch: Miroslav Djukić, Ariel Ortega and Goran Vlaović had started the game, and Claudio López had come on as a substitute. With Marcelinho Carioca, that made five.

As the Brazilian jogged on to the pitch, murmurs ran through the stadium. The fans had worked it out: Valencia were breaking the rules. A panicked Valdano tried to remedy the situation by pulling off Djukić, reducing Valencia back to four non-EU players, but he had already made three substitutions, so he could not send on another player to replace him. Valencia had to finish the game with ten men.

Roig had seen enough. People make mistakes, but not something like this. Not something as basic as counting to four. It was the excuse he needed to fire Valdano. Ranieri's name was put forward. Roig, by his own admission, didn't know much about him, but he asked around and called Valencia's Italian fullback, Amedeo Carboni, into his office and asked his opinion.

'What could I say?' Carboni recalls. 'I mean, I had never met the guy so I couldn't say anything bad about him. So I called some friends who knew him and they spoke well of him. But it was an odd situation to be in as a player.'

It was enough for Roig to fly to Rome a few days later to meet Ranieri and once again the Italian charmed a club owner on interview. Roig was smitten, in part because he remembered Ranieri's Napoli team destroying Valencia at the Mestalla 5–1 back in 1992. Ranieri was hesitant at first, but also keen on a new experience. He took the job.

Back in Spain the local media presented him as some kind of savant, but also a hard man, a polar opposite to Valdano. In part, this is what Roig – a fiery man who treated Valencia as if the club were his child – had told the press. The players were too spoiled, too lazy under the dreamy Valdano. They needed a drill sergeant, and that's what Ranieri would bring: discipline and order. That Ranieri could be characterised in this way might surprise those who saw him at Chelsea or Leicester, but that's because plenty goes on at a club to which the media are not privy. Often a narrative is built, a label created, and deviating from it is like doing a U-turn in an aircraft carrier: it takes a heck of an effort.

It should have been obvious at the time that Roig was not much of an expert on Ranieri because when the new manager was unveiled with much pomp and circumstance the president got his name wrong. Not once, not twice, but over and over again.

'Roig gets up and says "Meet Mr Rinaldi,"' remembers Carboni. '"We are lucky to have Mr Rinaldi with us ... Mr

Rinaldi was very successful in Italy ... Soon we will hear from Mr Rinaldi ... Now over to you, Mr Rinaldi ... Does anybody have any questions for Mr. Rinaldi?" I was laughing hysterically.' Roig continued to call him Rinaldi even after members of the media correctly addressed him. As for Ranieri, of course, he was too polite to correct Roig.

Ranieri, joined by the ever-present Antenucci and Pellizzaro, as well as fitness coach Roberto Sassi, tried to learn as much as he could as quickly as he could. What he found was a club that was like a club in the social sense of the word. There were favourites. Some players wouldn't train all week and yet, miraculously, were fit for the weekend. The veterans were treated like gods, the youngsters like interlopers. Ranieri knew he had to make serious changes and maybe even pick a few fights. The first thing that struck him was how unfit many of the players seemed. Many were extremely talented but seemed to think their skills meant that fitness did not matter. Sassi, a tough-minded coach, introduced extra fitness sessions, and often they trained twice a day. The players did not take it well, but maybe it was what they needed.

However, after two weeks Ranieri changed the training regime. He did it at the request of one of the veteran players, legendary goalkeeper Andoni Zubizarreta.'He came to me and said, with great humility, that he missed seeing his kids,' Ranieri said. 'With training in the late afternoon, by the time he got home, they were in bed. But he did it in such a sweet way that I could not say no.' A compromise was reached. Valencia would train just once a day, in the mornings as before, except the sessions would be far more intense.

Valencia were beaten on Ranieri's debut by Real Madrid, and a number of things struck Ranieri. Not only was there a

Left: Grappling with Zico whilst playing for Catania. Zico is one of Brazil's all-time greatest players and was the second most expensive player in the world at the time.

Top right: 'He managed to remain cool no matter what the situation.' Catanzaro teammate Piero Braglia on Ranieri.

Bottom right: Ranieri made six appearances for Roma in the 1973–74 season.

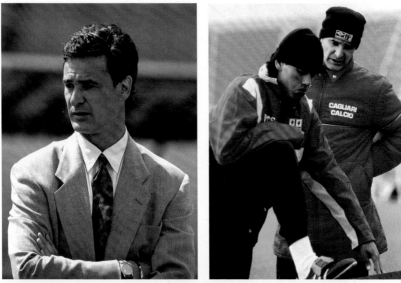

Top left: It was after joining Cagliari in 1988 that Ranieri truly made his name as a coach.

Top right: Crucial to Ranieri's success at Cagliari was the signing of 20-year-old Uruguayan striker, Daniel Fonseca.

Bottom: Ranieri was part of a new breed of emerging managers and the big clubs, including Napoli, had taken notice.

Top left: Stars of the mid-1990s Fiorentina team, Manuel Rui Costa and Gabriel Batistuta.

Top right: 'He opened our minds. And he was exceptional at creating a team, at man management, at giving players confidence.' Fiorentina defender, Stefano Pioli.

Bottom: In 1999, Atlético Madrid was a ticking time bomb.

Top: Premiership calling: in August 2000, Claudio Ranieri was unveiled by owner Ken Bates as the new Chelsea manager.

Bottom left: In his hotel room before his English lessons during the 2000–01 season at Stamford Bridge.

Bottom right: For the second time in his career, Ranieri calls on striker Gianfranco Zola to provide his team's firepower. Zola went on to make 229 appearances for the club.

Top: Talking with Chelsea captain John Terry during a press conference ahead of a 2004 UEFA Champions League match against VfB Stuttgart in Germany.

Bottom: Preparing the Chelsea players to face AS Monaco in the UEFA Champions League semi-finals. Ranieri would later go on to manage the French principality.

Chelsea supporters back Ranieri in 2004. The following year the club would go on to win the Premier League under José Mourinho, with a squad assembled almost entirely by Ranieri.

Left: As Valencia manager, Ranieri holds the UEFA Super Cup after his team defeated Porto in the Stade Louis II in Monte Carlo, Monaco.

Right: In 2008, Juventus' points total was the highest of a newly-promoted side in decades.

Top: Returning home. Of the managers available to Roma there were a few who had comparable charisma and ability, but only one who had three critical qualities: he was Roman, he was a Roma fan and he had played for Roma.

Bottom left: Club legend Francesco Totti has been in the senior Roma squad since 1992 and has played under 17 different managers.

Bottom right: 'I made a mistake when I was manager of Greece. I wanted to look because it is a different job at a club to a national team. I had four matches and for each game I trained the players for just three days. That is 12 days of training. What can I do in just 12 days? I had to rebuild a national team in just 12 days. What could I do? I am not a magician.'

lack of fitness, there was a lack of speed, both physical pace and execution.

'You love possession and keeping the ball and spreading it around,' he told the players. 'But I think you enjoy shooting and scoring goals even more. And I will prove to you that we will shoot more and score more if we take fewer touches and move the ball quicker.'

It was a challenge to the squad.

'We knew we had turn this team inside out,' says Antenucci. 'It had to start with professionalism.'

The two main challenges were Romário and Ortega.

Romário had been the star of the 1994 World Cup and the top scorer in Johan Cruyff's Barcelona 'dream team'. He was one of most lethal finishers in history. Short and squat, he didn't look like much and didn't appear particularly athletic either. He rarely broke out of a gentle jog unless the ball was around, at which point he'd take off, arrive before the defender and usually score. Now thirty-one, his appetite for hard work seemed to have abandoned him. His appetite for other things, however – most notably partying – was alive and well.

Ortega was an Argentine number ten straight out of central casting. Nicknamed El Burrito – the Little Donkey – he was wonderfully skilled and creative, but he too did not like to run. He liked tackling even less and was always demanding the ball. Ortega had been the star signing of that summer, while Romário had been Roig's big investment the year before. Neither was Ranieri's type of player.

'Both of them would come to training, and immediately there'd be something wrong,' says Antenucci. 'One day it would be the leg, the next the muscle, the next the groin. I don't think they ever trained before Thursday or Friday.'

Ranieri took stock and then sprang into action. Discipline was required and it was time for bad Claudio to make his first appearance in Spain. He stormed into the dressing room one day and went straight for Romário. The Brazilian had been talking about how this season was important because he wanted to defend the world title he had won with Brazil at the next World Cup in France.

'You keep talking about the World Cup and being champion again, but how do you expect to get there if you go out at 10 p.m. and don't return home until eight?'

On this point Ranieri had plenty of intelligence. Romário's habits were well known in Valencia. He'd come home at a time when most were going to work, get changed, show up at training and complain of some physical ailment or other. And then he'd take a nap, followed by lunch and then an afternoon siesta. Then, around ten, he'd go out again for dinner, followed by clubbing. And the next day he'd do it all again.

Romário mumbled something about how the national team was his business, not Ranieri's, but his coach's words had clearly stung.

Ortega received similar treatment. In some ways he was even more frustrating for Ranieri. Whereas Romário was thirty-one and had already achieved plenty in his life, Ortega was twenty-three and at a crossroads in his career. He could either kick on and live up to his talent or be led astray by others.

'I had a notebook in which I kept track of each training session – who trained and how they trained,' says Antenucci. 'Ranieri pulled it out and asked Ortega if he wanted to be told, in front of his teammates, the same ones who worked their rear ends off for him, how many training sessions he had missed. And, because I also kept a rudimentary count of various statistical events, he asked him if he wanted to be told how many times he had given the ball away and how many times he had tracked back in each match.'

Embarrassed, Ortega looked at the floor. Ranieri thought that Romário was probably a lost cause but hoped that Ortega could be salvaged. He appealed to his pride. He explained that his teammates worked hard for him but he did not keep his end of the bargain. If Ortega wasn't up for it, he was ready to cut him loose too.

Ranieri would say later,

I went to Roig and I told him we had a big problem and that he would soon need to make a decision. I told him I was going to promote some of the many gifted youngsters we had into the first team and make them starters because they actually followed my instructions and embraced my style of play. That meant that some veteran superstars were not going to be happy.

When that happens, Mr President, and it will, you will have a choice to make. You will either back me and stand with me, or you will need to fire me to keep your stars happy. It will be up to you.

Roig knew what Ranieri meant, but he also asked him to be realistic. 'What do you want me to do?' he said. 'I mean, I can't just go and sell somebody like Romário. Not unless he wants to leave . . .'

Even as he said it, the plan became clear. He was going to back Ranieri's decisions, and Valencia's veteran stars would either shape up or ask to be shipped out. Which is what happened. With the excuse that he wanted to be back in Brazil ahead of the World Cup, Romário was gone by Christmas.

When Ranieri took over, Valencia's first-team squad comprised more than thirty professionals. 'How were we even supposed to train thirty guys at once?' Antenucci says. Throughout those early months, the focus had inevitably fallen on the veterans, and the youngsters were overlooked, but now Ranieri made a point of seeking them out. And what he found was an extremely talented bunch. There were three twenty-year-olds, Juanfran, Miguel Ángel Angulo and Francisco Farinós, as well as a seventeen-year-old Barcelona cast-off, Gerard López, and the hard-running Gaizka Mendieta, who was twenty-three. Plus, a lightning-quick twenty-three-year-old winger/forward had arrived from Argentina over the summer, Claudio 'El Piojo' López. These were players who either languished on the bench or, if they got on the pitch, did the donkey work for the likes of Romário and Ortega. They represented what Ranieri wanted: hard work, tactical intelligence and a cutting edge created by moving the ball quickly and precisely.

This all represented a fundamental shift and took time to implement, but there were enough high points along the way, including a 4–3 win at the Camp Nou against Barcelona to give fans and, crucially, players faith that this might just work. They ended the season in eighth place. Given that Ranieri had taken over after three defeats in the opening three matches, it was not a bad result: winning just two of those games would have taken them into fifth place. What's more, they scored fifty-eight goals, evidence that, despite his defensive reputation, the challenge he laid down to the players – take fewer touches, play faster and follow my instructions and you will shoot and score more – had been vindicated.

'That first season was fantastic. We were all galvanised and felt we were working towards something,' says Carboni.

They had qualified for the Intertoto Cup. Often snubbed by clubs, Ranieri decided they would take this summer competition seriously. It was a route into the UEFA Cup, and he felt the club needed European football. They duly won their first match, but their run in Europe was halted by Liverpool. After a scoreless draw at Anfield, they were leading 1–0 on the return leg with ten minutes to go when Steve McManaman and Patrik Berger scored within minutes of each other. The game would end 2–2, and afterwards Ranieri took full responsibility. He said he was to blame and could not fault the players. It was the sort of gesture that cemented his authority over a young side that was willing to go to war for him.

In Ranieri's second season at Valencia they showed that they could more than hold their own against the big clubs, beating both Real Madrid and Barcelona in La Liga. But they would do even better in the Copa del Rey. In February they took on Louis van Gaal's Barca and defeated them home and away, 3–2 and 4–3. Sandwiched between these results was a Liga victory. In the space of three weeks they had beaten Van Gaal's mighty Barcelona three times, scoring no fewer than eleven goals. So much for Ranieri as a *catenaccio* manager.

López was particularly devastating against Barca. Van Gaal simply could not get to grips with him when he took off in search of space, and Ranieri made sure the midfield moved the ball quickly enough for him to receive it in areas where he could exact damage. Viewing some of López's runs and goals that season looks like watching Jamie Vardy in 2015–16, only wearing black and white.

Real Madrid, the reigning European champions, were up

next. Again Ranieri unleashed López, and the tie was over and done with in the first leg in Valencia, as they romped to an extraordinary 6–0 win. It was humiliating for Real Madrid. Spain had just beaten San Marino 5–0 and the crowd at the Mestalla serenaded Madrid by singing, 'You're just like San Marino!' That season Valencia finished fourth in La Liga, securing a spot in the Champions League, and in fact were just three points away from second place. And the best was yet to come: the Copa del Rey final against Atlético Madrid.

By this stage Ranieri had mixed emotions. Roig had left the club and his replacement, Pedro Cortés, was a different sort of character. Ranieri questioned some of the signings that had been made the previous summer. He was comfortable deferring to the club when it came to transfer decisions, but only as long as he saw a plan and as long as he was consulted. Judging by the signings, he wasn't sure this was the case. His opponents in the final had approached him, promising the earth, sun and stars. He wondered whether he had taken Valencia as far as they could go. Unsure of what the future held at the Mestalla, Ranieri told Atlético that he would be joining them.

But first he was going to beat them. And he did, as Valencia won 3–0 and López stole the show. By this point everyone knew he was leaving, but the general feeling was more one of sadness than betrayal. Ranieri had shown Valencia a different path. He had persuaded them to take it with him and they had been successful. For that the fans were always going to be grateful. 'I don't know why he chose to leave us,' says Carboni. 'Maybe he did not fully believe we could go on to greater things, maybe Atlético gave him a huge contract and wide-ranging powers. I don't know. But he built something special here.'

He left behind a legacy, a philosophy that endured. And

however grateful the fans might have been on the night of the Copa del Rey, their gratitude would increase in the following seasons. The very next year Ranieri's replacement, the Argentine Héctor Cúper, took Valencia all the way to the Champions League final, where they eventually lost to Real Madrid. The season after that they again made it to the final, this time falling to Bayern Munich, albeit only on penalties. In 2001–02, under Rafa Benítez, they won their first Liga title in thirty years. Two seasons after that they would win it again.

Clearly Ranieri would not necessarily have achieved those same results had he stayed, but the bulk of the team, that core of young players he had promoted, was the same. Angulo, Mendieta, Gerard López, Farinós and Juanfran would all go on to earn caps for Spain, and many in Valencia still credit Ranieri with breaking the mould of a team that had become so used to a certain type of football that it had stopped evolving. Without those two seasons of Ranieri, there would never have been the success achieved under Cuper or Benítez.

Still, at the time, it seemed a logical choice, a clear step up. Valencia's economic limits had become obvious to him, whereas Atlético were spending big year after year. This was Madrid, this was the big time, and the squad he inherited at the Estadio Vicente Calderón was very strong on paper. He had a bona fide goalscoring centre forward in Jimmy Floyd Hasselbaink, a refined assist man in Juan Carlos Valerón, the hard-working support striker Kiko and an Argentine international – who would go on to win the Champions League at Real Madrid – Santiago Solari in midfield.

Unfortunately, he had also joined a club that was a ticking time bomb. Atlético's controversial president, Jesús Gil, had a whole range of legal proceedings pending against him. Gil was an old-school hire-and-fire type of owner, a wheeler-dealer who cut corners. He was impatient, colourful and peremptory in his decisions. He famously shut down Atlético's youth academy in 1991, thereby depriving the club of a young striker named Raúl. He ended up travelling across town to Real Madrid, winning three European Cups and going down in history as one of Spain's all-time greatest players.

Gil had spent time in prison in the 1960s after a condominium he had built with cheap materials collapsed, causing the deaths of fifty-eight people. He ran for mayor of Marbella, founded a political party whose acronym was GIL and while mayor got the town to sponsor Atlético, hundreds and hundreds of miles away. At the time of Ranieri's arrival he was being investigated for fraud, false accounting and money laundering, and Atlético were in a dire financial state. To what degree Ranieri was aware of all this is unclear. One person familiar with the situation said that while they had read reports of Gil's difficulties, Ranieri and his assistants figured that, because the wheels of justice moved slowly, it would not affect the team.

Ranieri threw himself into the job. He lived in a hotel and devoted most of his waking hours to trying to fix a team that had started the season badly – with three defeats – and was clearly beginning to suffer from the dysfunctionality upstairs. Every day brought new rumours that Gil would be arrested, that the club accounts would be frozen, that players would not be paid. Nevertheless Gil and his family continually pledged their support to Ranieri and told him he had carte blanche to do as he saw fit. They told him not worry, that Gil was simply the victim of persecution by the Spanish prime minister. But there were at least four different cases pending against him, and the players were clearly distracted to the point that Ranieri could not focus them.

Nevertheless Antenucci maintains there was no excuse for the poor form of the team in the first half of the season. 'Sometimes that's how it is. You try your best; you think you've done everything right and the results simply don't come.'

That December things went from bad to worse. Gil was arrested and imprisoned, with a judge appointed to administer the club. His name was Luis Manuel Rubí, and he had a reputation for being fastidious and meticulous. He was there to represent the state and the club's many creditors. The problem was that Rubí also fancied himself as a football man. Or, rather, he thought that being a court-appointed administrator at a football club entitled him to make footballing decisions. Tensions mounted with club employees; the team went from bad to worse; Ranieri soldiered on, boosted by the fact that, in the UEFA Cup at least, Atlético had advanced to the last 16. But that's where the run ended. They fell to Lens, 6–4 on aggregate.

Rubí asked to speak to Ranieri and gave him an ultimatum. 'You need to win the next match,' he said. 'Otherwise you're sacked.'

For Ranieri this was a step too far. Bad Claudio returned with a vengeance.

He looked Rubí in the eye. 'A club president can give ultimatums, not you,' he said. 'Not an administrator sent by a court. And a club president can sack me. Not you.'

With that he walked out and submitted his resignation.

When he heard the news, Santiago Solari begged Ranieri to change his mind. He knew the club was disintegrating; losing the manager too would just accelerate its demise. But Ranieri was done. He could not work under those conditions. Nobody could.

8. Tinker Man to Proud Man

In two and a half seasons Gianluca Vialli had won an FA Cup, a League Cup and a Cup Winners' Cup at Chelsea. Plus, for those who consider them proper trophies, a UEFA Super Cup and a Charity Shield as well. At that point it was only marginally less than Chelsea had won in the club's whole ninety-five-year history. But Chelsea had concerns over whether their former striker, who had originally been appointed as player-manager and had no prior coaching experience, was knowledgeable enough to take the team to the next level. And there were differences of opinion in terms of personnel as well. They needed a poor run of results to let him go, and that's just what happened early in the 2000–01 season. After beating Manchester United in the Charity Shield and winning their home opener, Chelsea lost at Bradford and then drew three consecutive games.

It was the perfect opportunity. The club felt they needed what they called a 'truly continental manager' and owner Ken Bates turned to Claudio Ranieri. The Premier League was not what it is today, but it was certainly on its way. And having been happy outside Italy at Valencia and Atlético, Ranieri was up for a new challenge. He was joined by his usual crew – his right-hand man Angelo Antenucci, goalkeeping coach Giorgio Pellizzaro and fitness coach Roberto Sassi.

Chelsea were a mix of high-profile veterans such as Gianfranco Zola, Marcel Desailly and Graeme Le Saux, as well as promising youngsters like John Terry and Jody Morris, but the feeling was that they weren't firing on all cylinders. 'We were a very competitive team, but we had started badly,' Zola recalls. 'And there was a sense that we could go to the next level. Particularly certain individuals.'

Mario Melchiot was a right back in that team, and his words confirm that, initially at least, Ranieri delivered what they needed. 'Vialli was just starting out. Inevitably some of his sessions were not as coordinated as Ranieri's,' he says. 'He did a bit of tactics but he also wanted us to have fun and play football. But Ranieri from day one, he wanted to teach and teach us tactics. It was boring, but it was necessary.' He adds, 'The most important thing to him is what you do when you don't have the ball. Where do you go? What do you do? The funny part is that he'd have these sessions where he'd run around shouting "I am the ball! I am the ball!" and you were supposed to react to wherever he was. It was hilarious.'

One mistake Chelsea made, which put Ranieri in an awkward position, was retaining Vialli's staff while also hiring Ranieri's. Graham Rix, Ray Wilkins and Eddie Niedzwiecki stayed on and it was frustrating for them. Out of both sets of assistants, the only one who spoke English and Italian was Wilkins, and he ended up having to act as an interpreter, which he did not appreciate. Eventually, after about a month, the old staff quit, but their presence initially did Ranieri no favours.

The language issue soon proved to be more problematic

than originally anticipated and in more ways than one. Ranieri relied on forming relationships and weighing his words carefully for maximum effect as a means of team-building. But with limited English, that was always going to be difficult. 'He really did not speak a word when he first arrived,' recalls goalkeeper Carlo Cudicini. 'Especially for a manager like him, who relies so much on communication, it must have been hell.'

With Wilkins gone, he would often ask Gus Poyet to translate. It was a less than ideal situation which then got more awkward when Poyet started getting dropped. Eventually it boiled over, and it's not hard to see why: it's one thing to interpret for teammates, but when you're not playing, you feel as if all you are is a guy who happens to be bilingual.

Despite the language differences, his staff had settled well . . . apart from Sassi, the fitness coach that is. 'Sassi was very knowledgeable and professional, but he had replaced a fitness coach [Antonio Pintus] who was loved for his jovial nature,' says Zola. 'Sassi on the other hand was always serious, demanding, and many did not appreciate that. He had a way of presenting himself that was the opposite to Pintus whom everyone loved . . . There was a bit of conflict.'

More than a bit, judging from what happened one snowy day. The players would often chase Sassi, mainly to mess about, but one occasion Mario Melchiot got carried away. He tackled Sassi so hard that he broke his ribs. 'I mean, I really laid him out,' Melchiot recalls. 'I broke his ribs. Everybody was laughing, but he was crying.' Ranieri asked what had happened, and Melchiot told him Sassi was only pretending to be hurt. Ranieri gave him a quizzical look. For the good of the team he did not press the issue. Sometimes being a manager means learning how to ignore certain things. 'In fact, we wanted to get rid of the guy,' says Melchiot. 'He was annoying. We knew we could not complain to Ranieri because he was his guy, but we could beat him up.'

Ranieri lost six of his first eleven games, which wasn't exactly the great start he would have envisioned. On top of that, the British media started getting on his back, mainly for two things. One was Ranieri's lack of English. This was compounded by the fact that sometimes his statements in translation came out sounding silly or nonsensical. The other was his tendency to change players and systems from match to match and sometimes even in a single game.

'It took him a while to find the right balance and so he changed things around,' says Zola. 'I think people forget he was overseeing a massive generational change as well. But he did it to put guys in a situation where they could offer 100 per cent.'

Thus was born the Tinkerman moniker.

Actually the tinkering criticism made little sense. Anyone who bothered to take a close look at, say, the club that was far ahead of everyone else at the time – Manchester United – would have noticed that Sir Alex Ferguson also rotated frequently, sometimes even more than Ranieri. As for changing systems, part of it was to find the right fit, and part of it was to keep the opposition off balance and give his team an advantage. In his mind it was normal. Indeed, a team that can switch tactics efficiently has a huge edge and can create mismatches and exploit weaknesses.

But the Premier League in 2000 was in a different place to where it is today. 'You don't know what you're doing!' and occasionally 'They don't know what you're saying!' rang out.

Some of the tabloid press started calling him Clownio. Away to Ipswich on Boxing Day, Dennis Wise, the club captain, played three or four positions in the course of the game. Chelsea, who had been 2–0 up, ended up drawing 2–2. Wise took it badly, seeing it as lack of respect. Shortly afterwards he asked for a transfer. It was at that point that a portion of the crowd really turned on Ranieri.

That campaign finished with Chelsea in sixth place and many wondering whether the club had made a mistake. Vialli had been popular with fans and the media. Ranieri's English was almost as difficult for many to understand as his personnel decisions.

The club however recognised the work Ranieri was doing on the training pitch. They also recognised that he was trying to revitalise the side and oversee the transition from an ageing group of players.

Compared to Italy and Spain, where signings were often a wrestling match with the director of football, Ranieri had far more latitude at Chelsea. He brought in players he felt matched his vision: a veteran defensive midfielder with charisma and proven Premier League experience (Emmanuel Petit), an uber-athletic versatile defender (William Gallas), an elegant, intelligent winger (Boudewijn Zenden) and a young English midfielder who would go on to become a club icon (Frank Lampard Junior). Looking back, Gallas and Lampard belong among Chelsea's greatest players, Petit was slowed by injuries but nevertheless contributed, and Zenden tailed off after a positive start. The club backed Ranieri and he had helped deliver what would turn out to be one of Chelsea's best-ever transfer windows.

Preseason training, in keeping with Ranieri tradition, was

at Roccaporena. Not everybody appreciated the austere solitude of the place, Melchiot included.

> So you arrive in Rome and you're excited. And then you get in the bus and you drive half an hour, one hour, two hours, three hours, and you're still going. And then you end up in Alcatraz, although maybe that's disrespectful to Alcatraz. It was like a prison. It was so boring. There was nothing to do other than training and watching old people come to pray. I know he liked it, but he was there with his wife, his daughter and his dog. Well, I'd be happy in the middle of nowhere too if I had my family there.

The season started slowly. Chelsea were drawn to play Hapoel Tel Aviv in the UEFA Cup, but following 9/11 were told the safety of the players could not be guaranteed. Ranieri left it up to each squad member whether they wanted to make the trip. He probably could not have forced them anyway for contractual reasons, but he also felt it was the right thing to do. There was no point in going if you were not in the correct frame of mind. Five players, all regular starters, opted to stay at home – Marcel Desailly, Graeme Le Saux, Manu Petit, William Gallas and Eiður Guðjohnsen – and a weakened Chelsea side was knocked out of Europe early.

The league itself proved a slog, with the club hovering around sixth place. Zola was having a difficult time and Lampard was playing out wide, a decision for which Ranieri was getting hammered in the press. His changes did not help either: this was peak Tinkerman time. Things came to a head in the League Cup when Chelsea lost 5–1 away to Tottenham. It wasn't just defeat to a rival London club, it was defeat to a rival they had not lost to at home or away since 1990. Again the fans were not impressed.

Still, Chelsea went on a run in the FA Cup and got a measure of revenge, going to White Hart Lane and destroying Spurs 4–0. They would eventually reach the FA Cup final, where they faced Arsenal, who had already won the league. Chelsea lost 2–0, holding out until late in the game but were ultimately outclassed by a better side.

Chelsea finished sixth in the league, but Ranieri had seen plenty of promise. John Terry, a homegrown centre back whom he trusted enough to turn into a starter (diverting Gallas to left back) had emerged as a fan favourite and an excellent defender. Lampard, after a difficult few months, had been tremendous towards the end of the season. At a time when Chelsea were criticised for being a team full of foreigners, having two outstanding young Englishmen in the starting eleven was important. Zola had endured a difficult season, scoring just three league goals, and was entering the final year of his contract, but Ranieri was confident he would regain his mojo. And when he struggled, Guðjohnsen was proving a viable alternative.

Most of all, that spirit which Ranieri valued so much had been created. This was a team. His team. 'Ranieri was so good. Whenever the shit hit the fan, he knew how to keep control,' says Melchiot. 'He loves a joke, he was really cool. He knows how to break the ice and make people feel comfortable.'

Meanwhile Ranieri knew that Ken Bates had got into debt to redevelop Stamford Bridge, but it wasn't until closer to the summer, when Trevor Birch, a specialist in distressed companies, joined the club that the full extent of its financial difficulties became clear. The team did not need much, just two or three signings and time to let the youngsters improve, Ranieri figured. Get that right over the summer and they'd be shooting for a Champions League spot and maybe more. But all he got was a Spanish midfielder, Quique De Lucas, on a free transfer from Espanyol. Most contract negotiations – including Zola's – were also put on hold. Ranieri, on the other hand, did get a new deal, mainly because the club felt it was important to keep him happy.

Ranieri nevertheless managed to turn the situation into a positive. There was a sense that, finally, they knew where they stood. Times were tough, so everyone needed to come together and take responsibility. That was his message, and he felt that his team was growing and could step up to the next level. Ranieri relished the challenge, and in week one of the new season sensed that things were coming together. Zola looked exceptionally sharp in the 3–2 win at Charlton, while an eighteen-year-old kid from the youth team whom Ranieri had championed during preseason, Carlton Cole, came on to score the winner.

Chelsea spent most of the season in the top three and, with three games to go, found themselves two points in front of Newcastle United and one ahead of Liverpool, who they would host on the final day of the season. Ranieri knew the next two games were tricky – London derbies against teams fighting to avoid relegation – and Chelsea were poor in a home draw to Fulham and then lost away to West Ham. Everything hinged on avoiding defeat against the Reds on the final day of the season. And not just in terms of Chelsea's European future, but their future full stop.

New details emerged about Chelsea's accounts which revealed that they were extremely close to insolvency. In fact, if they didn't finish in the top four and get a share of that

Champions League money, there was a very real risk that the club would fold. The night before the game Birch visited the team hotel and personally told the players how dire the situation was. They were playing for the future of the club. They had to win.

Ranieri understood the situation as well as anyone. And he made a crucial, momentous decision before the game. He dropped Zola, the fans' favourite, the man who was enjoying a brilliant season after his struggles in 2001–02, and opted for a Guðjohnsen–Hasselbaink partnership. It was a move that took Liverpool by surprise and ultimately steered the game Chelsea's way. Despite going a goal down to Sami Hyypia's header, goals from Marcel Desailly and Jesper Gronkjaer gave Chelsea a 2–1 win. This changed the history of the club – and, perhaps, the Premier League.

A Russian named Roman Abramovich had watched his first football match, a Champions League game between Real Madrid and Manchester United, the previous month. That's when he caught the bug. He had decided he was going to own a football club and, because he happened to be a billionaire, he had the means to make it happen. He took a look around Europe, weighed up a few clubs and then settled upon Chelsea. His one condition was that they had to be in the Champions League. That was the competition that got him excited, and that's what was at stake when Chelsea faced Liverpool that day.

Ranieri knew none of this; he just knew that he had got Chelsea into the top four, and that meant some fresh cash coming into the club. Which in turn meant some breathing space. Not much. He worried that Hasselbaink or Gallas – who had plenty of suitors – might be sold. And he'd need to replace Zola. Even with the prospect of Champions League revenue, the club were in no position to offer him a proper contract extension. Quite the opposite: the deal they put together was seen as an insult by many, a pay cut of 45 per cent. This, after a stellar season which saw him feature in every single game and score sixteen goals in all competitions, all of them from open play.

But on 1 July 2003 Abramovich acquired control of the club from Ken Bates, and everything changed. Ranieri received a late-night phone call from Birch. Others found out in different ways. 'I was watching TV, and all of a sudden . . . BREAKING NEWS . . . I was shocked,' says Cudicini. 'I rang up John Terry. Neither of us knew anything about what would happen.'

A week later Ranieri met Abramovich for the first time. Ranieri expected to be let go because when a different boss rides into town, that's what usually happens. A new owner wants to make his mark straightaway, and that generally starts at the top. What's more, five days earlier Abramovich had met the England boss, Sven-Göran Eriksson, at his house in London. Plenty in the media put two and two together. It was hard not to, not least because Eriksson stopped short of denying that Abramovich had offered him a job. The FA put out a statement in which Eriksson simply confirmed the meeting, reaffirmed his commitment to England and explained why he was hanging out with a Russian billionaire who had just bought a football club.

'I have known Roman Abramovich for several months, and during that time have also enjoyed socialising with him when he is in London,' he said. 'However, due to the intense media profile given to Mr Abramovich's involvement with Chelsea, I accept that this meeting may create unfortunate speculation.' That's right. It's entirely normal for the England manager to 'enjoy socialising' with the owner of a football club eighteen years his junior who at the time did not speak good English. Nothing to see here, folks!

It's not hard to see why the first thing Ranieri did when he met Abramovich was ask him if he planned to replace him.

Abramovich said he had no such intentions. 'No, I want you to continue managing the team,' he told him. And then discussions turned to his ideas for the club. And they were massive. There had been rumours about what Abramovich, one of the fifty richest men in the world, was planning, but to be told then and there, to have it spelled out, was something else. The plan was simply to build the club into one of the best in the world and win the Champions League. Ranieri was floored.

The will was there, the funds too. The question was whether Abramovich was really committed to Ranieri. Sure, he was keeping him on, but this was a guy who hadn't even known he liked football until two and a half months earlier. A rash, impulsive owner might want to change things from day one. Someone who has been a fan all their lives, like many armchair supporters, might think he knows better than the guy stalking the sidelines. Abramovich was neither. He had no background in the game, he had not even been a casual supporter, and he had the humility to recognise this. Equally, he was canny enough to approach this the way he might have any other business venture.

If he had bought, say, a biscuit factory, and had never been in that business before, would he fire the factory foreman and change the production methods in the first week? Obviously not. He would learn the business first, maybe make some funds available for the current management team to invest as they saw fit, so he could assess their judgement. And then perhaps he'd bring in the chief executive of one of the best biscuit factories in the world and have him run it. All the while he'd be sitting back, watching and drawing his own conclusions. Only once he'd learned enough about the business would he act.

That's pretty much what Abramovich ended up doing. Unfortunately for Ranieri, as it turned out, Abramovich would get that top executive from one of the best biscuit factories – in this case football clubs – in the world: Manchester United's Peter Kenyon. And, as for that meeting with Eriksson, according to multiple sources no job was ever offered. Abramovich had no immediate plans for a new boss. He knew that trying to get Eriksson to break his contract with the FA would be difficult, expensive and would make him unpopular. And he did not yet feel ready to decide who should manage the team. What's more, Abramovich knew full well that the meeting had been very useful for Eriksson, who had made no attempt to hide who he was seeing. It felt as if he was using Abramovich to get a new deal, and, sure enough, a few months later, in November, Eriksson did sign an extension with the FA.

Meanwhile, for Ranieri the possibilities were endless. It was like assembling a Panini sticker collection. That summer in came a brand-new pair of fullbacks: Glen Johnson from West Ham and Wayne Bridge from Southampton. In came an equally new striker partnership: Hernán Crespo from Inter and Adrian Mutu from Parma. In came a whole gang of midfielders: Damien Duff from Blackburn Rovers, Joe Cole from West Ham, Geremi and Claude Makélélé from Real Madrid, and Juan Sebastián Verón from Manchester United.

Ranieri was playing fantasy football. He had what every manager wants, but few admit they do: two players for every position. The challenge in that situation is managing the sheer volume of players and keeping everybody happy. Most managers think they can do it; certainly Ranieri did. It would mean squad rotation, sure, but he'd already been through the wringer for doing that and lived to tell the tale. He could handle it.

For the survivors from the old Chelsea it was a tough summer. They were up in Roccaporena and each day brought somebody new. 'Every morning you open the paper and you were like . . . "What?! That guy is coming?!"' says Melchiot. 'It was crazy. Crazy, man.'

The one regret in all this was that Zola had gone. He had turned down the original contract extension with the pay cut and committed himself to Cagliari before Abramovich's arrival. He stayed true to his word, even though it was just a verbal agreement and Abramovich offered him a hugely lucrative deal to stay. 'I had made my decision. I wanted to return to Sardinia,' he says. 'I wanted my kids to live there and I wanted to leave Chelsea on a high. This mattered to me. Plus I had always dreamed of playing for Cagliari one day. Ranieri asked me to stay, but he respected my decision. Abramovich too.'

Chelsea raced through the first two months of the season, winning eight of nine and drawing the other. Ranieri was managing the rotation, and by and large it was working. As long as they kept winning, and everyone got the chance to play, there would be no problems. Even the first league defeat of the season, away to Arsenal in mid-October, did not cause major problems. For this game Ranieri had conjured up a new defensive partnership of Melchiot and Robert Huth.

'I had not played in three games,' says Melchiot. 'I had not even been in the reserve team. Suddenly, he tells me I'm starting. Not just that, I'm starting at centre half, where I have never played in my life! And it's against Thierry Henry! Henry! The best player in the league . . . I'm like . . . really, dude? Are you crazy?

'But then I realised what he was doing,' he adds. 'He was throwing me in at the deep end. He wanted to see if I could swim. And I said, you know what, that's what I'm going to do. I had an amazing game, even though we lost.'

In the meantime Kenyon had been appointed chief executive. That was in early September. Because of the terms of his contract with Manchester United, he had to go on gardening leave, so a temporary stand-in, Paul Smith, was put in place. Of course, all along there were stories that Ranieri too was a stand-in, filling in for the manager Kenyon really wanted – Eriksson. The rumours had been rumbling all summer. On multiple occasions Ranieri was asked flat out who was responsible for bringing in the new players.

'Did you sign these players? Did you? Who signed them? Who brought them in?' one particularly aggressive journalist asked him that August.

Ranieri, who'd had enough, pursed his lips and exhaled. 'I don't know . . .' he said. 'Maybe . . . maybe it was Eriksson?'

Eriksson's contract extension did little to quash the rumours. Later, after Kenyon was able to take charge at Chelsea, the club hosted a briefing for members of the media in which the summer signings, in particular Makélélé, were savaged and Ranieri was referred to as a 'dead man walking'.

The media lapped it up, but it's telling that Makélélé was singled out as the epitome of the past-it mercenary who had come to the Premier League for one last pay cheque and was contributing little. Ranieri valued Makélélé tremendously, as did most people who understood football. Certain members of Chelsea's club hierarchy at the time did not, to the point that they subjected him to ridicule. You can only assume they changed their minds when José Mourinho, Ranieri's successor, made him the midfield linchpin of his two title-winning sides. (Ranieri would get his own back when he said of Kenyon, 'We were never on the same wavelength, maybe because I don't know much about marketing and he does not know much about matters on the field of play.')

Ranieri wasn't oblivious to all this, but he made the best of it. He felt that if he delivered – and with the team he had, nothing was impossible – Abramovich might yet change his mind. That January transfer window the club had locked in two signings for the following June, Arjen Robben and Petr Čech. Ranieri signed off on both. Robben was primarily the club's doing, but it was Giorgio Pellizzaro who pushed hard for Čech. The fact that Ranieri was so involved in acquiring two players who would not play until the following season also fuelled rumours that he might stay. Even if he did not, the identification and signing of the players would be a tremendous calling card for his next job.

Beyond that though – and just as important – this was his fourth season at Chelsea, and he genuinely felt a bond with the club and their fans. He had won the supporters over, sticking with them through the tough times, and this season they had been fantastic, if a bit incredulous at what was unfolding in front of them. But back-to-back defeats to Arsenal in February put an end to Chelsea's FA Cup campaign and very likely the Premier League hunt as well. It wasn't so much that Chelsea were nine points behind with twelve games to go, it was more the fact that Arsenal were simply a cut above that season. Indeed, they'd go on to become the first English side since the 1880s to go an entire league season without suffering a single defeat, earning them the nickname 'The Invincibles'.

Attention thus switched to the Champions League. Chelsea had reached the quarter-finals and yet another date with Arsenal, and Ranieri had a dilemma with Crespo. By this stage they did not see eye to eye, and the Guðjohnsen–Hasselbaink pairing was his preferred option.

According to Crespo, Ranieri had said that he was going to keep him fresh for the Champions League, and the other two would be the regulars in the league. 'So then it's the Champions League quarter-final and I assume I'm starting,' Crespo says. 'But no. He drops me, even though he had said I'd play in Europe.'

Crespo demanded an explanation. The best Ranieri could do was give him a sheepish grin and say, 'Well, it's Arsenal. That's not Europe, that's London. It's sort of like a Premier League game.'

'I was ready to tell him to fuck off,' Crespo recalls, 'but he'd been so clever and so innocent ... I think the reality is that managing a big squad can put you in difficult situations. You have to reassure people, you have to calm them down but you also have to be ruthless and put the team first. As a player, you don't see it that way. But now that I'm a manager, I understand him a bit better. You have to have 360-degree vision.'

Still, Ranieri sent him on in the second half. 'Knowing that Hernán was angry with me for not including him in the starting line-up, I wanted to put his anger to good use,' Ranieri wrote in his account of the 2003–04 season. If it was a psychological ploy, it worked: Crespo started the move that led to Bridge's winner.

Chelsea overcoming Arsenal was not the only upset in that

season's quarter-finals. Real Madrid lost out to Monaco, and Deportivo La Coruña eliminated AC Milan after a stunning comeback. The fourth winning quarter-finalists were Porto, managed by Mourinho, who had won the UEFA Cup the previous season. Clearly all these teams were formidable, but if Ranieri had been told at the start of the campaign that he'd reach the Champions League final four and these three clubs would stand between his side being crowned European champions, he would have taken it with glee.

In the popular narrative Chelsea's next Champions League game, away to Monaco in the semi-final, sealed his fate. That may well be true, but maybe it's more accurate to say it eliminated the final shreds of possibility that he'd be sticking around. The day before the game he discovered Chelsea officials had met Jorge Mendes, Mourinho's agent. With Eriksson out of the picture, the Portuguese rising star was the name on everyone's lips.

'I had put up with a lot in these last few months, but this was really hard to take,' Ranieri wrote. 'It showed a lack of respect not just for me, but for the players and for all the effort we were putting in to try and achieve something historic at Chelsea.'

Ranieri has a point. There was simply no fathomable reason why the club could not have met Mendes in secret. Theories abound over who leaked news of the meeting, but the cynical view is that both sides had an interest in letting it come out. Mourinho's camp was turning the screws and letting it be known he was being pursued by the biggest-spending club in the world. Even if things did not work out, this would send a clear signal to his other suitors, among them Liverpool and Tottenham. As for Chelsea, those who wanted Ranieri gone were well aware that dismissing him after winning the Champions League would be that much tougher.

This is not a theory Ranieri necessarily shares, but the situation was obviously handled extremely poorly.

Ranieri takes full responsibility for what happened that evening. 'I had let myself be affected by anger over the meeting between the club and Mourinho's agent,' he wrote. 'I wanted to win as a way of retaliating and proving a point. But it was a mistake.' With the score tied 1–1, Ranieri made a string of decisions aimed at killing the game there and then but which instead blew up in his face.

He took off Gronkjaer for Verón despite the fact that the Argentine had played just thirty-four minutes of competitive football in the previous five months. Gronkjaer was having an off-night, but Verón was worse. Eight minutes into the second half Monaco's Akis Zikos was sent off, harshly, for a clash with Makélélé. Sensing his team was taking control, Ranieri made the fateful decision to take off Melchiot, a right back, for Hasselbaink, a centre forward. For seven minutes the team were all at sea. There was no recognised right back, though Scott Parker gravitated towards the flank. Crespo, Hasselbaink and Guðjohnsen crowded the area – and each other's paths – up front. Makélélé sat in front of the back four, while Lampard and Verón got in each other's way.

'We didn't know what the hell he was trying to do,' says Melchiot. 'It felt like he was in his own world and we were on a different planet.'

Ranieri tried to remedy the situation in the sixty-ninth minute by sending on a defender, except it wasn't Geremi – who was not a natural right back but at least had played there before – who came on, but Huth, the giant centre half. Chelsea now had three centre forwards, two attacking midfielders, a holding midfielder, three centre backs and a left back. With Chelsea all over the place, Monaco scored two late goals through Fernando Morientes and Shabani Nonda, the latter after a mistake by reserve keeper Marco Ambrosio, to win 3–1.

'Utmost respect for the opposition, the chance to take advantage of their misfortune and the events of the night before had combined to influence my judgement and I made the wrong choices,' he wrote. 'This was the first time such a thing had happened to me. But the fault was all mine. At my age and with my experience I should have been able to rise above situations like this, but in the end it was human nature that determined the outcome.' Rarely in the history of football has there been such a full and complete admission of responsibility.

It felt as if he threw in the towel after the Monaco defeat. At a press conference before the return game he was asked about his future. 'Oh, come on, my friend,' he said. 'I think we both know what will happen next year, regardless of what will happen tomorrow . . . You will be here, I really do not think I will be. Maybe I'll drop in and see you, we'll have a coffee together.'

In his book Ranieri says he was being honest and that he 'did not want to sound like a visitor from another planet'. Maybe so, but he must have realised how such a statement – as opposed to the typical manager script: 'We'll worry about next year when we get there,' or 'I'm only thinking about the present' – might affect the team. Monaco were a good side, but they were not Real Madrid or Manchester United. They were beatable. And the away goal from the first leg meant that a 2–0 result, hardly impossible, would see Chelsea through.

On the day of the match he gave an inspirational speech and had photographs of the Champions League trophy placed inside every player's locker, but his words from the previous day hung in the air. And yet Chelsea found themselves 2–0 up just before half-time, thanks to goals from Gronkjaer and Lampard. They were through. The joy lasted no more than 120 seconds. Hugo Ibarra – possibly with his hand – pulled one back. With the aggregate score now 4–3, Chelsea needed a third just to get to extra time. Instead, Morientes scored in the second half to fix the final score at 2–2 on the night, 5–3 on aggregate. Now it really was all over.

'When you think about it, forget the first game. We lost a chance to be in the final because of Ibarra's handball in injury time,' says Cudicini, perhaps taking for granted that Chelsea would never have let slip a 2–0 half-time lead. 'And the final, with all due respect, was against Porto, not Real Madrid . . .'

Ranieri's Chelsea would finish the Premier League season in second place, eleven points behind Wenger's Invincibles. It would be their second-highest-ever finish in history, after the 1954–55 title-winning side. In the Champions League, advancing to the semi-finals was further than they had ever reached in the game's premier club competition.

Chelsea would win the title the following year under Mourinho. Of Mourinho's eleven most frequently used players, all but three – Tiago, Paulo Ferreira and Didier Drogba – were either signed or developed by Ranieri in his four years at the club. Among them were Terry, Lampard and Čech, who would end up ranking third, fourth and sixth on the list of Chelsea's all-time highest number of appearances. This was his legacy.

9. Rock Bottom to Rebirth

They say you should never go back. And Claudio Ranieri nearly did not.

Chelsea sacked Ranieri on 31 May, but the writing had been on the wall for a long time, since well before that semi-final with Monaco. Ranieri was determined to take another job in the Premier League. He loved the environment and he had made a home in London. Several clubs sent out feelers even before he was released by Chelsea. On 1 June, the day after he was released by Chelsea, he met Daniel Levy, the Tottenham chairman, at the Hilton Hotel at Heathrow. Spurs were in the midst of a managerial hunt but would later insist that it was purely a courtesy meeting and that they had already identified Jacques Santini as their new boss, with the Frenchman appointed on 3 June. According to multiple sources close to the situation, Ranieri interviewed for the Spurs job that day but hours later took himself out of the running. Valencia had contacted him and things moved very quickly. The Spanish club wanted him to replace Rafa Benítez, now departed for Liverpool.

Ranieri let his heart rule his head. There was unfinished

business at the Mestalla. The team he had built had gone on to win two Liga titles and a UEFA Cup, while reaching two consecutive Copa del Rey finals. This was his chance to go back and write a different ending.

Except he returned to a very different club. Part of the reason Benítez had left Valencia was the disarray at the top. He rowed continually with the management over transfer decisions and demanded more investment. A cycle of success had clearly ended – Benítez said so himself in a surprise press conference when he announced his departure – and now it was time to rebuild, but the management did not see it that way. The fans were furious at Benítez's exit and blamed the club, which needed to do something to appease them.

'Benítez had been hugely successful, but he knew that the second title, in 2004, really was a miracle,' says Amedeo Carboni, who would go on to become Valencia's director of football. 'Management at the time figured it was cheaper to try to keep the fans happy by bringing in a guy like Claudio, who was hugely popular, rather than truly trying to strengthen the squad. In that sense, they simply used his name.'

Ranieri identified positions that needed to be strengthened but it soon became clear that the board had its own plans and they were not aligned with what the manager wanted. In a sense it wasn't their fault, as they had done a deal that had gone very wrong. Three years earlier, in the summer of 2001, they had sold Gaizka Mendieta to Lazio for some £40 million. The fee was to be paid in instalments, but Valencia had received less than half the agreed amount. Lazio went into administration in 2003, and the club's owner, Sergio Cragnotti, was arrested. The court-appointed administrators offered Valencia a deal. They told the club there was no cash available to pay the roughly £20 million Lazio still owed. Valencia had two options. They could file a legal claim, but the best-case scenario was that they would only get paid if the club was liquidated. Or they could take some players – thereby reducing Lazio's wage bill – in exchange.

Valencia chose the latter option and signed three footballers from Lazio: midfielder Stefano Fiore and strikers Marco Di Vaio and Bernardo Corradi. It would turn out to be a decision that backfired badly. They weren't bad players; they just weren't the players Valencia needed. Ranieri once again found himself managing an impossibly big squad and trying to keep everyone happy.

What's more, a rather ugly media narrative took over. Some papers spoke of an 'Italian invasion' – with Carboni, who by this point was almost Iberian after a decade at the club, and another newcomer, Emiliano Moretti, there were now five at Valencia. It set an unpleasant tone, and while Valencia started well, taking thirteen from a possible fifteen points in their first five games, they struggled mightily in the Champions League, suffering a 5–1 defeat to Inter at the Mestalla. Things got even worse when they lost at home to Werder Bremen in their final group game and were eliminated.

Exacerbating matters for Ranieri was that his relationship with two of the Italian players had become strained. Fiore was unhappy because he wanted to play in the hole, but Ranieri kept deploying him on the wing. During one game, while warming up as a substitute, he got into a shouting match with Ranieri well within earshot of the media and fans. The other simmering row was with Di Vaio. He and Ranieri simply did not see eye to eye. The striker did not take defeat well and had a habit of being critical of Ranieri in front of his teammates.

Ranieri fined him repeatedly, but the back and forth continued and was hugely destabilising.

Ranieri felt isolated. In an effort to settle the former Lazio trio, he gave them as much attention and playing time as possible. He was stuck with them, and he was going to make the best of it. But they were playing poorly, and Ranieri's tactic created resentment among some of the other players, who saw it as favouritism. Matters came to a head at Valencia's Christmas Party. A version of secret Santa had been organised in which everyone received an anonymous present from a teammate or a member of staff. Some of them were gag gifts. For example, Miguel Ángel Angulo, who had been linked to Arsenal, received an Arsenal shirt with his name on the back.

Ranieri's present? A self-help book: *100 Things to Do When You Retire*. If it was meant to lighten the mood, it clearly backfired. He never found out who gave it to him.

They were dropping way too many points, but were still alive in the UEFA Cup and third in La Liga. Ranieri went to the board and explained how he saw the situation. 'This club overachieved tremendously under Benítez, but we need a total rebuild now,' he said. 'I need your help. I've taken the heat for you after Benítez's departure; you need to help me.' He was told not to worry, that everything would be fine, but a few weeks later, after elimination from the UEFA Cup at the hands of Steaua Bucharest, he was fired.

What followed would be Ranieri's longest period out of work in his managerial career, nearly two years, although he stayed busy. He and Rosanna moved back to London, where they had kept a home since his time at Chelsea. He did some media work; he travelled; he watched a lot of football.

*

One day Ranieri got a call from Tommaso Ghirardi, the president of Parma. The club were second-bottom in Serie A with just fifteen points from twenty-two games. Ghirardi had sacked Stefano Pioli, who had worked under Ranieri in his Fiorentina days, and was desperate for a new manager, to the point that he had called from an airport car park.

It wasn't Ranieri's dream job. Not since Cagliari more than fifteen years earlier had he taken charge of a team whose sole objective was to avoid relegation. And if the rule of thumb in Serie A is that teams stay up with thirty-eight points, he'd need to get twenty-three in sixteen games, a tall order indeed. Nevertheless he flew to Italy the next day, and Ghirardi persuaded him.

Ranieri missed coaching, and didn't argue about money. The part of the contract which stipulated his salary was blank, but he signed it, agreeing to manage Parma until the end of the season. 'Look, I'm not coming for money, I'm doing this for the challenge,' he told Ghirardi. 'Why don't you decide how much you think I'm worth and how much you want to pay me.'

Ghirardi duly wrote an amount on the contract.

Ranieri frowned. 'I knew it was going to be a small number,' he said. 'I just didn't expect it to be this small.'

One of the first phone calls he made after signing was to Pioli, his old protégé.

'Getting sacked was a traumatic experience for me,' Pioli says. 'It was a shock to the system. I did not take it well. But then Claudio rang me, and he was very sensitive. He said, "Stefano, this is the job we chose; this is the life we lead. If I had not taken this job, somebody else would have." I really appreciated it. It still hurt, but it showed Claudio's humanity.

Not many would have done that. I was still hurt, but I desperately wanted Parma to succeed.'

Ten years had passed since Ranieri had worked in Italy. He left with Serie A still the gold standard in world football and returned to find a league on its knees. Napoli and Fiorentina, two of his former clubs, had gone into administration and been relegated. Perennial giants Juventus were in Serie B, following a corruption scandal that had shaken the Italian game to its foundation. And he had chosen a desperate, seemingly impossible task. But that stimulated him. In fact, he was so fired up that at one of his first press conferences he made a very uncharacteristic blunder, choosing language that was very unlike him and downright offensive to some.

'I told the president and I will be telling the players,' he said, 'we are either going to stay up or we will die trying. If we go down, there will be no survivors and nobody will be wounded. We will all be dead.' Not surprisingly, he soon apologised. 'I didn't want to offend or trigger people who deal with real violence,' he said. 'I apologise to everyone I have offended. What I meant was, from this moment you're either with us or against us. Between now and the end of the season Parma will be my life, and I expect my players to think twenty-four hours a day about how we are going to avoid relegation.'

Ranieri soon found that he had taken over a side which wasn't lacking in talent but had serious confidence issues. They'd start most games well, concede a goal and then fall apart. This would primarily be a psychological job, not least because there was no transfer window in which to tweak the squad and little time available on the training pitch.

He lost his first three matches, two of them UEFA Cup ties. Then came a five-match unbeaten run, a defeat to Inter and a streak of five games in which they secured thirteen of a possible fifteen points. He found a devastating goalscorer in Giuseppe Rossi, a striker who was keen to jump-start his career. An Italian-American born in New Jersey, he had only just turned twenty and had joined Parma on loan from Manchester United. He would score eight goals in the final three months of the season as Parma pulled off one of the more remarkable escape acts in recent Serie A history. Parma finished in twelfth place, with Ranieri's side taking twenty-seven points from sixteen matches. Had they been able to keep at that clip all season long, they would have finished third. Job done, he said farewell to Ghirardi and Parma.

His star was shining bright again. Manchester City, under new owner Thaksin Shinawatra, made an enquiry. Ranieri did not pursue it, not least because he had received another call, one from the biggest club in Italy.

Juventus were emerging from their darkest moment ever. They had spent the previous season in Serie B for the first time in their 110-year history. What made the experience even more traumatic was what had caused their relegation. After the 2005–06 campaign, club officials were found to have operated a sort of cartel in cooperation with the heads of the Italian referees' association. It has been described as match-fixing, but it was more subtle than that. Club officials were found to have exerted undue influence over the appointment of referees, vetoing the appointment of certain match officials and championing others. Those the club did not like – perhaps because they had made decisions that the club felt had been unfair to them – ended up being penalised by the referees' association. A cycle was created whereby if match officials wanted to build a career they tended to give Juventus the benefit of the doubt. If they didn't they would never get the biggest matches. No money was ever found to have changed hands, but according to the prosecutors it didn't need to.

In what came to be known as the Calciopoli scandal, Juventus were stripped of the titles they won in 2004–05 and 2005–06, relegated to Serie B and hit with a further nine-point penalty. The club's owners, the Agnelli family, took the punishment on the chin. They quickly parted ways with the three Juventus officials who were thought to have masterminded the affair – Luciano Moggi, Roberto Bettega and Antonio Giraudo – and sought to distance themselves from the shame brought on the club. (Since then, especially after the emergence of new facts, the club has taken a different stance. Its president, Andrea Agnelli, now insists that Juve's actions were no different from those of other clubs and that the trial and the club's punishment were a sham. He has begun legal action to have the titles reinstated, and to this day many Juve fans insist that the club have won thirty-four titles, not the thirty-two in the record books.)

Juventus turned to the French manager Didier Deschamps for their one season in Serie B. It made sense. He was a club legend but also a successful coach and, as a foreigner, somewhat untainted by the Italian game. He had left Serie A in 1999 and did not return until 2006. Still unsure about what the investigation – which was wide-ranging – might uncover, the club felt they needed to be sure that the new boss would not have any ties to the old regime. They needed to rebuild the club's image with fans, sponsors and media, and could not take any risks.

Relegation led to cost-cutting, and a number of stars of Champions League quality moved on. Zlatan Ibrahimović joined Inter; Emerson and Fabio Cannavaro moved to Real

Madrid; Lilian Thuram was sold to Barcelona. Still, Juve had plenty of talent left, and the club cruised to the Serie B title. Deschamps hit his target, but wanted a raise over the summer with the club back in Serie A.

'Didier felt his contract wasn't sufficient, so we parted ways,' Jean-Claude Blanc, Juve's French chief executive, said. 'Everyone is free to make their own choices.'

Within a few days, the club had turned to Ranieri. He was an obvious choice. Other than the three months at Parma, he had been away from Italy for the past decade and had held important jobs abroad. That was an assurance that he was both competent and clean. His past as a Roma player and the fact that he remained a Roma supporter were seen as further guarantees, not least because of the fierce rivalry between the two clubs and the fact that Roma often felt victimised by Juventus: Giallorossi fans over the years saw vast conspiracies aimed at favouring the Turin club over their own. Most of all it was Ranieri's image and style that mattered. He was a gentleman, a guy who never complained about referees, who was liked and respected by all. Nobody could cast aspersions on Ranieri – and nobody ever has.

Juventus would later estimate the economic damage caused by relegation – loss of Champions League income and sponsorship above all – in the hundreds of millions. They were very much on a budget, both in terms of fees and wages, but – Blanc said – the ambition was clear: a return to the international stage. That summer they spent a hefty £35 million net in the transfer market. There were no superstar newcomers, just a bunch of hungry, hard-working players with a very clear idea of the immediate task at hand. Which is what Ranieri wanted, mainly because many of the pre-Calciopoli stars were still around: Gigi Buffon in goal, Giorgio Chiellini in defence, Mauro Camoranesi and Pavel Nedvěd in midfield and David Trézéguet and Alessandro Del Piero up front.

With no European football to worry about, Ranieri got the side into the top three early, and they stayed there all season long. There was no real question about challenging for the title. Inter had taken the Scudetto the previous year and were miles ahead of everyone. Roma too had a first-rate squad, and the goal was to settle and consolidate back in the top flight. Juve's points total was the highest of any newly promoted side in decades, and Del Piero was the league's top goalscorer.

Ranieri had achieved exactly what was expected of him, if not a little more: the club's original projection had budgeted for a top-six finish; instead he took them to third. Now, knowing there was more Champions League revenue to come, the club could kick on and start thinking about challenging for the title the following season. To do this, they needed to strengthen in key areas, particularly midfield. This is where tensions arose.

The aim was to sign an experienced defensive midfielder, and there were three options: Arsenal's Mathieu Flamini, Sevilla's Christian Poulsen and Liverpool's Xabi Alonso. Flamini was a free agent and though he would need to be paid well, he would cost nothing to bring in. Poulsen was in the £8 million range and Alonso was at least twice that. Filling the role was a club priority, but there were other targets too. If the cheaper Poulsen – or even the free Flamini – could be secured, more resources could be devoted to strengthening elsewhere. Flamini quickly committed to Milan, leaving Poulsen and Alonso as the options.

'We reached a deal with both players and their clubs, so it

was a straight choice for Claudio to make,' Blanc would say later. 'We did not want to impose our will on him. And Claudio chose Poulsen.'

It's a version of events that Ranieri disputes strongly. 'Blanc did ask me who I preferred,' he says. 'But I also told him that I liked Xabi Alonso about twenty times as much as Poulsen. That's who we wanted. But then, even though they never said it explicitly, it emerged that actually we could not afford Xabi Alonso. And so that's when I told him it was fine to go with Poulsen.'

It's normal for there to be disagreements within clubs when it comes to signings, particularly when the players concerned cost very different amounts, but Ranieri felt hung out to dry when it came to Poulsen. Suggesting he genuinely thought Poulsen was better than Xabi Alonso is simply insulting, as anyone who has watched the two play for Liverpool will confirm. Moreover, it was uncomfortable and unnecessary to talk publicly about who wanted who. Transfer decisions are made, for better or worse, together.

This incident foreshadowed a relationship that would grow increasingly tense during the 2008–09 season. Worse still was Ranieri's relationship with a Serie A newcomer that year: José Mourinho.

Mourinho is often depicted as some kind of arch-villain, picking fights and playing mind games. In fairness to him, when it comes to his battles with Ranieri, it wasn't the Special One who opened fire. Mourinho, freshly installed at Inter, was trying to sign Frank Lampard, who had played for him (and Ranieri) at Chelsea. Roman Abramovich refused to let him go. Ranieri joked that if *he* asked to sign Lampard, Roman Abramovich would let him have the English midfielder. In a less jokey way, referring to Mourinho, he said, 'I am not like him. He needs to win to convince himself that he's doing a good job. I don't.'

It wasn't intended as a barb; it was a reference to Mourinho continually talking about winning and victories and titles and how much he'd won. It was about the fact that Mourinho set the bar extremely high. Ranieri, who had been around the block, felt that you could not judge your own work solely by results because sometimes they were out of your control. You had to put the hard graft in, do the best you could and learn to accept what happened.

Predictably Mourinho fired back at a press conference.

I want to tell Ranieri that I'm here to work; I'm not here to get into a war of words with him. I just want to focus on Inter and forget about what he says. But maybe he's right. Maybe I do need to win to have the reassurance that I'm doing my job well. Maybe that's why I've won so much in my career.

Ranieri on the other hand says he doesn't need to win to be happy. Well, that's obvious. Maybe that's why, at nearly seventy years of age, with this sort of mentality he hasn't won anything significant, just a couple of throwaway trophies. Maybe he needs to change his mentality. But, at his age, I doubt he can manage it. After all, he lived in England for a long time and still struggles to say 'Good morning' and 'Goodnight' in English.

The media lapped it up. Ranieri of course had won more than 'a couple of throwaway trophies'. And he was fifty-seven, twelve years older than Mourinho but hardly 'nearly seventy'.

But his English was a sore point, and maybe that's why Ranieri couldn't resist continuing the back-and-forth. 'I think it's going to be tough for Mourinho to take over a team that won back-to-back titles and go on and win everything.'

Mourinho responded almost straightaway.

'Ranieri spoke once and he was happy,' he said. 'Then he spoke again and he was happy again. Then I spoke and he got very angry. It's as if he won 2–1 but I scored the best goal.'

To be fair, in his first season at Inter, Mourinho took pot shots at everybody, from his predecessor Roberto Mancini to the chief executive at Catania, Pietro Lo Monaco, of whom he said, 'Lo Monaco? Who is that? The only Monaco I know is the Grand Prix.' This tension in his relationship with Ranieri would rumble on over the years before they settled into a rather staid mutual respect, which suited both.

On the pitch, things were going well for Ranieri. After a rocky start, Juventus had found their stride, going on two runs of five consecutive victories and winning their Champions League group, beating Real Madrid at home and away. They were drawn to face Chelsea in the last 16. After losing the first leg, they dominated the return and were unlucky to lose to a side that the previous year had only missed out on becoming European champions on penalties. But there was turmoil in the dressing room after the match.

'Ranieri took me off when we were chasing the game,' said striker David Trézéguet. 'I don't understand it. We need to score and he takes off a forward?'

Ranieri's response was vitriolic, perhaps the culmination of tensions that had built up behind the scenes. '[Trézéguet] is a spoiled baby,' he said. 'We were already a man down because Giorgio Chiellini had been sent off. Frankly, with Trézéguet on the pitch it was like being down to nine men. He betrayed me on a human level.'

Behind the scenes, things were unravelling even though results, by and large, continued to come in. By early April they were in the semi-final of the Coppa Italia against Lazio and second in Serie A, seven points behind Inter. The club were pleased with progress but then the wheels really came off. They went eight games without a win in all competitions, including a home defeat to Lazio which knocked them out of the cup. In the league it was six draws and one loss, and the margins were slim. Twice they conceded injury-time goals and on another occasion gave away a goal with two minutes to go. Two victories turned into draws and a draw turned into a defeat, five points which Ranieri's Juve had tossed away in the dying minutes. Juventus slipped to third.

If they had secured those five points, they would have been second, eight behind Inter, and nobody would have been saying, 'Ranieri hasn't won since March.' As it was, following a 2–2 draw with Atalanta, which again saw the opposition come from behind, Ciro Ferrara, the club's youth team coach, got a call from Blanc. 'I never expected it, but he offered me the job and asked if I would finish out the season,' he says. 'I felt uncomfortable. Maybe it's normal for veteran coaches, but I was new to all this. Still, I felt I had to accept.'

Years later Ranieri would dispute the narrative whereby he was let go because of the run of poor results. That was merely the club's face-saving excuse. He says the relationship had broken down earlier over transfers.

'The truth is that things ended when I decided that they would end,' he said in an interview with *Corriere dello Sport*. 'We no longer saw eye to eye. I was told from day one that we'd be making transfer decisions together. It would be me, Blanc and the director of football, Alessio Secco. And we would all need to agree. Instead, they told me they had made a signing for next season. I told them I did not agree, but the two of them were in agreement. And so I told them that I would be leaving.'

The signing of which Ranieri did not approve was that of former club captain Fabio Cannavaro. He had left to join Real Madrid after relegation in 2006 and was now a free agent. Cannavaro was charismatic and had captained Italy to the 2006 World Cup while winning countless trophies with Juventus, but he would also turn thirty-six the following September.

For Ranieri it was a matter of principle. Long before his dismissal after the Atalanta game his mind had been made up. He could no longer work at Juventus.

10. Coming Home

The summer of 2009 passed and Claudio Ranieri was again ready for a break from football after his Juventus experience had ended sourly. He had done his job well but, he felt, without the support of the club. It was probably no coincidence that Juventus would only rediscover success in 2011–12, once the likes of Blanc and other senior Juve management had moved on.

Ranieri had decided to be more careful in the future about accepting jobs, but then the next opportunity came and it was an instant decision. There was nothing to think about because it spoke to his heart. Thirty-five years after leaving Roma, he would be going back.

The club were in a very difficult situation financially, debt-laden and still very much family run. Luciano Spalletti had delivered three consecutive second-place finishes despite lacklustre summer transfer campaigns and tight budgets, but the previous season Roma had fallen to sixth. In the summer of 2008 the club's long-time owner, Franco Sensi, had passed away. His daughter Rosella took over, and a clearer picture of Roma's financial situation emerged. They were hundreds of millions of euros in the red and were forced to sell prize assets like Cristian Chivu and Alberto Aquilani just to service the debt.

Morale was sinking fast, and after losing the first two games of the season Spalletti suddenly quit. He'd had enough and there were plenty of clubs around Europe ready to speak to him. Rosella Sensi knew she had to act fast to placate the fans. Of the managers available there were a few who had comparable charisma and ability, but only one who had three critical qualities: he was Roman, he was a Roma fan and he had played for Roma.

There was no negotiation. Ranieri said yes straightaway. And while the package wasn't quite the bare bones it had been at Parma, it wasn't that much better. Though he'd be coy when asked about his decision later, the reality was that he was fulfilling a dream. And, thinking back to the words of his old coach Carletto Mazzone, who had said that no Roman could call himself a manager until he had managed Roma, he was finally getting his stripes.

Later Ranieri would say he felt more than a little apprehension. 'What if it doesn't work out? After all, this is my home . . .' he said in a Gazzetta TV interview. All of that however paled in comparison to being able to manage the red and yellow of Roma. It soon became obvious why Spalletti had left. The team was in disarray, as if he had squeezed every last ounce of quality out and they had nothing left to give. By late October they were fourteenth in Serie A.

'He arrived at a very difficult moment,' recalls Simone Perrotta, a 2006 World Cup winner and a midfielder in that Roma side. 'The Spalletti cycle was clearly over. We simply could not do what he asked us to, and it was our fault. We needed a change.'

Ranieri, as new bosses often do, tried to settle the defence. It was hard work. Eventually things came together when he asked more-attacking players, like Perrotta, to help out at the back.

Basically, he told us that we had good strikers so sooner or later we'd find a goal. But it wouldn't do us much good if we were down by several goals at that stage, so we all had to work harder and make the defence watertight. Take my case. I was used to playing behind the striker. I'd start every game in that position, but after five minutes or so I could hear Claudio shouting at me and telling me to retreat and go wide left, to help stop the opposing fullback and help Mirko Vučinić, who was our left winger but was not particularly gifted defensively.

This happened time and again and underscored the challenges Ranieri faced. Vučinić did very little defensive work, and Roma would get killed on his flank, yet Ranieri could not drop him because he had no alternatives. And so he asked guys like Perrotta to do two jobs.

'He'd always apologise afterwards and say, "I'm really sorry, but we needed you in that position,"' recalls Perrotta. 'It was for the good of the team, so I did not mind. Especially once results started to turn.'

Roma would roar into life, winning eighteen of their next twenty-four Serie A games, taking an incredible sixty from seventy-two possible points. When the run began, they were fourteen points and thirteen places behind Mourinho's Inter. It was an unbelievable ride made all the more emotional for Ranieri by the fact that he was the man at the wheel, in his own city, with the team he had supported all his life.

'He fixed our defence, and that was critical,' recalls Francesco Totti, the club captain, who would go on to complete twenty-four years in the Rome first team. 'He understood us. He understood me. He's just like me. He's Roman, he's a *Romanista*, and he played for the club. Of course he only made six appearances in a Roma shirt; I made a few more . . .' Seven hundred and fifty-two more, as of September 2016.

The match that stands out is the Rome derby – the final victory of the run. The week before, the Giallorossi had pipped Inter to the top of the table when they beat Atalanta 2–1, while Inter had to settle for a 2–2 draw at Fiorentina. It was Mourinho who was frittering away points and had the critics doubting his winning mentality. Ranieri was sitting pretty and said little as Mourinho railed against the media and the referees, producing his usual string of conspiracy theories.

Ranieri knew he could not get the Rome derby wrong. It was obviously better to win, and he knew his side had the strength to bounce back from a defeat if it came to that, but this was the *Rome derby*. This was something on another level, which few of those who haven't grown up in the capital of Italy can fully appreciate. Rome is a city whose passion for football far outweighs the historical triumphs of Roma and Lazio. When it comes to football, Rome is one of the most insular cities in the world and one which engages in daily ritual self-examinations of the most granular kind. It's a place where everybody has an opinion, where three different sports radio stations pore over every aspect and angle of the two clubs 24/7, where nightly three-hour shows on local television dissect every last detail on a daily basis. And those who are from

Rome, who have grown up supporting either side, feel the weight of their allegiance every day.

Two of Ranieri's regulars that season were Rome born and bred, Totti and Daniele De Rossi, the Captain (with a capital 'c') and the man they call Captain Future. The only jersey – other than the red and yellow of Roma – either one had ever worn was the blue of Italy. They were the soul and the heartbeat of the team. Totti had already delivered Roma its third Scudetto, back in 2001. De Rossi, seven years younger, was expected to do the same at some point. There's an old saying about AS Roma: *'La Roma non si discute, si ama'* – 'One doesn't debate Roma, one loves Roma.' On a personal level the adage applied even more to Totti and De Rossi. They weren't to be questioned. They weren't to be debated. They were to be loved. And that's what made events at the Stadio Olimpico on 18 April 2010 so remarkable.

Lazio came out of the gates quickly. Wanting to win a Rome derby doesn't require any additional incentive, but in this case for Lazio there would be the bonus of derailing Roma's title bid. The old joke about the match is that both teams would rather finish one spot above relegation and win the derby than win the league but lose against their perpetual rivals. It's an exaggeration of course, but there's more than a grain of truth to it. Lazio were actually in danger of drifting towards the relegation zone, but stopping Roma from winning the title was its own reward.

Tommaso Rocchi gave Lazio the lead, largely against the run of play. Roma were frustrated and predictable. 'All we seemed to be able to do was hit long balls looking for [target man Luca] Toni,' Ranieri explained after the game. 'We had to find a different solution.' The tension from the stands weighed heavily on the players. Two of the worse affected were De Rossi and Totti. Both had been booked. But surely Ranieri would not contemplate taking them off . . . would he?

When the pair did not emerge for the second half, rumours spread like wildfire in the Stadio Olimpico. Surely something must have happened in the dressing room? Had they been poisoned? Kidnapped by aliens?

Nope. The loudspeakers announced that they had been substituted. In their place on came Jérémy Ménez and Rodrigo Taddei.

'If things had gone wrong after that, I'm not sure I'd be here to talk to you today,' Ranieri would joke years later. To paraphrase Billy Joel, he'd either walk away a king or he wouldn't walk away at all.

'We were literally walking out of the dressing room and back on to the pitch when he told us,' says Perrotta. 'That meant we had no time to metabolise it or to even think about the enormity of what had just happened.' But the change worked. It was a different Roma after the break. Aggressive, direct, confident. Two goals from Mirko Vučinić gave the Giallorossi a historic 2–1 victory.

Ranieri's hugely courageous decision had been vindicated. Perrotta explains:

Given his background and history he knew better than most what he would have faced even if we had only just drawn that game. He would have been crucified. Literally. But he had the courage to do what he thought was best for the team.

And it wasn't just a tactical move. It had a huge psychological effect. For those of us who were out in the second half it was a way of saying, 'Your leaders are gone. Now it's up to you to take responsibility.' The fact of the matter is that for far too long De Rossi and Totti were the lightning rods – they shielded Roma, it was all about them. Now we had to step up.

Ranieri didn't gloat after the match. Asked about the substitutions, he was extraordinarily honest:

What did I explain to them? Nothing. I just told them they were going to rest in the second half. They had been booked and they simply felt the weight of the occasion too much. They weren't in the right frame of mind, it was too much of a burden. And that meant they couldn't contribute in the way they usually did. I am from here. I grew up at this club and in this city. I understand how things work. And the better you understand it, the more it became obvious that we had to take them off.

Now the pendulum had swung firmly in Roma's favour. The last four fixtures were all eminently winnable. Mourinho and Inter were behind them and, what's more, were preoccupied with the Champions League. Sampdoria were the next visitors. They were having a good season and challenging for a Champions League spot. Roma, however, dominated the first half, taking the lead through Totti. It looked as if the impossible was truly within reach. And then Sampdoria scored twice, both against the run of play. The Stadio Olimpico was stunned into silence. What had just happened?

'That first half was the best forty-five minutes of football we played that year,' says Perrotta. 'We created tons of chances; we should have scored far more. Maybe we felt as if the game was already won.'

That same weekend Inter beat Atalanta 3–1, and Mourinho once again had his nose in front. Most believed Inter would win each of their last three games – particularly away to Lazio the following week. All week long Lazio supporters had been putting pressure on their team – who incidentally were not yet mathematically safe from relegation – to lose to Inter so that Roma would not get back in front. When Inter went a goal up late in the first half many Lazio fans cheered. Others displayed a sarcastic banner which read, OH, NO! It's a testament to the mentality of Roman football supporters that many Lazio fans have fond memories of that season – which ended with their own side in twelfth place – simply because Roma came so close to the title and got burned at the finish.

Spoiling your neighbour's party is often more fun than celebrating your own.

Roma had also made it to the Coppa Italia final. With it came the chance to do some spoiling of their own: Mourinho was chasing the treble and this was the first leg. But by that stage Roma had run out of gas. It finished 1–0 to Inter and could have been more. Totti lost his cool and was sent off for an ugly and dangerous late foul on Mario Balotelli. It was a night to forget.

This was a chance for Mourinho to resume his verbal sparring with Ranieri. The media reported that Roma players had watched the Russell Crowe film *Gladiator* to psych themselves up ahead of the Coppa Italia final. Mourinho said,

You know, if the day before a major final I had told my players to go and watch *Gladiator* one of two things would have happened: either they would have started laughing or they would have called the doctor wondering if I had lost my mind. What did I watch? I watched the last six Roma games and took notes. And I spent eighteen hours preparing for the match. But of course it's easier to prepare just by putting on a movie. I think Ranieri forgot that he's not coaching children, he's coaching great players.

I never said I was the best, but it's not my fault that when I asked Chelsea in 2004 why Ranieri was being replaced, they told me 'Because we want to start winning and as long as we stuck with Ranieri that was not going to happen.' That's certainly not my fault.

Ranieri fired back.

'Mourinho's words are ticking time bombs,' he said. 'It's too easy to motivate and be a unit by simply pretending you're under attack at all times. I think Mourinho is a good manager, it's the media that depict him like some sort of genius. We would rather win in another way: by playing football and playing good football.'

Roma had certainly done that in 2009–10. You could not argue with the numbers. If you take out the first two weeks of the season, when Spalletti was still in charge, Ranieri actually won more points than anyone, even Mourinho. Reaching the Coppa Italia final and galvanising a city and a fan base – his city and his fellow Roma fans no less – was a huge achievement as well. In the popular narrative that defeat to Sampdoria cost them the title and, strictly speaking, it did. But Ranieri and his players felt the real reason they came up short was their performance against the small sides. Above all, Livorno.

'That's where we lost it,' says Totti. 'They beat us at the Olimpico and held to us a 3–3 draw at their place after we'd been ahead three times. Those are five points right there that we left on the table.'

Perrotta agrees and goes further: 'We didn't have that ruthless winning mentality,' he says. 'That mentality where a big team will go and pummel a weaker one. We were strong against the strong and weak against the weak. But that is an age-old problem for Roma.'

As a fan, this was a problem Ranieri was determined to fix. As a realist, he wasn't sure it could be done. Money was still hugely tight and, sure enough, the club would be sold at the end of the 2011–12 season. The summer before Ranieri's second campaign, the club could only wheel and deal in loans and free transfers.

'Even during preseason I could tell things weren't the same. We had lost something,' he would say later. 'I even went to the players and asked them if there was a problem. If they weren't going to tell me as a coach, I joked that they needed to tell me because I was a Roma fan. But . . . nothing. They told me not to worry.'

Nevertheless the financial chickens were coming home to roost. The mismanagement of previous seasons was biting hard. Results did not help Ranieri either. It was a season of fits and starts. It began badly – winless in four – then they managed a run and got as high as fourth in January. Along the way they beat Lazio twice: once in Serie A, once in the Coppa Italia. To some fans that was already enough to make a good season. After the derby win in November, annoyed by constant questions about officiating and the state of his team, Ranieri broke into some colourful language at a press conference, switching to Roman dialect to make his point.

'What do you want?' he said. 'I'm in Rome now, aren't I? So I'm going to start acting like a Roman.'

Ranieri may have said that his second season at Roma was different, that things had changed and not for the better, but in truth it was still there to be salvaged in early February. They were third – Milan were just six points clear – but drew at home with little Brescia and followed up with defeats to Inter away, Napoli at the Stadio Olimpico and Shakhtar Donetsk in the Champions League. To avoid going into free fall they needed to win away at Genoa. Early in the second half they were 3–0 up and cruising to victory. Then the seemingly impossible happened: Genoa somehow scored four times in thirty-nine minutes, and Roma folded. It was a collapse and a humiliation. Ranieri decided to resign on the long walk from the bench to the dressing room. At the club training facility he told the players, 'This team needs to find itself again. I can't take that journey with you. You need to do it on your own.' He then saw every player and member of staff individually to say goodbye.

He knew he had made the right decision.

As a Roma fan, as a manager and as a human being.

11. Chelsea 2.0

Claudio Ranieri enjoyed a long summer off, but in September 2011 the call came again. And this time it was Inter Milan.

There were more than a few reasons to be wary. For all their recent success under José Mourinho and Roberto Mancini, Inter had a reputation as a notoriously badly run club, and since Mourinho's departure – the very night he won the treble in Madrid against Bayern – things had stuttered. Rafa Benítez came in, lasted six months and then left, complaining about a lack of signings. Leonardo, an AC Milan legend, took over and took the team to second place and victory in the Coppa Italia, but he too was dispatched at the end of the season. Next up was Gian Piero Gasperini, a former Genoa coach known for his 3-4-3 formation. One point from five games in all competitions did for him.

Now it was Ranieri's turn, and many felt he was ignoring the warning signs. This team was clearly underperforming, and when a side underperforms for three different managers in the space of a year, doesn't it suggest that it's best to steer clear? Ranieri did not feel that way. He was hungry for another go, especially given the way things had ended at Roma. He even got a boost from none other than Mourinho.

'Unlike some people who are pseudo-Inter fans, I am a real Inter fan,' Mourinho said. 'I always want Inter to win, regardless who the manager is. I will be happy if Ranieri does well and, as an Inter fan, I hope he's as happy there as I was.'

Many of the treble-winners were still at the club: Javier Zanetti, Dejan Stanković, Samuel Eto'o, Wesley Sneijder, Lúcio, Maicon, Diego Milito and Walter Samuel. But perhaps that was part of the problem. This group had been there and had done that. They were almost all the wrong side of thirty, which did not help either. And there were arguably reasons why his predecessors had come up short. Benítez arrived right after the treble; the players did not feel like listening to him, and it was always going to be difficult to follow Mourinho. Leonardo was too soft and cuddly. Gasperini's tactical schemes were unnecessarily complicated.

Ranieri would be different and was bullish at his first press conference. 'I've worked at a number of big clubs, but Inter is unlike every other place I've managed,' he said. 'Seen from the outside, this team is going through a tough spell, but some of it is down to injuries and some of it is down to bad luck. I'm convinced Inter have it in their DNA to bounce back.'

This was going to be above all a man-management and motivation job. That was meant to be his forte and after an inconsistent start, Inter did indeed begin to fire on all cylinders, winning seven games in a row and rising from fifteenth in the table to fourth. But key mistakes were made that January, above all the sale of Thiago Motta to Paris Saint-Germain.

'He gave us balance, like he has given every team he's played for,' Ranieri would say later. 'But the club needed to sell. I wasn't going to fight them over it. As a manager, I have a glaring weakness: I understand the needs of the club and the people who bankroll it,' he added.

Injuries hit Inter hard too, though Ranieri is reluctant to use them as an alibi. What did happen is that, like at Roma, an exceptional streak was followed by a horrendous one. At one point Inter had lost seven of eight in all competitions. This was a team of veterans, many of whom were counting down the days left on their contracts. On top of that, after splurging in the Mancini and Mourinho years, Inter were trying to cut costs. And that meant cutting wages. In the circumstances it was hard for the players to stay motivated. Ranieri would be dismissed on 26 March, following defeat to Juventus the day before. Some of the changes he made in the second half against Juve backfired badly, and he was heavily criticised.

'We had an awesome run of wins and then a long streak of defeats that were, on the whole, difficult to explain,' Ranieri would say later. 'This was an unusual season for Inter, there were still ghosts of the past hanging around. Let's say I jump-started the car but then it broke down, and let's leave it at that.'

He's certainly right about the ghosts. Inter have been a haunted club, underachieving ever since Mourinho. Ranieri arrived as a cycle was ending, when Inter had allowed the players who had been part of that cycle to stick around, rather than shipping them out elsewhere. There was no Inter to speak of any more, just a bunch of weary, battle-worn ageing stars raging against the dying of the light.

'Inter remains my greatest regret,' Ranieri says.

This is understandable. He took over a team he had not built and, without the benefit of preseason training, took them seven places up the table by the time he left. With more time he could have stabilised the team even further, but the truth is it would have merely been a case of kicking the can down the road, for now Inter were done. And, as far as Italian football was concerned, so was Ranieri.

At least that's what he thought. While his next job wasn't strictly speaking in Italy, it was about as close as you can get without actually being there. The Principality of Monaco is a microstate, bounded on one side by the Mediterranean Sea and on the other three by France. It sits just eight miles from the Italian border and its culture is a mix of native Monegasque, French, Italian and, more recently, Russian. With a population of around 37,000, it's without question one of the smallest cities in the world to boast its own top-flight club. AS Monaco play in the French League – if they had their own league, they'd have nobody to play against – and have won seven French titles.

In December 2011 a Russian billionaire named Dmitry Rybolovlev acquired a controlling share in the club, which had slipped into Ligue 2. The plan was to not only gain promotion, but to relaunch Monaco as football's equivalent of a boutique, luxury brand. After all, the principality has more millionaires per capita than any other nation on earth. Sponsors like to sell to rich people, who tend to have more disposable income. While other clubs pursued the mass market, Monaco would aim itself squarely at buyers of luxury items. That was the idea, anyway. First, they had to get back into the top flight.

Given that they were stuck near the bottom of the second division, it was obvious that they'd need to wait until next year. The club had also been in turmoil, losing money hand over fist, and needed to find themselves a new manager, not least because the current boss, former AC Milan striker Marco

Simone, did not actually have coaching badges. They drew up a profile of their ideal manager and figured it ought to be somebody who had worked in a variety of countries, who spoke several languages, who was used to working with strong, autocratic, self-made owners and who was willing to work with what he had rather than demanding a whole new squad.

This described Ranieri perfectly. He met Monaco's director of football, Tor-Kristian Karlsen, at the Airport Hilton in Rome and immediately turned on the charm. 'What struck me was his personality,' Karlsen says. 'He was extremely likeable and gave off a positive, charismatic vibe. You could see him being a leader. And he was very well prepared. He had watched many Monaco matches and was already very familiar with the squad.'

Ranieri had two more meetings – one in London and one in Monaco, where he met both Rybolovlev and Prince Albert, the principality's head of state, who retains a one-third share in the club. Everything was agreed, and Ranieri was hugely enthusiastic. He did not necessarily buy into what he had been told – that the club's objective was to win the Champions League in the next five years (easier said than done) – but he sure as heck was going to try. Indeed, he could not wait to get started.

'I basically had to force him to go on holiday. He could not wait to start working,' Karlsen says. 'And still, every morning he'd be on the phone, asking about transfers and how we were preparing for the season.'

The French second division is a peculiar league. It regularly ranks among the lowest-scoring tournaments in Europe and is marked by a lot of physicality and tactical rigour. 'If you want to play out of the back, you get nowhere in the French second division,' Karlsen says. 'So we wanted someone who could be direct and play quick, transition football with the right tactical organisation. That was Ranieri.'

While Rybolovlev's wealth meant that Monaco could have attracted superstars, Ranieri and Karlsen felt it was best to seek out specialists, players who would fit into the Ligue 2 style of play. Ranieri's adjustment wasn't quite seamless, but by the halfway mark Monaco were neck and neck with Nantes at the top of the table.

That winter they added an experienced midfielder, Mounir Obbadi, who had plenty of Ligue 2 experience under his belt, and the team took off in February. They lost just once in the second half of the season and won promotion with several games to spare. Part one of the task had been completed. Now came part two: rebuilding the squad for the top flight.

While heavy investment was always expected once promotion was gained, nobody at the club was quite prepared for the scale of what actually happened. The original plan had been to promote a few youngsters from Monaco's excellent academy. Ranieri had given debuts to two players who would go on to bigger things, midfielder Nampalys Mendy, who would later join him at Leicester, and winger Yannick Ferreira-Carrasco, who would help Atlético Madrid to the Champions League final three years later. A hugely promising but very raw nineteen-year-old winger named Lucas Ocampos had also been signed from River Plate for close to £20 million. The idea was to let them develop, add four or five international-standard players and push for a place in the Champions League.

A man named Vadim Vasiliev changed all that. A former diplomat who had spent several years in Iceland, and a business associate of Rybolovlev, Vasiliev became the club's director of football ahead of the summer. He wanted to step on the gas and start spending money straight away. Ranieri obviously wasn't averse to Vasiliev delivering stars, though there was some concern about the fact that he had no footballing background and seemed particularly close to a certain group of agents. Ranieri had coped with clubs buying players on a whim or without consulting him in the past, but if that was going to happen in Monaco, they were going to be talented players.

Barcelona and Real Madrid were raided for Éric Abidal and Ricardo Carvalho. There was no doubting their quality and experience, though, at thirty-four and thirty-five respectively, Monaco weren't exactly building for the future. João Moutinho joined from Porto, and Geoffrey Kondogbia, who had been a revelation in La Liga, arrived to bolster the midfield. Further up the pitch, in came Anthony Martial, James Rodríguez from Porto and Radamel Falcao from Atlético Madrid. When the dust settled, this newly promoted side with an average gate of under 10,000 had spent in net terms more than £150 million. And there would be more to come: in January they would also pick up former Manchester United striker Dimitar Berbatov.

It was like being at Chelsea all over again, Ranieri must have thought. Russian owner, massive spending, hordes of new world-class talent walking through the door every day. However getting the pieces to fit together was a challenge. The newcomers had to get used to Monaco, a place that, at least until the end of September, looks more like a holiday resort than a real town. There was also some resentment from the players who had actually got the team promoted. And while there was no explicit pressure put on him, Ranieri felt the burden of expectation to accommodate all the high-priced signings, which meant altering the tactical blueprint he had originally drawn up. As it turned out, nine of his starting eleven would be entirely new that season. For any manager, getting such a large proportion of new recruits to gel is a huge ask.

The other problem was that, while Monaco were one of the five biggest-spending clubs in Europe, Paris Saint-Germain also had wealthy foreign ownership – the Qatari Sovereign Fund – and they matched Monaco's summer 2013 spending blow for blow. The difference was that PSG had already spent at least as much, if not more, the previous season. In other words, Rybolovlev found himself competing against someone wealthier and in even more a hurry than he was.

Put another way, it's a little bit like buying a BMW to race in, only to discover your opponent is showing up in a Ferrari. Monaco battled PSG to a 1–1 draw in September and at the midway point of the season were just three points back. The return fixture, in Monaco, also ended in a draw. Nevertheless it had become obvious that PSG were on another level. It would take a superhuman effort to catch them.

By January it was clear this would not happen. Not after Monaco lost Falcao to a cruciate injury. The Colombian had scored sixty-nine goals in all competitions in the previous two years. He had eleven for the season when he got hurt on 22 January, and looked to be getting stronger. Berbatov and Antony Martial came in to replace him, but both were entirely different players with a different skill set. What's more, Berbatov was thirty-three and, even in his younger years, had never been the most dynamic player on the pitch.

Now Ranieri became a victim of Monaco's early-season success. Vasiliev and Rybolovlev seemed to forget that this was still a newly promoted side competing against a genuine powerhouse which had been even more expensively assembled and, crucially, had come together over several years. It was clear that, short of winning the title, there was nothing that would keep Ranieri in his job for the following season. In fact, maybe even winning Ligue 1 would not be enough to do the trick.

If there's one thing Ranieri had learned in football it's that wealthy owners are surrounded by a whole range of intermediaries, advisers and hangers-on, all of them with an eye on their money, all of them offering advice. This was the situation at Monaco, and it wasn't just tough on Ranieri; it affected the squad. Players were looking over their shoulders. Even though Ranieri got on well with the squad, his authority was inevitably undermined when many started to believe he would not be back the following year. He became isolated, and this affected Monaco's performances, if not their results.

Still, their second-place finish was never in doubt, and it came with the highest-ever points total for a team finishing second in the top division of the French league, evidence that PSG truly were on another level. Perhaps in the following years Ranieri would take satisfaction in his own performance, when his replacement, Leonardo Jardim, the man who was going to modernise the club and take them to the next level, could only manage third place in each of Monaco's next two campaigns.

12. Faroe Islands Shipwreck

The writing was on the wall at Monaco in the spring of 2014 and so the usual recruitment channels – clubs, agents, football associations – sprang into action. People often describe this level of management as a carousel, and in many ways it is. But it's also a continuous selling job. In the same way that a US president effectively starts campaigning for re-election halfway through his first term, a manager needs to sell his story as well, in a way that goes beyond results.

Results spoke of a Ranieri-led Monaco that won Ligue 2 handily, spending the entire campaign in the promotion spots, and then went on to finish second in Ligue 1 in their first season back in the top flight. Most seasons, their eighty points would have been enough to secure the French championship. By any measure these were excellent results.

Of course, then you temper that with the club's spending – both in wages and on transfers – and you may conclude it's no great achievement. Ranieri did what his resources suggested he would do. But that's why it's highly reductive to only look at results without considering the context.

Ranieri had shown the strength and personality to integrate

the newcomers – or, more aptly, take his new Panini-sticker collection of stars, real or supposed – and quickly turn them into a unit capable of getting results. These qualities resonated with a number of potential suitors. Among them were Southampton, who had just lost their talented coach Mauricio Pochettino to Tottenham Hotspur.

Southampton had become something of a model club. Eschewing the traditional old-school British paradigm of the omnipotent manager, they had set themselves up to weather the inevitable turnover on the bench and on the pitch. This meant having a strong structure in place that was not dependent on the moods of the manager and could do what was best for the club in the medium term. It also insulated the club against success. Southampton understood that they were not going to become Manchester United or Real Madrid. If they did well, other clubs would come calling for their star players and their manager as well. Which, incidentally, is exactly what happened. In addition to Pochettino, they lost goalscorer Rickie Lambert and attacking midfielder Adam Lallana to Liverpool, left back Luke Shaw to Manchester United and defender Callum Chambers to Arsenal. The sales brought in some £70 million, and the money would be reinvested by the club in concert with the new coach, rather than simply handing him a chequebook and telling him to go and spend.

Ranieri was well accustomed to this way of working, which is why he was on Southampton's shortlist. They were impressed with the way he had handled the turnover of players at Monaco: he didn't complain when new guys arrived, he simply found a role for them and man-managed them in such a way that everybody was happy. Ultimately Southampton opted for well-travelled former Ajax, Valencia and Benfica manager Ronald Koeman, who had resigned his post at Feyenoord, and back-to-back seventh- and sixth-place Premier League finishes following his appointment suggest that executive director Les Reed made a good choice.

Ranieri was hoping to return to England, and Southampton was a very appealing option for him simply because it was such a well run club. He was open to taking time off post-Monaco, but, equally, if an opportunity arose, he had the hunger to get back into the fray. It was the old Ranieri dichotomy, the two Claudios inside him, the one who accepts defeat and the one who can't stand it and demands an immediate rematch.

With Southampton no longer an option, his mind turned to another opportunity, one which intrigued him for different reasons: managing a national side. The Greek Football Association, via intermediaries Giannis Bethanis and Giorgos Kazianis, had first reached out in May as part of a wide-ranging search for a manager. Fernando Santos had taken them all the way to the quarter-finals of the 2012 European Championships, but his contract was due to expire after the 2014 World Cup and the Portuguese was ready to move on.

Ranieri's response was lukewarm at first, partly because he was still under contract with Monaco and partly because he felt there might be better options, such as Southampton. The Greeks themselves had a range of names on their shortlist, including their preferred option, Francesco Guidolin, the former Udinese boss who would go on to take charge of Swansea in 2015–16.

Guidolin turned down the opportunity, and as the 2014 World Cup unfolded, the Greeks realised they needed a big name to replace Santos. Outwardly dark and dour, inwardly emotional and prone to tears (as he would show at the 2016 European Championships), he had developed a special rapport with the players and the Greek fans, which reached a new level in Brazil. Greece qualified for the knockout stage thanks to a dramatic winner from Giorgios Samaras deep in injury time against Ivory Coast. This earned them a place in the last 16, where they faced Costa Rica. After going a goal down, they snatched a last-ditch equaliser in injury time through Sokratis Papasthatopoulos. This led to extra time and eventually penalties, though by that stage Santos had been sent to the stands. He clashed with referee Ben Williams at the end of extra time and was later given an eight-game ban (reduced to six on appeal) for abusing the match official. Greece went out and were left to ponder what might have been.

The Greek FA therefore wanted someone who could replicate Santos' qualities of outer calm and inner fire – though perhaps minus the sending-off in crucial moments. The Santos era had been an emotional roller coaster, but he also squeezed every last drop of effort out of his team. The bottom line was that Greece had only made it past the group stage of a major tournament three times in their entire history and twice it had happened under Santos. (And, to prove this wasn't a fluke, Santos returned to coach his native Portugal and ended up winning Euro 2016 in equally dramatic circumstances.)

Ranieri was now firmly in the Greeks' crosshairs and, given their heightened expectations after the 2014 World Cup, they knew they had to push the boat out. They met him in Rome and offered a two-year deal worth around £1.2 million a season, making him one of the ten highest-paid national team coaches in the world.

It was a very good offer and, because it was now July, Ranieri figured it was worth taking with an eye towards Euro 2016. He flew to Athens a few days later, and on 25 July 2014 he put pen to paper, becoming the new head coach of Greece. He was unveiled to loud fanfares, maybe a bit too loud. He was put up in one of the finest hotels in Athens, blessed with stunning views. All around were blue skies and sunshine even as – in the real world – Greeks were coming to terms with the aftermath of their bail-out referendum.

One individual close to Ranieri at the time revealed that he did not fully appreciate how different this job would be. On paper it was all downhill, the easiest of rides. Under the new rules, the top two sides in each six-nation group would automatically qualify for Euro 2016, while the third-place team would enter a two-legged play-off. FIFA rankings may be imperfect, but they aren't entirely meaningless. Greece were ranked 13th in the world and had been drawn in a qualifying group that included Romania (27th), Hungary (34th), Finland (55th), Northern Ireland (95th) and the Faroe Islands (183rd). It was as close to a dead certainty as you're likely to get in modern football.

'Ranieri made a great first impression on all of us,' says Papasthatopoulos, the Borussia Dortmund centre back and defensive leader. 'He was looking to build on Fernando Santos' work; he was humble and explained things clearly. He was a gentleman in every sense of the word.'

With the Greek league only beginning in late August, he did not have much time to prepare for his inaugural game, the visit of Romania, on paper one of the toughest fixtures in the qualifying run and with no discernible home advantage as it would be played behind closed doors because of fan trouble in a previous competitive international. Giorgos Sarris, the president of the Greek FA, had outlined the task ahead. He told Ranieri that he was expecting a generational shift. Much of the Greek side that had done well at the World Cup was ageing and had played together for a long time. There were promising youngsters itching to break in. This was the perfect time to usher out the old and bring in the new.

Indeed, Greece had lost the seemingly immortal playmaker Giorgos Karagounis, who had retired aged thirty-seven with a record 139 caps. Another long-time mainstay, Giorgios Samaras, had left Celtic after his contract expired and was a free agent, training on his own. Thirty-five-year-old Kostas Katsouranis, also a free agent post-World Cup, was on his way to India to join Pune City. It was the perfect opportunity to freshen up the squad, so Ranieri gave a debut to Petros Mantalos, a twenty-three-year-old midfielder who had just joined AEK Athens, and, in the second half, he would send on another debutant, Olympiakos striker Dimitris Diamantakos.

It all backfired badly.

After just ten minutes veteran left back Jose Holebas brought down Alexandru Chipchiu in the box and referee Mark Clattenburg had no choice but to point to the spot. Up stepped Ciprian Marica, who buried the penalty to give Romania the lead. It was a poor start and made worse by the somewhat surreal circumstances at the empty Georgios Kariskaikis stadium. Other than the players, some officials from UEFA, the two national FAs and the media, there was nobody there. You could hear the players' shouts echo across the stadium. You would have heard Ranieri's too, except not having yet learned Greek, he was somewhat subdued. Early in the second half the goalscorer, Marica, went off injured. Down a man, Romania closed ranks in midfield and Greece were unable to capitalise, though Vasilis Torosidis did hit the crossbar late in the game.

'It was a bad day at the office, nothing more,' said defender Kostas Manolas. 'We'll learn from it. Nothing really worked for us today, but we will still qualify for the Euros. I'm not worried about that.'

Ranieri himself took it on the chin, saying that his side simply weren't prepared and made mistakes. He added they were still favourites to win the group. And yet perhaps there was a bit of foreshadowing at work too. He envisioned a key role in this team for Verona midfielder Panagiotis Tachtsidis. At six feet three inches tall and weighing some 189 pounds, Tachtsidis is very much an atypical midfielder in the modern game. He's an unusually good passer for a man his size, but lacks the quickness and athleticism to be the shield in front of the back four. Karagounis, of course, was also a deft passer who – in his case because of age rather than athleticism – had recently not been able to perform this task in front of the defence. Ranieri felt Tachtsidis could fill a similar deep playmaking role and make Greece less of a one-dimensional side. While he'd been around the Greek team for several years, he did not play a single minute at the World Cup and in fact had only ever featured in one competitive game for Greece – against Liechtenstein, hardly a powerhouse.

The problem was that while the rest of the Greek midfielders were happy to run themselves into the ground for a legend like Karagounis, they seemed less inclined to do the same for Tachtsidis. And so, as the Greeks racked up more and more minutes of sterile possession with the big man in the playmaking role, frustration grew. Tachtsidis' own words after the game – 'We did not do what the manager asked us to do' – also seemed like a veiled dig at some of his teammates.

However, the initial media reaction was not particularly harsh. The empty stadium, the fact that it was the very first match . . . everything contributed to the critics withholding judgement until the next internationals: a trip to Finland and the visit of Northern Ireland.

Ranieri again rolled the dice, giving opportunities to newcomers. Out went his front men – Samaras, Dimitris Salpingidis (who had captained the side against Romania) and Kostas Mitroglou – and in came Stefanos Athanasiadis, Nikos Karelis and Charis Mavrias. The contrast was stunning. The three veterans who were dropped had nearly 200 caps between them. Athanasiadis had played twenty-nine minutes of competitive international football. Mavrias had been capped twice two seasons earlier and had begun the year with the under-21 side. Karelis was making his debut.

It was a huge gamble. And, after an early scare when Finland hit the woodwork, it looked as if it might pay off. Karelis, the debutant, opened the scoring in the twenty-fourth minute. Greece were firmly on top, but in the second half a sensational volley by Jarkko Hurme brought Finland level and it stayed 1–1.

Ranieri, understandably, was bullish after the game.
'We wanted to win and we played well,' he said. 'We improved greatly from the first game. I took risks with the youngsters like Karelis and Mavris and we were rewarded.' And then he raised the stakes. 'I said it from day one, our goal is to qualify.

If we don't, then it's simply a disaster. For me, for the players, for everybody in Greece.'

You could understand the confidence. Northern Ireland had lost every time they'd been to Greece. Ranieri brought back Mitroglou and Samaras and fielded an even more attacking formation than against the Finns.

Again, though, it was uphill early on. Corry Evans' corner kick sailed across the box where it was met by Jamie Ward. It was an odd finish, part scuff, part redirection, and the ball ricocheted into the Greek goal. Ranieri's men pushed on but lacked cutting edge in the final third despite plenty of sterile possession. Just before half-time Kyle Lafferty received the ball in space with Kostas Manolas all over him. Lafferty seemed to slow down for a beat or two before accelerating away from Manolas, galloping into the Greek area and hitting the crossbar.

You can only imagine what Ranieri thought. Here was Manolas, one of the quickest centre backs in Europe, being thoroughly burned for pace by – with all respect – Lafferty. But the big Irishman fully deserved his goal in the second half. A delicate touch befuddled Konstantinos Stafylidis on the counter, and a composed finish gave Northern Ireland their historic 2–0 win. The progress shown against Finland had clearly been wiped out. Ranieri blamed a lack of focus and concentration, but the verdicts from some of his senior players were more cutting.

'It's not the defeat that hurts, it's the display,' said his captain, Torosidis. 'We don't play the way we used to. We have lost our identity.'

Samaras went even further: 'In our last three games something has been missing.'

Everybody who heard those words knew what was different about the last three games: Ranieri was in charge.

Bubbling in the background was another issue. Ranieri's openness to promoting new talent was proving to be a double-edged sword. These were turbulent times in Greek football, with the country coming to terms with the Koriopolis corruption scandal. A number of club and FA officials (including Sarris, the man who hired Ranieri and was later accused of being part of an organisation called the System, which communicated using SIM cards registered to Chinese and Pakistani immigrants) were under pressure. Throw in the financial crisis and the possibility of Greece leaving the European Union and the situation was desperate. Clubs and agents lobbied hard for their uncapped players to get a chance with the national team; a footballer who has played for his country will not only command a higher fee, but international football is a shop window which can help bring in hard cash.

Ranieri would call upon a total of thirty-six players for the national side during his tenure. Inevitably, he had to rely on reports from scouts for some of those choices, as there was no way he could personally view players multiple times, especially those from the smaller clubs.

Meanwhile there was a month to go before the next qualifier and Ranieri knew the situation could yet be salvaged. Bumps in the road, nothing more. There were twenty-one points still at stake; Greece had played their three toughest opponents in the group and, hand on heart, he knew the team was up to it. It was simply a question of getting some confidence and assimilating his style of play. Surely a big win over the Faroe Islands at the Karaiskakis would give everyone a spring in their step. And then, when qualifying began again in March, it would be a different story.

If you've got this far in this book, you probably know what happened.

But if you don't, here's some context.

The Faroe Islands are a semi-independent nation and part of the kingdom of Denmark. What this means in practical terms is that the Danes provide the islands' military, police and justice systems as well as the currency, while the Faroes look after their domestic matters. Which makes sense, given that Denmark and the islands are some 900 miles apart. The Faroes are marooned in the North Atlantic somewhere between Norway and Iceland. Ask Google Maps for directions from the nominal capital, the Danish city of Copenhagen, to the Faroes, and it will suggest either a two-hour flight or a forty-seven-hour surface trip that includes a forty-one-hour ferry ride. And, in case you're wondering, there is no Google Street View option in the Faroe Islands.

The entire population of the Faroes is around 50,000. According to UEFA, the Faroes have some 6,000 male footballers to choose from, and that number includes children and the over-forties. The vast majority of the side is semi-professional, though some are amateurs and some ply their trade in the Danish football league. Ahead of the Greece game, they had played 121 competitive matches and lost 102 of them, with ten draws and nine victories. Other than a freak win over Austria twenty-three years earlier, they had never beaten a team that had qualified for a major tournament at any point in their history, let alone former European champions like Greece.

Ranieri again revolutionised his team. In fact, of the twenty outfield players in the squad that took on the Faroes, just eight had been part of the World Cup team in Brazil, only five months earlier. Still, this was the Faroes, including one guy just a month shy of his thirty-seventh birthday, Frodi Benjaminsen, in the middle of the park.

The first half saw plenty of chances – worryingly for Ranieri – for both teams. Panagiotis Kone sent a header wide and Karelis and Christodoulopolos both had opportunities, but the Faroes hit the post with Brandur Olsen, while Greek keeper Orestes Karnezis had to make two saves before the interval. Everyone expected Greece to come out all guns blazing in the second half. Instead, the Faroes hit the woodwork once more, thanks to the ageless Benjaminsen. And then, in the sixty-first minute, they broke through. Olsen latched on to a cross and fired at goal. His shot was going well wide, but Joan Edmundsson stuck out a boot to steer it past Karnezis.

It wasn't a sucker punch. It wasn't against the run of play. It was fully deserved for the visitors. And while Kone hit the woodwork late on, the harsh reality was that Greece deserved to lose. Torosidis summed it up when he said, 'I can't explain what is wrong with us . . . We lost to a weaker team that played better than us.'

Ranieri too appeared stunned. 'I have no words to explain what happened,' he said. 'We are last in our group because that is what we deserved.' Pausing a moment, he then added, 'The coach is always responsible.'

He clearly knew what was coming.

A few hours later the Greek FA sacked him. The statement on the official website by President Sarris left no room for interpretation. 'Following today's devastating result for the national team, I take full responsibility for the most unfortunate choice of coach, which has resulted in such a poor image of the national team being put before the fans.'

It was a total humiliation. And, perhaps, the Greek FA's reaction was exacerbated by domestic events. The day before the Faroes match the deputy head of the Greek referees' organisation, Christoforos Zografos, was attacked by two men who beat him with wooden clubs. It was seen as an intimidation attempt in a league already beset by match-fixing scandals. As a result, the Greek Superleague was suspended. In such a climate nobody was in the mood to be forgiving.

Ranieri had come up short. And while he was willing to stay on and put right the damage, he accepted the Greek FA's decision. So determined were they to see the back of him that they paid the remainder of his contracted salary immediately. Ranieri was left to reflect on what had gone wrong.

In interviews at the time he put the focus squarely on the differences between international and club football. 'I coached Greece for a total of fifteen days,' he said in various media interviews, though in some versions it's twelve and in others fourteen. 'This was a key part of why things went wrong. I didn't have the time to transmit my ideas. I'm not a magician. Greece has some very good players, but if you don't have time to work with them everything becomes more complicated.'

Without question it was a valid point and the key to his failure. A club coach can introduce new concepts and tactical schemes because he has the time to do it. An international coach simply does not. There isn't enough time and there is often too much turnover in the squad. That's fair enough. But several sources familiar with the situation add two other factors into the mix.

One was a collective underestimation of the issue of

language. Ranieri did not speak Greek and neither did his staff. While it's true that a chunk of the squad – Papasthatopoulos, Karnezis, Kone, Manolas, Torosidis, Tachtsidis – had played in Italy and understood Italian, it was clearly not enough. The other is that a certain narrative – the high-priced foreign manager, only there to make a buck – quickly took hold and Ranieri struggled to break it. His critics pointed to the fact that he was only living in Athens part of the time, which was not entirely relevant, considering the bulk of the Greece team played abroad, many of them in Italy. The local media was also critical of all the assistants who accompanied him – four in total – which seemed excessive to them and a case of 'jobs for the boys'.

These are factors whose importance is typically tied to results. Win and nobody cares if you can't speak the language or employ a giant staff. Lose, however, and they become central to your underachievement.

'I think this was a wake-up call for Claudio,' said one long-time associate. 'He realised of course that this was a different job and a tough one at that. But I think he mostly understood that international football was not for him. Let's face it, it's a retirement job. You work a couple of days a month and then a month every two years. Had he been ready to semi-retire, it would have been perfect for him. But Claudio is not like that. He needs to work.'

Still, several of the Greek players stood up for him. 'I think he ran out of time,' said Papasthatopoulos. 'He didn't have much time before the first game, not even a friendly; he didn't have time on the training pitch, and after the poor results he ran out of time entirely. I think if he had stayed, we would have gone to the Euros. It's just my opinion, and I know sometimes things turn out worse in reality than how you feel inside. But the work he did was top-notch. So much so that I wasn't surprised by what happened in his next job.'

By February 2015 the paperwork had cleared and he was free to seek a new job. Again he kept his options open, never hiding his wish to return to England.

13. Claudio Ranieri? Really?

In March 2015 Ranieri gave the mandate to represent him in England to a man named Steve Kutner, perhaps best known for being Frank Lampard's long-time agent. Ranieri and Lampard had known each other since their Chelsea days and Ranieri held Lampard's judgement and opinion in high regard. He told friends he was 'going to give Lampard's guy a go'.

This meant breaking a long-standing relationship with another agency, Base Soccer. According to multiple sources, Ranieri was a gentleman about it. He could have done what many others do: cast a very wide net and then pick whichever agent brings the best deal to the table, jettisoning his existing representative with an email or letter. The fact that he chose not to do this and instead picked up the phone was appreciated.

While Ranieri obviously preferred a job in the top flight, his desire to give England another go was such that he was also open to managing in the Championship, the second tier of English football. And that was a very significant point because one of the clubs Kutner felt might be interested in him appeared to be heading straight for relegation. That club was Leicester City. In mid-March they were bottom of the Premier League table, six points from safety. Much as clubs like to deny it, they make contingency plans and operate in the real world. And the reality here was pretty clear. Leicester weren't just in serious danger of relegation, they were severely underachieving relative to the investment the owners had made in the club. The pressure was clearly mounting on manager Nigel Pearson.

The King Power International Group, which operates duty-free franchises throughout Thailand, had acquired control of Leicester City in 2010, and its founder and chief executive, Vichai Srivaddhanaprabha, had become chairman in the October of 2011, when the club was in the Championship. The owners had remained loyal to Pearson when Leicester finished that first season in tenth place and followed up with sixth place in 2012–13. That led to a place in the play-offs and a dramatic defeat to Watford which included a late penalty miss and conceding a last-ditch winner to the Hornets. But in 2013–14 Pearson's Leicester dominated the Championship, amassing an incredible 102 points, the second-highest total ever, and returned triumphantly to the Premier League.

Throughout the Pearson era the owners had been supportive, and their loyalty had been vindicated by results as the side steadily improved. But the summer after promotion saw the club spend close to £20 million in net terms, a total surpassed by just eight Premier League clubs. King Power knew the step up was going to be tough, but they also expected results to reflect their investment.

What's more, Pearson's behaviour had grown somewhat erratic. According to individuals familiar with the situation, the concern wasn't so much with his relationship with club officials and members of his squad: he could be demanding and idiosyncratic, but he commanded respect and genuine admiration. Rather, there was concern that several incidents were tarnishing his image and, by extension, that of the club.

A home defeat to Liverpool in December 2014 saw him react to fan abuse on the touchline. Pearson turned and told the supporter to 'Fuck off and die.' It's the sort of thing that can happen to managers (and players), who routinely endure all sorts of insults and abuse; the problem here was that it was captured on video. The clip did the rounds on social media and, watching it again, it's hard not to have some sympathy for Pearson, who simply had the misfortune of being immortalised on someone's smartphone.

The club backed him, as you'd expect, though his reaction seemed to some proud and pig-headed rather than clever. 'I have had run-ins with fans in the past and in the heat of the moment these things happen and there won't be an apology,' he said. 'Let's put it like this: it's best if we don't speak about what happened on either side. I am very keen to protect my players and myself, and I'm more than happy to stick up for myself in that situation and, more importantly, protect my players – that's the root cause of the problem. If people were offended by what happened in some ways that is regrettable but there's no need for me to apologise to someone of that ilk.'

Pearson had a point. He had responded to verbal abuse with verbal abuse and without getting particularly aggressive either. Whatever apology he produced would likely have seemed empty, of the if-I-have-offended-anyone variety. Indeed, nobody who attends professional football matches could honestly claim to be offended by such language. And yet someone who represents a football club with image-conscious owners is expected to play the media game with all its faux humility. Pearson refused to do that. And while it may have been commendable on one level, it also showed a man who, to the outside world, was seeming increasingly stubborn.

Another bizarre turn, one that would have an especially unusual coda, came on 7 February in a home defeat to Crystal Palace. Palace midfielder James McArthur tackled Leicester winger Marc Albrighton near the touchline. In so doing, McArthur fell into Pearson, who was looking in the other direction, and took out his legs. ('I didn't see it coming,' Pearson would say later. 'If I'd seen it, I would have gotten out of the way.') The Leicester manager fell to his knees over the prone McArthur and his hands went around his throat while he appeared to exchange words with him. Pearson then seemed to help McArthur up, all the while talking to him, and as the Palace player tried to return to the pitch, Pearson continued to hold on to his arm, refusing to let him go.

The whole incident only lasted a few seconds, but it was deemed so odd that it received plenty of airtime on BBC's *Match of the Day*. Gary Lineker, the *Match of the Day* presenter, Leicester born and bred and perhaps the club's best-known supporter, called it 'a bizarre piece of behaviour'. Jermaine Jenas and Danny Murphy, the two guest pundits, seemed to agree, with the former saying he was a 'bit shocked' and the latter questioning Pearson's reaction after the match. Indeed, his post-game interview did him no favours. When asked by the reporter whether it was a 'friendly' incident, Pearson, who seemed to go out of his way not to smile or to minimise events, said, 'It was OK. Don't worry about that. If there's anything to say about it, I'll say it.' He then added somewhat ominously, 'I'm more than capable of looking after myself, there's no doubt about that.' With his six-foot-plus frame, broad shoulders and crewcut, Pearson does look like the sort of guy who can take care of himself.

As curious as his post-match words were, events took a further turn when rumours began to spread that he had been sacked, although the club issued a statement denying these reports. Multiple sources with knowledge of what transpired that day provide conflicting versions of events. Whatever the case, Pearson was rattled. And he made another poor decision by taking on the media, specifically *Match of the Day* and Lineker. 'I don't care what they think of me, I pay my tax bill,' Pearson said. 'It's not helpful when the three fountains of knowledge on *Match of the Day* make a mountain out of a molehill.'

It's not a good idea to take on a national treasure like Lineker, particularly when he has five million Twitter followers, and especially when you're in charge of his former side and you sit dead last in the table.

Lineker mocked him on Twitter: 'Ah Nigel Pearson is blaming *MOTD* for making a mountain out of a molehill. We'd best be careful in the future, the fella can look after himself.' He also tweeted, 'If I was [a fountain of knowledge] I'd tell you he was sacked by one of the owners' family and reinstated by another, but then I'm not.'

Sources disagree, but this is most likely when Leicester's owners began looking for a Plan B. And the desirability of finding an alternative to Pearson became even more apparent after another ill-advised media performance after a draw with Hull City on 14 March. Pearson appeared both annoyed and awkward when a reporter asked him whether Leicester's season was 'waxing or waning' in a post-game press conference. He came across as dismissive and impatient. And when it was over and he was getting up to go, he muttered to himself while still well within range of the microphones, 'Waxing or waning, my arse . . . Fucking hell . . . Prick!'

Leicester enquired about the availability of Martin O'Neill, who had managed the club in the late 1990s, but O'Neill was coaching the Republic of Ireland national team, who were in the midst of the qualifying process for Euro 2016. He was committed to the job and had already gained an impressive away draw with world champions Germany. Kutner, who also represented O'Neill, put Ranieri's name forward as an alternative, and it was one of several the owners considered, along with that of Guus Hiddink, the Holland coach, who was similarly involved in trying to qualify for Euro 2016.

The fact that Leicester's owners compiled a shortlist which included O'Neill, Hiddink and Ranieri gives a clear picture of the profile they were looking for: all three were vastly experienced men in their sixties who tended to avoid controversy, got along well with the media and acted as a calming influence.

However, Pearson's departure was not a done deal. According to people familiar with Leicester, there was also a belief in the club that Pearson had been unlucky. Football is a low-scoring game: victories can easily turn into draws and draws into defeats. From a footballing perspective, letting him continue – even in the case of relegation – seemed the right thing to do. Then the decision got taken out of the owners' hands for the simple reason that Leicester began winning. And winning. And winning again.

Actually, the run began following a 4–3 defeat to Tottenham, which proved several things to the owners. One was that the players were clearly still united behind Pearson, as they battled back from a two-goal deficit. Another was that they were unlucky. Spurs scored a goal after being awarded a highly dubious penalty. They notched up another after an unfortunate ricochet led to a Jeff Schlupp own goal. And then came a run of four straight victories in April that saw Pearson being named Manager of the Month and Leicester rose from the bottom to safety with a one-point lead over Sunderland (who nevertheless had a game in hand).

Sacking Pearson was out of the question at this point, though his behaviour again raised eyebrows the following week after a home defeat to table-topping Chelsea. Pearson complained about criticism directed at his players and a Leicester journalist asked him to what he was referring.

'If you don't know the answer to that question then I think you are an ostrich,' Pearson said, glaring at him. 'Your head must be in the sand. Is your head in the sand? Are you flexible enough to get your head in the sand? My suspicion would be no . . . I can [get my head in the sand] . . . You can't.' On and on it went, increasingly bizarre and uncomfortable, with Pearson calling the journalist daft and mimicking his voice. It ended with Pearson walking out of the press conference.

This time Pearson apologised and he did so in public, three days later, ahead of Leicester's next game, against Newcastle United. His apology was immediately accepted and in normal circumstances that would have been that. Except there was nothing normal that day.

A Midlands-based reporter named Pat Murphy decided to take the opportunity to grill Pearson about his behaviour. Pearson made the mistake of engaging with him. What followed was an excruciatingly painful seven minutes and twenty-two seconds exchange that will live on for ever on

YouTube. It was like one of those made-for-TV legal dramas, with Murphy in the role of the sharp-tongued prosecutor and Pearson the overmatched, squirming defendant. You can see Pearson's chest rising and falling, as if he's controlling his breathing in an effort to stay calm, while Murphy, off-camera, challenges his every answer.

Watching it back, it's as remarkable as it's uncomfortable. Pearson, flanked by empty chairs, looks like the loneliest manager in football. Murphy tells him that he's 'in danger of appearing a bully and paranoid' and that 'someone's got to tell you'. He asks him if he's 'thought of taking anger management courses'. And he adds that what happened 'didn't need to be a big story but it's now a 24/7 story and it's [Pearson's] doing'.

On the last point Murphy was 100 per cent correct. Pearson was showing time and again his inability to handle the media. In 2015 that was a problem. It's a trite cliché to describe football as a business rather than a sport, but it's true. And it's not just any business; it's a media entertainment business. Money flows to the clubs based not just on their results, but also on their image and their ability to attract interest. Sponsors paid a lot of money to be associated with Leicester City, and those brands were being juxtaposed with a man who appeared passive-aggressive, uncomfortable and unpleasant. Every manager can lose his cool, make mistakes or be put in difficult spots by the media at some point, but Pearson was at once reacting badly to those moments and drawing them out from one news cycle to the next.

Months later, in an interview with *The Times*, Pearson acknowledged that perhaps adopting a different public persona might have been to his benefit. 'Do I wish I had composed myself better in that instance? Yes, which is why I apologised to the journalist in question,' he said. 'In my next job maybe I'll try to do things a little differently . . . but I certainly don't intend to take a crash course in projecting an image that I am not. That's pretty shallow. I am what I am.'

What he was, was a guy who had put his club in a difficult position, because despite the concerns about his image, the football side was flourishing. As awkward as Pearson was being in public – not through malice – the owners were increasingly convinced he was getting the job done on the pitch. For the time being, Plan B was put on hold. Football-wise there was a firm conviction that Pearson was the right man to keep them up. Image-wise the jury was still out.

As it happened, Leicester roared up the table. They notched up consecutive wins against Newcastle (3–0) and Southampton (2–0), before a goalless draw at Sunderland guaranteed safety with a game to spare. And they won their final match too, a 5–1 hammering of Queens Park Rangers.

Pearson's footballing nous was vindicated, as was the owners' faith in him and the team. Several factors contributed to the end-of-season rally, among them the switch to a three-man defence, the arrival of centre back Robert Huth in January and the form of midfielder Esteban Cambiasso, as well as the fact that Leicester had been reaping less than they had sowed in terms of performance. The team's self-belief and unity also played a huge part. These were qualities that would be critical the following season as well.

Meanwhile, the club's dramatic comeback had drawn plenty of attention in the Srivaddhanaprabhas' native Thailand. Given the owners' strong links both to the Thai royal family and the business community, including the tourist authority, an end-of-season visit was hastily arranged. Leicester's visit was meant to be all about photo opportunities, glad-handing and strengthening commercial ties, but it boomeranged due to the antics of three young men who had very little to do with the first team.

During the tour three junior Leicester players – goalkeeper Adam Smith, defender James Pearson and striker Tom Hopper – filmed themselves engaging in sex acts with several Thai women. They provided a running commentary which included sexist and racist slurs. The video circulated among friends and acquaintances and ended up in the hands of a tabloid newspaper, which published the story on 30 May 2015.

The tale was hugely embarrassing to the club's owners, even though it did not cause quite as much of a splash in Thailand as it might have, thanks to some sterling PR work in the local media. It was pointed out that the trio had, between them, made just one appearance for the club in 2014–15, and that was in an early-round League Cup game. Still, it was deeply disappointing for the Srivaddhanaprabhas. After an internal investigation all three had their contracts terminated on 17 June.

A statement from the club read: 'Leicester City Football Club is acutely aware of its position and that of its players, as a representative of the city of Leicester, the Premier League, the Football Association and the club's supporters. It is committed to promoting a positive message of community and family values and quality, and to upholding the standards of a club with its history, tradition and aspirations.'

Had the three been just any players, the problem might have been put to rest then and there, but the James Pearson in question happened to be the son of the manager. Less than two weeks later Pearson himself was dismissed. A statement released by Leicester spoke of 'fundamental differences in perspective' between Pearson and the club. Did his son's dismissal play a part in the decision? Plenty in the media speculated that it did. Sources who claimed inside knowledge offered conflicting accounts. One said that Pearson resented the fact that he had not been involved in the decision to sack the three players. Another insisted that the incident had little to do with his departure, which had become inevitable amid concerns over his erratic behaviour.

What most agreed on was that Pearson was not sacked for footballing reasons, and many did not take it well. Despite his earlier criticisms of Pearson, Lineker, front and centre, tweeted, 'Leicester City have sacked Nigel Pearson! Really? WTF!' On social media he added, 'So, after not only getting LCFC promoted but pulling off the most miraculous escape in PL history, Pearson is sacked. Those who run football never cease to amaze with their stupidity.' A poll in the *Leicester Mercury* revealed that 70 per cent of respondents disagreed with the club's decision.

At this point you might be tempted to conclude that football fans only care about the football side, and that Pearson's odd public behaviour was irrelevant to them, as were the reputation issues raised when his own son was involved in the orgy video. But the fact that nearly one in three Leicester supporters agreed with the decision suggests that they understood the position in which the Srivaddhanaprabha family found themselves. Or perhaps they remembered that while Pearson did engineer a great escape, he had also guided the club to last place in the table in March. Maybe they felt letting someone else have a go was not entirely a bad thing.

Much was made of the fact that Pearson's sacking came on

the eve of the transfer window officially opening and less than a week before the club's preseason training camp in Austria. At some clubs losing a manager at that stage would have been disastrous, but Leicester were set up differently to many traditional English clubs, where there is an omnipotent top-down manager who oversees every last detail from signings to training sessions to the colour of the napkins in the canteen.

Instead, Leicester had a strong scouting and recruitment operation, involving Director of Football Jon Rudkin, Assistant Coach and Head of Recruitment Steve Walsh and Technical Scouting Coordinator Ben Wrigglesworth. They had arrived at the club in different ways and at different times. Rudkin, a former Leicester youth team player, had been a coach at the club since 1998 and responsible for the academy since 2003. Walsh, a former schoolteacher and part-time scout for Chelsea (curiously, he overlapped with Ranieri), had been working with Pearson since 2008 and was retained after his sacking. Wrigglesworth, still in his mid-twenties, was considered something of a technical scouting prodigy who had worked his way up from a work experience position.

The club felt the infrastructure was there to press on, and while Pearson's departure obviously mattered, it would not require a whole new blueprint as is often the case when a manager moves on. Reverting to the Plan B shortlist of a few months earlier, and with O'Neill and Hiddink not showing much interest in the job, they arranged to see Ranieri. According to sources familiar with the situation, while they valued his experience, they were ready to cast the net wider if they weren't wowed by their initial meeting. Instead, the interview went well. Exceptionally well. So much so that within a few days he had been appointed manager.

For Ranieri it wasn't a difficult decision to make. He was nearing the stage of his career where he'd experienced most of what football had to offer. He'd managed thirteen clubs in four countries and eight divisions. He'd managed a national team. He was pretty clear on what he did – and did not – enjoy. He doted on English football and loved, to use his own expression, the daily smell of the fresh-cut grass on the training pitch. Odds are, he would have taken the Leicester job even if he hadn't walked into what he would later describe as one of the most impressive and efficient set-ups he had known in football.

Still, taking over such a well established and well run club and replacing a manager who had finished the season on a high and had been let go for non-footballing reasons was very much a double-edged sword. The club were clear on the fact that they believed in their blueprint. That meant transfer decisions were largely out of his hands. Indeed, a fair chunk of the club's incoming players were already signed or on their way. This also meant that Ranieri would not be bringing an entire new coaching team with him; Paolo Benetti and Andrea Azzalin were the only ones who joined with him, Giorgio Pellizzaro had to step down for health reasons. It's hard to overstate the significance of this. This was a very different Ranieri to the manager who had joined Chelsea fifteen years earlier. Back then, as was his custom, Ranieri had taken with him an assistant coach (Angelo Antenucci), a goalkeeping coach (Pellizzaro) and a fitness coach (Roberto Sassi).

There are obvious pros and cons. On the one hand, it means a manager is surrounded by trusted advisers who are very much on his wavelength. They know the way he works, they know what he wants and they can act as his eyes and ears.

On the other, it can isolate the new boss not just from his players – particularly when the manager is foreign and there is a language barrier – but also from the rest of the club. It may create an us-versus-them situation which can be distinctly unhealthy. Equally, a manager with his own staff is far from ideal from the club's perspective. When the manager moves on, there is a real risk that he will take his crew with him, meaning the club must start from scratch. That was a very real concern when Leicester sacked Pearson, particularly vis-à-vis assistant bosses Steve Walsh and Craig Shakespeare. Would they remain loyal to Pearson? Would he demand their loyalty? Would Ranieri even want to work with them?

It's a credit to all involved that Ranieri had the humility to learn and work with Walsh and Shakespeare, and they had the humility to accept their new boss – particularly one who was so different to Pearson – and the open-mindedness to work with him. Benetti was Ranieri's most trusted adviser given their long-standing relationship, but he wasn't a second in command. Shakespeare and Walsh had more influence than he did. Azzalin came in but worked under Matt Reeves, Leicester's incumbent head of fitness and conditioning. Pearson too deserves credit: after all, he had hired them during his first stint at the club in 2008 and he had taken them with him to Hull City and then back to Leicester.

Whatever the circumstances, it's fair to say that Ranieri had tiptoed his way back into the Premier League. And part of that had to do with his experience and personal growth over the past fifteen years. He understood he was not in a position to make demands. Fifteen years earlier, when he took over a pre-Abramovich Chelsea, he may have nurtured ambitions of going on to manage the biggest clubs in the world. As it turned out, he never got to take charge of a Real Madrid or a Bayern Munich or a Manchester United, but for pressure and prestige the likes of Juventus, Inter and Roma weren't far behind. Now he just wanted to work, and to do so in a country and a footballing culture he had come to love.

'The footballing culture that I feel best represents me and my view of the game? It's English football,' he said in an October 2015 interview. 'They have the same spirit as I did when I played football. I wasn't a star, I wasn't talented, but I never gave up, I was always there. If I got knocked down, I got back up. That was my idea of football and it was pretty close to the English game.'

Yet the general reaction to his appointment ranged from the underwhelmed to the downright angry. Lineker summed up the thoughts of many when he famously tweeted, 'Claudio Ranieri? Really?' He then added, 'Claudio Ranieri is clearly experienced, but this is an uninspired choice by Leicester. It's amazing how the same old names keep getting a go on the managerial merry-go-round.'

You can understand the scepticism. For all the talk of globalisation, most football cultures remain inward-looking. To much of the English public Ranieri remained frozen in time as the guy from 2004, the Tinkerman who had struggled with the English language and whose Chelsea side suddenly became dominant after he left. The main difference was that he was now eleven years older.

The fact that in the intervening years he had managed three of the greatest football clubs in Italy mattered little, nor that he had finished second in Serie A with Roma, nearly derailing José Mourinho's treble-winning Inter Milan and doing so on a limited budget. Or that he took Juventus, in their first season back in the top flight, to a third-place finish. Or that his Monaco team, newly promoted to Ligue 1, recorded the highest points total ever of a second-place side, beaten only by the biggest-spending team in the history of the French game. Or that maybe, just maybe, he had learned something in the past eleven years, that perhaps some of his mistakes had taught him some lessons and that he was now a better manager than before. Instead, all you got from some quarters – mostly Wikipedia warriors – were giggles at the fact that his Greece side had lost to the Faroe Islands.

This shouldn't surprise us. Once you leave the Premier League – or, to be fair, Serie A, La Liga or the Bundesliga, because to varying degrees they too are distinctly insular – it takes something hugely special to get back on the radar. Short of winning European silverware and a slew of league titles, you remain, for better or worse, what you were when you left. It's a bit like the geeky guy who was mocked by everyone returning for his high school reunion. He may have become hugely successful, started a family, done many worthwhile things, but the first reaction remains based on the perception folks had of him back when he was in their midst.

Ranieri was a bit odd. He was too nice. His English was rubbish. He was a lovable loser. And, above all, he was the Tinkerman, a manager who meddled needlessly. Which may explain why those who paid attention to his very first press conference – and it probably wasn't that many outside Leicester – were slightly surprised when he said, 'I am sure I don't want to change too many things. [And the things I want to change] I am going to change very slowly, so that everyone understands me.'

He would be true to his word.

14. If It Ain't Broke . . .

Leicester City had been doing their preseason training in the spa town of Bad Radkersburg, right across the Mura river from Slovenia, in the south-east corner of Austria. It was the sort of place that coaches love: quiet, remote, no distractions. Craig Shakespeare and Steve Walsh had been in charge during the search for a new manager, and Ranieri immediately flew out to join them. He knew first impressions were crucial. He didn't want to be seen as a pushover, but he also didn't want to disrupt what had been a very successful team. Particularly on the recruitment side, where the likes of Christian Fuchs and Shinji Okazaki had been brought on board.

Ranieri told Shakespeare and Walsh that for the first few days he'd simply watch the way they took training. He wasn't going to jump to conclusions, either about the squad or the staff. This decision had its risks. When a new boss comes in and says something like 'You go ahead and do what you normally do; I'll just watch and then draw my own conclusions' it can be distinctly unnerving. Coaches know their positions are under continuous review, that they can be let go at any time. But it's one thing to work under the guidance of a manager who will stick up for you because you've been together for nearly a decade, as had been the case with Pearson; it's another to have one's work scrutinised by a new boss, one who sits on the sidelines and simply watches while you get on with your work.

Yet Ranieri, with the support of the club, was able to create an atmosphere of trust. And he liked what he saw from day one. The players were motivated and hard-working, the input from Shakespeare especially was sound, the vibe and ambience excellent. 'I saw the way they worked and I quickly came to the conclusion that there wasn't much to change,' he said. 'They were very good, very professional. And I knew we could work together.' Ranieri had made up his mind about his new staff. And for their part, even if they had reservations about Ranieri, they were willing to give him a go.

His first few days of training camp were marked as much by getting to know his new staff and squad as they were by monitoring the club's efforts to re-sign its 2014–15 Player of the Year, Esteban Cambiasso. The Argentine veteran had arrived late in the transfer window the previous summer. He was thirty-four years old and had spent a decade at Inter. Prior to that, he had been at Real Madrid. Not surprisingly a few had scoffed that this was just yet another case of a veteran has-been looking for one final payday in England. As instant judgements go, this one was particularly wide of the mark.

Cambiasso had gone on to make thirty-three appearances for Pearson's Leicester and had proved particularly instrumental in that dazzling end-of-season run when the Foxes gained twenty-two of a possible twenty-seven points and ascended from bottom to comfortably avoiding relegation. The supporters had had no hesitation in naming him Player of the Year, and after Pearson's departure there was even talk among some that he might be named player-manager, such was his charisma and popularity.

He had only signed a one-year deal at the King Power, and while negotiations to extend this had begun earlier in the year – with the club willing to keep him even in the Championship, as that was where it appeared Leicester were headed – they had stalled. There were reports that Cambiasso was reluctant to commit until a new boss was named, and the club hoped that when Ranieri was announced on 13 July it would help make up his mind. After all, the pair had worked together quite well during Ranieri's time at Inter in 2011–12 and Cambiasso had been pretty much an automatic choice in the starting eleven.

Instead, negotiations dragged on. Cambiasso's representatives requested a final offer from Leicester. A day after it arrived, on 21 July, he took to Facebook to say he would not be returning. And he was replying very quickly to the offer because he did not want to drag things out further for the club, but aimed to give them as much time as possible to sign a replacement.

There are different accounts as to what prompted this decision. According to one source, it was a family matter: they had a daughter nearing school age, so location was becoming increasingly important. Another insists that the prospect of Champions League Football with Olympiacos – he would sign with the Greek giants a few weeks later – and the lifestyle in Athens was too good to pass up. A third maintains that, while he admired Ranieri as a person and as a coach, he wasn't sure about his new manager's prospects in the Premier League after so many seasons away. Whatever the truth – and it may well have been a combination of all three factors – it was a blow to the club and to Ranieri, who hoped to build his midfield around Cambiasso. And it meant that they would need to find a replacement.

The club were already working on a central midfielder, one whom Steve Walsh had been excited about for some time: N'Golo Kanté. In the popular narrative he is one of those gems plucked out of obscurity, a tribute to outstanding recruitment. In fact, that's only partly true. While he did play for an amateur side in the ninth tier of French football, Suresnes, until he was nineteen, by the end of the 2013–14 campaign he had worked his way up to Caen, in the French second division. He had plenty of suitors that summer, but Caen, who had earned promotion to the top division, insisted on keeping him. When he once again shone in Ligue 1, as Caen finished mid-table, interest in him only ramped up further. Marseille, Olympique Lyonnais, West Ham United and Watford all took long hard looks at him, but in the end Leicester signed him for around £5.6 million in what would turn out to be one of the deals of the summer.

And yet Ranieri was somewhat sceptical; Walsh had to insist that Kanté was worth pursuing. What was it that put Ranieri off? Possibly a combination of factors. Football is not a perfect meritocracy, but it's highly unusual for a top-class player to get to the age of twenty-four – Kanté's age when he arrived at LCFC – and have just a single top-flight season under his belt. Not unless he has been injured or has had major off-the-pitch issues, like drinking, drugs or disciplinary problems – none of which applied to Kanté. Sure, you do get the occasional late bloomer in football, but for £5.6 million – not an insignificant sum for Leicester – you wanted somebody reliable.

After all, it wasn't as if Kanté was unknown. He hadn't grown up in some remote part of the world, but rather in Paris, a place teeming with scouts and so-called experts. Plenty of people would have seen him at Suresnes, and in fact by the time he was eighteen he'd had dozens of trials with bigger teams, including the likes of Rennes, Lorient, Sochaux and, most notably, at the French FA's national academy in Clairefontaine. All of them had rejected him. When he did get a move, at nineteen, it was to Boulogne, a yo-yo club between the second and third divisions. And even then he spent two seasons in the reserve team, only establishing himself as a starter in 2012–13. (Ironically he had actually made his debut the year before, when Boulogne were in the second flight – against table-topping Monaco, then managed by . . . Ranieri!)

This was a man who had not played a single minute of professional football before his twenty-first birthday. There isn't a great track record of players like that making it at the top level, especially when they're five feet seven inches tall. Sure, he'd enjoyed two outstanding seasons at Caen, but one was in the second division and the other could have been a fluke. Still, Ranieri placed his trust in Walsh, and he was able to deliver the player. Not necessarily because Leicester outbid the opposition or because it was a more appealing destination, but largely because of the legwork Walsh had put in the previous two seasons and the relationships that had been built with Kanté's entourage. That's a part of scouting and recruitment that often gets overlooked.

The Frenchman arrived on 3 August and first impressions were underwhelming, at least until he stepped on to the pitch. *Leicester Mercury* correspondent Rob Tanner tells a wonderful story about how the small and youthful-looking Kanté was mistaken for a lost teenager in the club car park, with a security guard asking him, 'Are you OK? Are you waiting for your parents to pick you up?'

On that same day Leicester made another signing, one who would leave less of a mark than Kanté but would cost roughly the same: Yohan Benalouane. Ranieri had taken stock of the team in the preseason friendlies and felt they were somewhat undermanned defensively, particularly if he was to continue using the back three formation that had brought Pearson success the previous year. At that stage there were only four centre backs in the squad: Robert Huth, Captain Wes Morgan (who had forgone his holidays that summer, opting to play for Jamaica in both the Copa América in Chile and the Gold Cup in the United States), Marcin Wasilewski (who had just turned thirty-five) and Liam Moore, a twenty-two-year-old who had spent half the previous season on loan.

Benalouane was twenty-eight and came with a reputation as a hard man. The year before, at Atalanta in Serie A, he had contrived to rack up fifteen yellows and a red in twenty-nine appearances in all competitions. But he was a grafter, a battler, and Ranieri felt he was right for the Premier League. And he had drawn attention from a number of bigger clubs. Plus, he could be deployed at both centre back and right back. According to multiple sources, he was the one player Ranieri really lobbied for.

Benalouane was also significant because by this stage Ranieri had decided to abandon the back three in favour of a traditional back four. His original plan had been to continue Pearson's work, applying the oldest principle in the world: if it ain't broke, don't fix it. But he was noticing how the back three often left Riyad Mahrez, arguably Leicester's most talented player, with insufficient room to operate. 'In most of the friendlies I'd start with a back three and switch to a back four at half-time,' Ranieri said later. 'And it was really simple. We just played better with a four.' In his mind he had not yet settled on what sort of back-four formation it would be, 4-4-2, 4-2-3-1 or 4-3-3 – he felt he had players flexible enough to employ any one of them – but what he did know was that the base had to be a straight back four.

By this point the 2015–16 season opener against Sunderland was just a few days away. When it came Ranieri was still getting to know what he had, and his first starting eleven was made up entirely of players from the Pearson era, bar Okazaki up front. The other new signings – Fuchs, Kanté and Benalouane – were all on the bench, though in the event all three would come on.

Leicester raced to an early 3–0 lead and went on to win 4–2, with Mahrez stealing the show. He scored two – one from the spot – and hit the woodwork. He walked off to a standing ovation. Another win followed – this time away to West Ham – using a similar blueprint. Leicester, with an unchanged eleven, hit on the break early, going two goals up through Okazaki and Mahrez and then hanging on to win 2–1. Two games, two wins and first place. Not a bad start, but Ranieri still felt he needed to sort out his midfield. Andy King and Danny Drinkwater had done a fine job in the opening games, but over the course of a full season there were going to be situations where he'd need to add an extra central midfielder. Carrying a front four with two strikers and two genuine wingers was going to be a burden for the middle of the park. Plus, if he switched to a three-man midfield against bigger opponents – something he was willing to do – he'd need an extra body.

And while he had been willing to roll the dice on Kanté,

who had impressed in his substitute appearances and in training, he still needed that replacement for Cambiasso, someone with experience and personality. Swiss midfielder Gökhan Inler had been tracked for some time, and Ranieri okayed the deal. Inler was thirty-one and coming off an injury-hampered season at Napoli. A few years earlier he had been considered one of the most promising box-to-box midfielders in Europe, which was why Napoli had spent £11 million to sign him in 2011. Four years later the club were ready to move him on, and it was felt, just as with Cambiasso, that he'd relish the challenge of relaunching his career in a new league. At just under £5 million he looked like a safe bet. He arrived on 19 August 2015 and made his debut off the bench in a draw with Tottenham a few days later.

The final game in August saw Kanté's starting debut and Ranieri's first use of 4-3-3. Okazaki was dropped and Kanté joined Drinkwater and King in midfield. A 1–1 draw meant Leicester were second in the table, three points behind Manchester City. As the international break rolled around, Ranieri took stock of his team. While he now felt Leicester had enough cover in central midfield, the wide areas were more of a concern. Mahrez and Marc Albrighton had both had a tremendous start to the season, but the club needed more options on the wings, not least because neither player was particularly durable: Mahrez had never started more than twenty-five league games in a season and the most Albrighton had managed was twenty. This had been less of an issue earlier in the summer, when Ranieri was considering persevering with Pearson's wing-back system, but in 4-4-2 or 4-3-3 it was different. He had no options on the wings, other than moving Shinji Okazaki out there or playing Jeffrey Schlupp when he wasn't needed as a fullback.

Leicester had been linked with a number of wingers that summer: Birmingham City's Demarai Gray, Sporting Lisbon's André Carrillo and Hull City's Ahmed El Mohamady. Apart from their position on the pitch, the three had very little in common. Gray was an exciting fleet-footed winger who had lit up the English Championship the previous season, but he was also only nineteen years old and it wasn't clear whether a season of part-time duty at a higher level would help him or the team. Carrillo was an elegant winger who, at twenty-four, looked ready for a step up from the Portuguese league. Yet he was a year away from becoming a free agent and had let his contract run down, suggesting a spiky relationship between Sporting and his representatives, and it was unclear how quickly he would adapt to the English game. El Mohamady was the safest option of the three and a proven top-flight performer who could provide cover at fullback as well.

Leicester knew there were pros and cons to each player, and took this into account when assessing how much they'd be willing to pay. Rather than viewing them as interchangeable – which they weren't – they were comfortable with the notion of getting the best player available, but only at the right price. As it happened, Leicester got none of them that August, but stuck to the task and ended up settling on Nathan Dyer, a reliable veteran dribbler, who arrived from Swansea on loan for a small fee.

We often think of team-building and recruitment in terms of the players a club can attract, but sometimes it's about getting the right player to fill the right role and not overpaying. Every new signing is a gamble. It's about assessing risk and how much you're willing to bet on that risk. In this case Leicester played it perfectly.

They avoided a bidding war for Gray early in the summer – when Birmingham City were turning down £5 million bids – and instead waited for him to sign a new deal with a release clause of just £3.7 million. With Birmingham in financial difficulties, Gray's representatives made the release clause a condition of extending his contract. Leicester ended up signing him a few months later in the January window. As for Carrillo, Sporting were still holding out for around £10 million, but when a player is only a season away from free agency, the price normally reduces significantly, so it made more sense for Leicester to wait and try their luck at getting him on a free transfer. (Carrillo would subsequently become embroiled in a nasty spat with Sporting, who would punish him for letting his contract run down rather than signing an extension so that they could obtain a fee when he was sold: they simply stopped playing him after mid-September.) On top of that, he picked up an injury while on international duty in mid-October and did not play at all for the rest of the season. Bullet dodged. El Mohamady had played all but one minute of Hull's Premier League matches the previous year. The club had been relegated, but his durability and reliability made him a valuable commodity and Hull knew it. Leicester had their own valuation and ended up walking away when the price got too steep.

In any case Ranieri now felt he had cover in all areas. Of course what he couldn't have known at the time was that he needn't have worried. Far from lacking durability, Mahrez and Albrighton would miss just one game between them all season.

15. Pizza Party

The vast majority of football folk are by nature superstitious. Some are happy to talk about it, others are not. Some take the attitude that they don't really believe in bad luck but, heck, you never know. Others allow it to dominate their lives more than it probably should. Claudio Ranieri isn't in the latter category. But he's human. And he's a football man. And sometimes incidents assume outsized importance because in the backs of our minds we tend to think they happen for a reason.

Leicester returned from the international break in October to host Aston Villa, and Ranieri gave Gökhan Inler his first Premier League start. He and the club still believed in the notion of an experienced midfield general to direct traffic and provide leadership, just as Esteban Cambiasso had done the previous season. Inler thus took his place alongside Danny Drinkwater, with N'Golo Kanté on the bench.

As it turned out, for sixty-four minutes Leicester were disastrous. They went two goals down to Villa, a side that would end up finishing bottom of the Premier League. It wasn't Inler's fault necessarily; it was collectively a poor performance. But it wasn't lost on anyone that after he came off, along with Marc Albrighton, it looked like an entirely different Leicester. Ritchie De Laet pulled one back in the seventy-second minute, and Jamie Vardy equalised with eight minutes to go. Then, in the eighty-ninth minute, Nathan Dyer, the latest acquisition and smallest man on the pitch, grabbed a dramatic winner. The five-foot-five-inch winger squeezed himself between Micah Richards and Alan Hutton and threw himself at Riyad Mahrez's lofted ball into the box. Villa keeper Brad Guzan – nearly a foot taller – rushed out to meet him. Dyer's head nudged the ball past Guzan and into the back of the net just as the two collided.

The King Power stadium erupted even as Dyer lay still on the turf for a second or two. It was the classic moment that made you fear the worst: a high-speed collision and a player not moving, often a worse sign than seeing someone writhe in pain. On the sideline Ranieri went from jubilation to fear and then back to elation as Dyer slowly got up. He was going to be fine. Dyer – and Mahrez, who continued in scintillating form – were the story of the day. Ranieri admitted his team had been outplayed overall but praised their performance late on.

The following week would take an eerily similar turn. Inler got another crack in the starting line-up, away from home to Stoke. Again, Leicester found themselves two goals down at half-time. Ranieri's post-game comments – 'We were making too many mistakes, losing a lot of balls in the middle of the pitch' – were confirmation of what everybody had seen: Inler was really struggling, perhaps more than against Villa. Off he came at the break and on came Albrighton. And on charged Leicester.

Mahrez converted a penalty early in the second half, and Vardy, scoring in his third straight game, made it 2–2 with twenty minutes to go. Leicester were second in the table, behind Manchester City, but it was not lost on Ranieri that in the 120 minutes that Inler had been on the pitch Leicester had conceded five goals and scored just once.

That may not have been down to Inler, but management isn't just about numbers and facts and things you can measure empirically; it's also about feelings and sensations. And with Inler – at least the current version – Leicester simply weren't as good. That Stoke game would be his last league appearance for three months. Ranieri appreciated him and kept him involved as long as Leicester were in the League Cup, but he also understood chemistry. And, for whatever reason, it wasn't working with Inler on the pitch.

Arsenal visited the King Power next, and this match would be in many ways a watershed moment. It was Leicester's first game against a Champions League side, and it marked the first time that Ranieri lined up what would become his trademark front six: Drinkwater and Kanté in midfield, Mahrez and Albrighton wide, Okazaki and Vardy up front. Look only at the scoreline – Arsenal won 5–2, Leicester's first loss in five months – and you'll see a heavy home defeat. Look back at the goals and you'll note some poor defending and some outstanding play from Gunners forward Alexis Sánchez.

But Ranieri saw something different, as did others on his staff. Leicester were by no means intimidated. And his players came out of the gate quickly and with purpose, the opposite of what had happened against Stoke and Villa, when they found themselves down and had to come from behind. Vardy opened the scoring – his run was now at four games – and hit the woodwork soon after. De Laet also came close. Leicester could easily have been 3–0 up in the first fifteen minutes. What followed was in many ways a collapse, but as Ranieri pointed out, the first half was very open. If Leicester could bottle that early performance, if they could play like that against a much better opponent, maybe they were on to something after all.

Not everybody saw it that way. Those who believed that Leicester would regress to the mean and begin their inevitable slide down the table thought that the five goals shipped against Arsenal were a sign of things to come. At this stage Leicester had conceded fourteen, the second most in the Premier League. There was a reason why Pearson had opted for a back three, they argued: Robert Huth and Wes Morgan on their own were bound to be vulnerable to pace, and if you were going to insist on a back four then surely you needed a three-man midfield. Kanté and Drinkwater on their own could not possibly be sufficient in the Premier League. Why not call upon Andy King, who had served Leicester so well the previous year? Or bring back Inler?

Ranieri took all this into consideration. His side had yet to keep a clean sheet, and this was bothering him, more so than the five conceded against Arsenal. He had even joked about it in public, announcing at the press conference ahead of the Stoke game that he would take his team out for pizza if they managed to keep a clean sheet. Thus far they had shown enough attacking firepower at the other end for the results to roll in, but it was unrealistic to rely on the heroics of Vardy and Mahrez to bail them out every game. At some point they would need to tighten up.

Ranieri knew this and was by no means averse to either 4-3-3 or 3-5-2. After all, he had pushed a three-centre-back system in preseason and had added Yohan Benalouane for that express purpose. Equally, Inler had arrived to give extra depth to the midfield, so they could easily switch to either formation. He was ready to make the changes if needed. Thirty-plus years in management had given him a tactical comfort level sufficient to make almost any system work. And perhaps the Ranieri of the past would have sought shelter in conventional wisdom, switching to what the critics were suggesting and choosing the path of least resistance.

But this Ranieri was different. Football wasn't just about systems or personnel, it was about execution. There were other ways to stiffen up the defence without necessarily compromising an attack which so far had looked impressive. There were players who deserved an opportunity. And, while he was loath to admit it in public, the good start to the season had given his team a bit of a cushion. This was not the time to batten down the hatches. He did decide to make changes for Leicester's next match, away to Norwich City, as many had predicted, however they weren't the ones his critics had expected.

Ranieri dropped Mahrez for the first time in the 2015–16 season. It would be the only time he did not feature at all in a league match. This decision seemed counter-intuitive – why would you leave out your most skilful player? – but was based on two factors. First of all Mahrez needed a breather, as had been obvious in the second half against Arsenal. This was a chance for the Algerian to clear his mind and rest his body. Just as important, Ranieri felt that directness and pace were the keys against a Norwich side that liked to keep possession at home but which didn't have a lot of cutting edge. The threat of a counter would be the best way to control the game, and so he moved Jeffrey Schlupp on to the wing. Now, in Vardy, Schlupp and Shinji Okazaki, Leicester had three of the fastest players in the league ready to bear down whenever Norwich lost the ball.

It worked a treat. Schlupp (twice), Vardy and Drinkwater all had clear chances to score early on, as Leicester's counter-attacks tore through Norwich. Vardy in the first half (the goal streak was now up to five consecutive games) and Schlupp in the second gave Leicester the cushion they needed to withstand a late Norwich siege. It finished 2–1, and the goals reflected what would be Leicester trademarks all season long. Vardy's was a penalty which he won under a questionable challenge from Sébastien Bassong. It wouldn't be the last time Leicester's top goalscorer would be accused of going down too easily. And Schlupp's goal came after some relentless pressing, which resulted in Norwich losing the ball in their own half and ended with Kanté setting him up.

Ranieri was vindicated across the board. Not just with his tactics or the decision to drop Mahrez, but with what he did defensively, giving two new fullbacks, Christian Fuchs and Danny Simpson, their first starts of the season. Thus was born the back four that would serve Leicester so well for the rest of the season. They may not have kept a clean sheet on the day, but they showed the kind of solidity and versatility Ranieri craved.

He kept the same line-up at Southampton for the following match, once again leaving out Mahrez. This time the script would follow that of the early games. Leicester went 2–0 down; Ranieri brought on Mahrez for Okazaki and Dyer for Schlupp at half-time, and they stormed back to grab a draw, while possibly deserving even more. It was Vardy who took the headlines – his two goals extending his scoring run in successive games to six – but it was Mahrez who changed the game, as Ranieri acknowledged afterwards. So too did Southampton boss Ronald Koeman, who commented, 'The half-time changes made all the difference . . . Mahrez created many difficulties for us.'

'We believe everything could be possible,' Ranieri said after the match. This was the first time he strayed, even slightly, from what would be his post-game refrain, that Leicester were simply trying to avoid relegation and aiming for forty points. He'd later say he was referring simply to their self-belief in getting back into games that appeared lost, though you wonder to what degree the twinkle in his eye said otherwise.

The next game, against Crystal Palace, was a bump in the road, one Leicester managed to negotiate and win – 1–0, with Vardy making it seven on the bounce – in an entirely different way. Ranieri would describe it as 'an Italian match more than an English one', and he wasn't referring to tactics or improvisation. It was tight and niggly, with Leicester more effective at shutting down Palace than creating chances at the other end. The winner came after a defensive mistake by centre back Brede Hangeland. Vardy, lightning quick, was there to pounce. The final whistle was greeted more with relief than joy, and Ranieri reacted by racing on to the pitch to congratulate his players. In so doing, he had violated one of the English game's unwritten traditions: the post-match handshake between managers.

Palace boss Alan Pardew, not the kind to let such a slight go unremarked, commented after the match, 'I thought Claudio Ranieri was goading our players, and he didn't shake my hand at full time, which is disappointing,' before adding ominously, 'They've got to come to our place and we'll remember that.'

And Pardew, like everyone else, was aware of Ranieri's penchant for handshakes – by this point his habit of shaking every journalist's hand before a game had become routine.

A younger Ranieri might have responded in kind. This one knew better. 'I was so happy at the final whistle, I went to celebrate with my players at the centre circle,' he said in his post-game interview. 'I am so sorry. I think he is going to come into my office now for a glass of wine. I'm sorry. I'm sorry. I'm sorry to him.'

Four sorrys in fifteen seconds or so. No opposing manager could ask for more. Ranieri will respond when provoked, his history shows this. The two sides of his personality he references – the placid, mature one who knows how to accept defeat as long as there is maximum effort, and the warrior, harking back to his playing days, who would rather die than surrender – are very real. And the match had been nervy with plenty of reasons for bad Claudio to appear. But Ranieri knew it was best to smother Pardew with kindness and unreserved apologies rather than point out that his complaint was silly. There's not much you can say back to someone who smiles and says, 'You're right. I was wrong. I apologise.'

The story went away very quickly, which is exactly what Ranieri wanted and Leicester needed. Best to focus elsewhere. Not least because Leicester had finally kept a clean sheet, which meant one thing: pizza.

What had begun as a throwaway comment before the Stoke game had turned into a public-relations masterstroke. You only had to hear the crowd at the King Power counting down the final minutes of the Palace game and singing, 'We want pizza! We want pizza!' Although go back and you'll note Ranieri says, 'I offered them pizza [to keep a clean sheet] but maybe it's not enough. Maybe it has to be pizza and a hot dog.' At a time when football clubs are brands and brands seemingly spend half their time trying to concoct attention-seeking initiatives (check out any club website; they're full of them) Ranieri's pizza meme had gone viral.

Sure enough, the club jumped all over it. The following Thursday lunchtime the players joined Ranieri at Peter Pizzeria in Leicester, accompanied of course by media and cameras. Ranieri announced that they wouldn't just be eating pizza, they'd be learning how to make it too. It became part team-building, part reward, part media event. The tale captured the imagination and provided fodder for Internet photo galleries of Mahrez flipping dough.

It made its way into all those 'How Leicester won the Premier League' stories that mushroomed all over the media at the end of the season. It became some kind of work/reward/team-building metaphor and evidence of Ranieri's psychological mastery at nurturing and maintaining team spirit.

With hindsight, it was more likely one of those fortuitous things that took on a life of its own. Offering players rewards for reaching objectives – or in corporate speak, key performance indicators (KPIs) – is nothing new. And guys who bank pay cheques in the mid-five figures every week aren't necessarily going to be motivated by a free meal. Equally, while it was no doubt a fun day out and a bonding opportunity, clubs do things like this all the time. Whether it's paintball, white-water rafting or the old British stand-by of a booze-fuelled lock-in at a pub, events like this are fairly common. There are companies who specialise in this very thing. And yet, for whatever reason, Leicester's pizza party resonated in a way that other more contrived team-building activities did not. Maybe because it was born out of an off-the-cuff joke. Or perhaps it was because Ranieri – both before and during the event – made it disarmingly innocent. Whatever the reason, it became part of the Leicester tale.

Meanwhile the club had entered the zone, that Midas moment when everything seems to go right and turn twenty-four-carat. They dominated West Bromwich Albion, went a goal down against the run of play and stormed back for a 3–2 win, with Mahrez bagging two and Vardy scoring another, to make it eight matches in a row. They played poorly away to Watford but eventually won 2–1, thanks to a late Vardy penalty, won when his umpteenth lung-bursting run was rewarded by an error from Heurelho Gomes, who hauled him down for a spot kick. Vardy put it away, and the magic dust was still there the following week, away to Newcastle, with Vardy equalling Ruud van Nistelrooy's record of scoring in ten consecutive Premier League matches when he slotted the ball past Rob Elliot in first-half injury time. Leo Ulloa and Okazaki rounded out the scoring in a 3–0 win.

Leicester were top of the table again, and Vardy was on the verge of making history. The media narrative focused more on the centre forward than it did on the club, whose run was seemingly chalked up to momentum and a hot streak, riding Vardy's coat-tails and perhaps some good fortune as well. This may have been true to some degree, but what some forget is that Ranieri didn't simply sit back, watch his men perform and enjoy Vardy's otherworldly form. Each game brought a series of tweaks and changes – those who dubbed him the Tinkerman back in the day would have been proud – that helped create the conditions for Vardy and the team to do their thing.

Against West Brom, known for their players' size and

set-piece prowess, he had dropped the diminutive Okazaki and played Ulloa, a legitimate centre forward, alongside Vardy, giving the side brawn and inches. For Watford's visit, after the first half had seen Leicester's game largely neutralised, he switched things around by sending on Okazaki for Schlupp and switching Mahrez from a central position to the wing, where he found fertile ground against Watford's inexperienced fullback Nathan Aké. And away to Newcastle he had again played Vardy and Ulloa together, but dropped the Argentine deeper, creating a physical mismatch between him and Newcastle's small holding midfielder Vurnon Anita. This allowed Ulloa to participate in the lead-up. Indeed, it was Ulloa who played a key role in the build-up to Vardy's record-equalling goal.

While pizza and Vardy dominated the headlines, there was a lot going on beneath the surface, much of it Ranieri being Ranieri: keeping the squad on an even keel and making the kind of adjustments that come from reading games in a way only someone with five decades' experience in football can.

16. Electric Vardy

Manchester United's visit provided Claudio Ranieri and Leicester with a perfect storm of attention. Already the Foxes were the story of the season, with the narrative extending back to the great escape under Nigel Pearson the previous April. And obviously there was the opposition. Manchester United aren't just one of the two most popular clubs in England, they are also natural headline generators. United fans love reading about their club all the time; those who dislike United love reading about them in bad times because there's nothing quite like *Schadenfreude* to cheer up a football fan. And while United's season hadn't been horrendous, despite massive spending they had not won anything in the past two campaigns and manager Louis van Gaal's ways were beginning to come under fire.

Most of all though, it was about Jamie Vardy and his pursuit of Ruud van Nistelrooy's record of scoring in ten consecutive Premier League matches. The twenty-eight-year-old striker had become the face of Leicester's early-season run, and the fact that he had only made his top-flight debut the season before and was unknown to the general public made his a very compelling story.

Vardy had come up through the ranks at his local club, Sheffield Wednesday, but was released at the age of sixteen. 'When I was released it was hard to take,' Vardy told Rob Tanner of the *Leicester Mercury*. 'It was a real heartache. The academy director told me I was too small.'

The game is littered with stories of players who go on to achieve great things but are let go at a young age by clubs and the men whose job it is to assess talent. The 'too small' or 'too frail' rationale has been lobbed at many players over the years. Many kids develop good footballing technique and physical coordination when they are still relatively small, and the big concern is that they will never fill out and won't be able to cope with the physical demands of the professional game.

Vardy was quoted in the *Guardian* in May 2016 as saying he was four feet eleven inches tall at the time of his release. Today he's listed at five feet ten inches, which he explains by saying he had a massive growth spurt at sixteen, just a few months after being let go. That would make him something of a freak of nature. According to charts used by the Royal College of Paediatric Health, a sixteen-year-old boy of that height is in the bottom 0.1 per cent and is projected to grow to just five feet two inches. Professional footballers under five six are exceedingly rare in England. Indeed, the smallest Premier League player in history, Aston Villa fullback Alan Wright, was listed at five feet four inches.

Sheffield Wednesday made a mistake in letting Vardy go, but given the improbability of him growing to a viable height, you can understand their decision. There were likely other factors too. That was in 2003. A top football club these days will be able to call on a wider range of technologies to help project a young player's likely growth. Certainly more so than Wednesday, who at the time were a club in severe financial difficulties and falling through the divisions. A wealthier club might have decided to carry Vardy for another year, just in case he did miraculously experience a growth spurt. But given the numbers and the circumstances, it's hard to fault Wednesday's call.

Because what happened to Vardy physically – the sudden massive growth spurt two months after his release – was improbable to the point of bordering on the miraculous. And, in that sense, it's fitting that he would end up as the face of a football club that would achieve something equally unlikely many years later.

And the Vardy story took another turn after his release: for seven months he simply quit football altogether. At that age this could well have been fatal to Vardy's development as a footballer. A friend eventually persuaded him to join the youth team of a local club, Stocksbridge Park Steels. Founded in 1986 as a result of the merger of the works team of the British Steel Corporation and another club, they were in the eighth tier of the English football pyramid. There were six levels and 188 clubs between Vardy's current team and his old club.

He progressed from the Stocksbridge youth team to the reserves and on to the first team, where he made his debut as a nineteen-year-old in 2006. Three years later he moved to Halifax Town, one tier above Stocksbridge in the Northern Premier League, for £15,000. After a season in which he bagged twenty-seven goals, he was sold to Fleetwood Town in the National League, the highest level of non-League football and a two-tier jump from Halifax, for a whopping £250,000. He was very much a phenomenon, at least at local level.

Vardy wasn't the first discarded player to prove his doubters wrong. The difference was his background and the way it affected his development. The vast majority of Premier League players follow a fairly standard career progression. They are identified at a very young age; they make the grade; they then spend the years between the ages of sixteen and twenty-one honing their craft under highly qualified supervision at state-of-the-art academies. Then a lucky few will make their professional debuts.

Vardy's experience was entirely different. At Stocksbridge he didn't have the benefit of top coaches, fitness specialists, dieticians, masseurs – all the things kids at the best academies take for granted. Nor did he spend time on the training pitch, doing the kind of drills and building up the knowledge and muscle memory which, we're often told, is crucial to developing top-level professionals. Even at Halifax they only trained twice a week, on Tuesday and Thursday evenings. And of course he didn't get paid until he got into the first team, and even then it was the princely sum of thirty pounds per week. That meant he had to work, so he found a job in a factory which made carbon-fibre splints. It was manual labour, lifting and transporting items on a noisy factory floor in long shifts. He stuck at this until midway through his time at Halifax. But the early scoring spree he went on there convinced him that maybe he did have a future in the game. At the very least he owed it to himself to give it a shot. The factory work was giving him back problems too, but mostly it was the demands on his time that forced the decision.

'Up at 7 a.m., in for work, finish work at 4.15, 4.30 p.m., straight into the car to meet up with the other lads from Halifax, and we were training and not getting home until 10 p.m. or 11 p.m. Then straight to bed.' That's how Vardy described his days. 'It was dinner at work then stop off at the service station before we met up with the lads. The England chefs probably wouldn't approve, but back then it was whichever fast-food stop was at the service station. You needed to get a bit of food down you. It was simple as that.'

Complicating matters was an incident that threatened to derail his football career. It happened in 2007 and was the sort of trouble that would instantly cause many clubs to steer clear: a conviction for assault. Vardy's version of events, as recounted to Tanner, makes his actions seem almost benign, but the court apparently did not see them that way.

'I was out one night with a friend who wore a hearing aid and two lads for no reason thought it would be funny to start knocking him and attack him,' he told Tanner. 'I am not proud of what I did but I stuck up for him and defended him as I would for any mate. It ended up getting me into a bit of trouble.'

Vardy was ordered to wear an ankle tag and observe a 6 p.m. to 6 a.m. curfew, which can be problematic when you play football in England, given the sacrosanct three o'clock Saturday kick-off time, particularly away from home. There were a number of away games when he'd need to be substituted so that he could make it home in time for curfew. He'd sprint off the pitch straight into his parents' car and hope there was no traffic on the way home.

Such experiences mark a young man, for better or worse. We'll never know if Vardy would have turned out to be the same player – or maybe even a better player – if, say, he'd joined Manchester United's academy aged ten and spent his entire career there, gaining a traditional football education. Many professional footballers probably could not cope with what Vardy went through. But, conversely, there is little question that his experiences helped give him the character and drive he has today. Vardy himself realises this, which is why he helped set up the V9 Academy, an organisation aimed at identifying non-League players in his former circumstances and helping them along. He has the humility to know that he can not possibly be the only gifted player outside the ranks of professional football to be overlooked year after year.

The season at Fleetwood marked yet another turning point. Vardy scored thirty-one league goals, proving that he could deliver at a far higher level. As a result Nigel Pearson, Steve Walsh and the rest of the Leicester recruitment staff approved his signing for £1 million. At the time it was a record for a non-League player. After a season of transition in the Championship, he played a key role as Leicester won promotion in 2013–14. His first year in the top flight then saw Pearson often deploy him wide, and his scoring output was limited to five goals.

From the very first training sessions Ranieri was struck not just by Vardy's pace and instinct for how play would unfold, but by his rapacious desire. By now the slight sixteen-year-old had grown into a sinewy mass of lean muscle, eager to launch his body into space, not just to pursue a loose ball, but to give teammates a target to hit. Ranieri quickly decided that Vardy belonged closer to the goal, if only for the havoc he could cause. If on top of that he could finish consistently – and his track record in previous seasons suggested he could – then he was tailor-made to be a centre forward or second striker.

Ranieri saw an obvious parallel between Vardy and the player who, perhaps more than any other, had influenced his first spell at Valencia, Claudio 'El Piojo' López. He too began as a wide player and was turned into a central striker by Ranieri.

He too was blessed with pace, desire and a north–south directness that stunned opponents. López had changed the face of Valencia. Ranieri felt Vardy could do the same for LCFC nearly twenty years later.

He was proved right. Vardy had scored thirteen goals in Leicester's first twelve games, and now he had the opportunity to break Van Nistelrooy's record of scoring in ten consecutive Premier League matches. Van Nistelrooy, ever the class act, tweeted, 'Records are meant to be broken. Go on @vardy7, all the best and good luck!' The moment came with twenty-four minutes gone, and it was a typical Vardy goal – pure directness. Christian Fuchs collected the ball straight from goalkeeper Kasper Schmeichel, galloped on the counter just past the halfway line and delivered the ball inside to Vardy, who took it in his stride and fired home from the edge of the penalty area. Manchester United equalised at the end of the first half, but the focus, as you'd expect, was all on Vardy.

Ranieri had been through this before. He had been in charge of Fiorentina back in 1994–95, when Gabriel Batistuta scored in the first eleven games of the season to set a Serie A record. As the hype had grown, whatever fears there might have been of it destabilising the side melted away. Batistuta was so popular with his teammates – and so intent on continuing to put the team first – that it did not affect their performances. Ranieri saw the same dynamic with Vardy. Nobody faulted him for pursuing the record so aggressively and everyone remained supportive. In fact, it felt like the record belonged to the entire squad.

Looking back on Leicester City's 2015–16 feat, you're struck by the number of incidents and narratives that went their way. Some were unanticipated, some slightly more calculated, yet the Vardy tale stands out. The scoring record gave the world his remarkable story. It shifted a lot of the attention on to him and away from the team, and that's something for which Ranieri was grateful. And Vardy, who was living through a blessed period in his life, could clearly cope. 'My friend in Italy asked me about Vardy,' Ranieri said after the record was broken. 'To explain I said I believe if Vardy grabs a light bulb, the bulb will switch on. He is electric. Jamie is electric. It is good energy . . . I should bring him to my house so I don't pay for electricity!'

If Vardy's achievement was incredible, it was also something of a media creation. Most football fans can probably tell you that Alan Shearer is the all-time leading goalscorer in the history of the Premier League and that Peter Shilton has the most England caps. But how many even knew of the existence of Van Nistelrooy's record at the start of the 2015–16 season, and of those how many realised that it was a bit of an artifice? It was a Premier League record; not an English top-flight record. That was set by Sheffield United's Jimmy Dunne, who scored in twelve consecutive games for Sheffield United back in 1930–31. And, during the 1950–51 season, the Blackpool legend Stan Mortensen scored in fifteen successive appearances, though the run was broken by injuries, and he missed several games. Why Van Nistelrooy's mark – which by the way was over two seasons – or Vardy's record should be held in higher regard than Dunne's or Mortensen's is inexplicable, other than the fact that the Premier League hype machine knows no bounds and it's easier to sell and market records with contemporary players.

Vardy failed to equal Dunne's feat in Leicester's next outing, away to Swansea (though he came close), and the limelight shifted back to Mahrez. The Algerian scored a hat-trick against the Swans, notched up another goal in a 2–1 win over Chelsea and hit two in a 3–2 victory away to Everton. He now had thirteen and, ironically, he looked to be one of Vardy's main challengers for the Premier League Golden Boot.

The wins against Swansea and Chelsea were followed by the sacking of their respective managers, Garry Monk and José Mourinho. Obviously, the latter event resonated with Ranieri. The four seasons he had spent at Chelsea were as long as he'd been anywhere as a manager, matching the four years in Florence. He still had a house in London, a long goal-kick away from Stamford Bridge. And he had a roller-coaster relationship with Mourinho. He says he took no pleasure whatsoever in Mourinho's misfortunes in 2015–16 and his ultimate sacking, but you wonder whether he's just being diplomatic. *Schadenfreude* is a very human emotion. And Ranieri is nothing if not human. Maybe more so than most.

Asked directly about his turbulent history with the self-styled Special One, Ranieri did not bite. 'I said it before and I'll say it again,' he stated in an October 2015 interview. 'I want my former clubs to do well. As for my history with Mourinho, I think that story is well past its sell-by date. Indeed, you could say it's an ancient relic.'

The run meant Leicester were top of the Premier League at Christmas, two points clear of Arsenal and six ahead of Manchester City. It wasn't a guarantee of ultimate success – indeed, the team top at Christmas had actually won the Premier League just nine times in the previous twenty seasons – but it was obviously impossible to ignore.

Conventional wisdom suggested Leicester were due a slip-up. They had been largely injury-free and had two guys – Mahrez and Vardy – performing way above preseason expectations. They were bound to regress at some point. Ranieri kept doing what he always did, stressing how far away they were from the forty-point mark, the magic number at which Premier League teams are pretty much guaranteed safety, but that was more showmanship and superstition. Deep down, while he knew his team could achieve more – much more – he also knew they would have a wobble at some point and have luck, particularly in terms of injuries, go against them. The key would be limiting the damage when it happened.

He knew the Christmas period would be critical. There was an away trip to Anfield on Boxing Day, where Jürgen Klopp had galvanised Liverpool. There was the visit of Manchester City, a potential classic six-pointer, with Manuel Pellegrini's men within striking distance of the Foxes. Also visiting the King Power were Bournemouth, a newly promoted side gaining plenty of plaudits, who had won three games on the spin in December, among them victories over Chelsea and Manchester United.

It began with defeat at Liverpool, as Klopp's crew flew through the ninety minutes, out-hustling and out-playing a listless Leicester side in every department. The 1–0 scoreline flattered Leicester. The only consolation was that Arsenal, beaten 4–0 at Southampton, failed to capitalise. Ranieri knew he could budget for an away defeat in those circumstances. But Manchester City was a different matter. A win by the visitors would see Leicester slip to third, since Arsenal had defeated Bournemouth to go top the previous evening. Again conventional wisdom had it that this was where the wheels would come off the Leicester bandwagon and the quality of the opposition would start to emerge.

'We live in a basement; they live in a villa with a swimming pool,' is how Ranieri described the disparity of resources and he wasn't far off.

The difficulty was figuring out how to avoid defeat against City. Their form had been inconsistent, but most agreed they had the best squad in the Premier League and could turn it on at any time. They had won two of the previous four Premier League titles not by being models of consistency but by raising their game against big opponents. And in the circumstances Leicester were big opponents. Ranieri's main concern was deciding whether the Liverpool performance was a post-Christmas-dinner aberration or a sign that cracks were starting to appear. The feedback from his fitness people suggested that it was a one-off rather than fatigue, but if the dip was psychological, how to remedy it?

He opted to recall Inler into the line-up. The Swiss midfielder had played just nine minutes of league football since September, a late substitute appearance against Chelsea. But he had experience in spades and he could stiffen up the middle of the park. He hadn't been happy about not playing, but had not created problems either. Ranieri rewarded him with a start in place of Okazaki. He switched to a 4-3-3 and appealed to Inler's big-game pride.

If this really were a Disney fairy tale, the reintroduction of Inler would have been decisive in helping Leicester to the scoreless draw which kept them second only on goal difference to Arsenal. But it's not. It's real life. And Inler's performance was fine, though not decisive. Yet the game's worth mentioning to show how Ranieri dealt with adversity, how he picked his spots – knowing when to gamble, knowing when to play it safe.

In the end, the difference came from the collective. It wasn't Mahrez or Vardy, who both missed chances, but rather N'Golo Kanté (who monstered his way around the pitch), the defensive pairing of Wes Morgan and Robert Huth (who kept Sergio Agüero at bay), goalkeeper Kasper Schmeichel (who shut the door against the club where he started his career) and Christian Fuchs (whose experience and quality gave Leicester a continued safe and creative outlet down the flank) who were the difference and earned the point. Most of all, Ranieri got a reaction in terms of spirit and personality. The players showed that the team on display at Anfield hadn't been the real Leicester. They had worked hard to capture the top spot and were not going to relinquish it without a fight. Not to Manchester City, anyway.

Nevertheless they threw away victory in the third and final game of the Christmas programme. Against Bournemouth at the King Power, they enjoyed a man advantage for the last half-hour. Vardy hit the post. Mahrez missed a penalty. Bournemouth keeper Artur Boruc made a series of excellent saves. Leicester were anonymous in the first half – the City game had evidently taken a lot out of them – but did more than enough to win in the second. And yet they were thwarted. If luck is something that ebbs and flows during a season, this was low tide. But after so much good fortune, Ranieri could live with it, at least outwardly.

'Sometimes everything goes right and sometimes some things go wrong,' he said afterwards. Inwardly though you wondered what the other Claudio – the rotten loser, the one who can't accept anything other than success – was thinking. Fortunately, most of the world did not get to see him.

Top: Premiership return: many pundits and former players were surprised by the appointment of Ranieri at Leicester.

Bottom: First game, first win: Ranieri directs his new team from the touchline during the Premier League match against Sunderland at the King Power Stadium on 8 August 2015

Top: Jamie Vardy was integral to the team's success. Just three seasons before, the 29-year-old had been plying his trade with non-league Fleetwood Town.

Bottom left: Jamie Vardy is congratulated for setting a new Premier League record by scoring in 11 consecutive games. The record of 10 games had been held for 12 years by former Manchester United striker, Ruud van Nistelrooy.

Bottom right: A delicious incentive: Christian Fuchs and Shinji Okazaki tuck into their home-made pizza: an imaginative reward for keeping a clean sheet against Crystal Palace.

Left: Danny Drinkwater celebrates with defender Robert Huth after the German defender's crucial goal against Tottenham Hotspur in January.

Top right: Riyad Mahrez was an outstanding performer throughout the 2015–16 season. The Algerian went on to collect the PFA Players' Player of the Year and Fans' Player of the Year awards at the end of the season.

Bottom right: Club captain Wes Morgan and Danny Simpson celebrate after beating Manchester City 3–1 at the Etihad Stadium. It was a win that inspired real belief in Leicester's prospects for a serious title challenge.

Top left: Ranieri offers some direction to Danny Drinkwater during the home game against West Ham.

Top right: Sharing a joke with former boss and Chelsea owner Roman Abramovic in the corridors of Stamford Bridge. The game finished 1–1.

Bottom: Late euphoria: Argentine striker Leo Ulloa celebrates after scoring an injury time penalty to earn the Foxes a point at home to West Ham.

Top left: Ranieri is mobbed by fans as he leaves an Italian restaurant, he had lunch with the team the day after winning the English Premier League title.

Top right: Let the party begin: Christian Fuchs can't resist the temptation to add a little fizz to Leicester's celebrations.

Bottom: We did it! Enjoying the celebrations at the King Power Stadium.

CHAMPIONS: The squad celebrates after being crowned English Premier League Champions 2015–16.

Top: 240,000 fans turn out to see the team's open top bus parade through the city centre.

Bottom: Young fans gather on the streets, preparing to welcome their hero, Claudio Ranieri

17. True Believers

Claudio Ranieri's Leicester had reached the forty points he had spoken about all season and done it with eighteen games to spare. There was no point pretending this wasn't a phenomenal achievement, though he did his best to tread the fine line between dampening expectations and ensuring Leicester would give their best shot at making the most of an opportunity that might never arise again.

'I think what we did [thus far] is a miracle, but if we finish in the top four it won't be a miracle,' he said. 'It will be something bigger, out of this galaxy . . . We're like a volcano that has exploded, but the explosion continues and the lava keeps coming . . . I don't know how this is possible,' he added. 'But now we must continue.'

As luck would have it, the third round of the FA Cup had paired Leicester with Tottenham Hotspur at White Hart Lane, and three days later they would return to north London for their league meeting. Mauricio Pochettino's young Spurs team had crept up the table into fourth place, just four points off the top. Ranieri knew that they were very much in the title race at this stage, with a chance to cut the lead to just one point.

Pochettino knew it too, so it's not surprising that both managers fielded largely second-string sides in the FA Cup. There was no point risking injury or showing your hand ahead of what would be a critical league clash. It finished 2–2, which meant there would be replay.

For Ranieri this was also an opportunity to give some of his starters a breather and the chance to recover from niggling injuries. Or, in the case of Vardy, a rather more serious one. For the previous month he had been unable to train properly due to a groin injury. The club decided to have him undergo a surgical procedure right after the Bournemouth game. It meant he'd miss the Tottenham clash in the FA Cup and probably the match in the league as well, but to risk aggravating the injury was not an option for Ranieri. Much as he admired Leo Ulloa, he needed Vardy.

Ranieri's priority was the unity and cohesion of his squad. This was a break from the past, from the Ranieri who at Chelsea said he'd ideally have two options for every position. Twelve years on he viewed things a little differently. He knew from the Inler experience that a senior professional who doesn't get playing time could be problematic, and he did not want to unsettle the remarkable spirit that ran through the side. He had learned that unlimited resources don't always bring the benefits you might expect.

And so it was that Demarai Gray, who Leicester had chased in the summer, arrived in January to provide another option on the flank. And later in the month they would sign Daniel Amartey, a utility player who could play both centre back and right back as well as in midfield the next season, from Copenhagen for £6 million. Those additions, Ranieri felt, were essential, but in both cases he made it clear to the newcomers that there was a hierarchy: they were there as back-ups. They would have a chance to become regulars, but most likely it wouldn't be until next season. Amartey's arrival meant Ritchie De Laet was allowed to join Middlesborough on loan. And striker Andrej Kramarić was also loaned out, to Hoffenheim in the Bundesliga.

Kramarić's case is an illuminating one. Twelve months earlier he had become Leicester's £9 million record signing, arriving from Rijeka in Croatia, where he had averaged more than a goal a game. Steve Walsh and the recruitment team were excited about him and viewed him as a long-term asset, but he struggled for playing time under Pearson, making just six starts at the end of the 2014–15 season. And with Ranieri he saw even less of the pitch, appearing in two league games for a total of just twenty-four minutes. It wasn't that Ranieri had anything against Kramarić; he was a technically gifted striker with an eye for goal. It's just that Vardy wasn't going to be dislodged from the centre forward position, and Leo Ulloa, who was better in the air, was a more appealing option as back-up because he brought something different to the table. And then there was Shinji Okazaki, whose work rate Kramarić simply could not match. (Nor could anybody else for that matter.)

Again, the old Ranieri might have acted differently. He might have been so impressed with Kramarić's talent and so unwilling to risk losing him that he would have kept him around as an insurance policy or as a long-term project. He would perhaps have rotated his forwards, telling himself that this was a way of keeping everyone fresh and motivated. This Ranieri felt differently. Whatever problems Leicester's forwards might have had, motivation was not one of them. They had built a delicate but hard-working balance, and while an equally hard-running winger like Gray could be inserted into the group without upsetting the balance, the same could not be said for a service-dependent striker like Kramarić.

The club agreed – for business reasons as well. Kramarić would start the final two years of his contract the following summer, which is usually when clubs decide to either sell or renew a player's deal. The way things were going, they would have very little to help them decide if he was worth extending, because he wasn't getting playing time. That also meant that, should they decide to sell him, his value would be severely depressed because clubs tend not to spend big on guys who are not getting on the pitch. Kramarić himself wanted playing time, not least because he didn't want to jeopardise his place in the Croatia squad for the Euros. So he was loaned to Hoffenheim in Germany. It was a deal that worked out well for all concerned: he scored five goals for Hoffenheim, and in the summer they bought him on a permanent basis. The fee was £8.5 million, meaning the club got most of their money back.

Vardy was back for the Tottenham game in the league, which would turn out to be one of the matches that defined the season, though maybe it did not seem that way at the time. Mauricio Pochettino's men had the bulk of the chances and possession, as you'd expect – they were at home and on paper the classier side – but they squandered their opportunities. Leicester looked to hit on the break, but Vardy and Mahrez were quiet, and so – as would happen time and again during the season – it was down to the rest of the squad to make the difference. With the game scoreless and seven minutes to go, big Robert Huth of all people slipped his marker and guided Christian Fuchs' corner kick past Hugo Lloris. It wasn't pretty, and Tottenham's marking wasn't great (it can't be when you lose a man of Huth's size in the penalty box), not that such details mattered to the delirious Leicester faithful packed into a corner of the ground. Pochettino had plenty to complain about. 'We deserved more, we deserved to win the game,' he said. 'In football you can get punished for one little mistake . . . We were unlucky tonight.'

Ranieri praised Leicester's performance in public; in private he knew this was the tough spell, the wobble that everybody was talking about. Vardy and Mahrez were bound to have off days, it was inevitable. It would be up to the others to step up, but they could only give what they had. And the simple fact of the matter was that on paper other teams had better players. But luck plays a role in football too. Teams need to be prepared to seize it when it arises. On this cold January evening in north London that's exactly what they did. Between that and Tottenham's finishing it amounted to a six-point swing. Come the end of the season, as Spurs continued their relentless challenge, these were the points that would make all the difference.

Those who point to Leicester's luck at White Hart Lane that night might want to look at what happened in the next match. LCFC travelled to Villa Park to take on Aston Villa, bottom of the league, and dominated for much of the game. They took the lead through Shinji Okazaki, wasted several opportunities, and then Mahrez had a (rather generously-awarded) penalty kick saved. The game looked in the bag until Rudy Gestede's late equaliser for the home side.

'Yes, we lost two points,' Ranieri said after the match. 'But we played well and I also told the players the performance is more important than the result.'

Managers say stuff like that all the time. They find the positives to give their players and fans confidence and make themselves look better in public. And of course you could juxtapose this game with the previous one, when Leicester played badly and deserved to lose but ended up taking all three points. For Ranieri to be consistent, he should have been unhappy after White Hart Lane, because while the performance was poor, the result was good. In fact, Ranieri was being rather honest. There had been a drop in performance in the previous month, as many had predicted, but he felt they had come through it, and the Villa game was hugely encouraging in that regard, despite the draw, the missed penalty and the dip in the second half. The old Leicester were coming back.

Ranieri fielded a largely second-string team in the FA Cup replay against Tottenham and duly lost 2–0. In a different season, in a different context, he would have gone for it, but few would fault him for conserving energy and focusing on the league. Leicester were level on points with Arsenal, Manchester City one behind. Tottenham were five back and Manchester United seven back. Ranieri knew how quickly a lead could crumble, particularly with sixteen games to go. He wasn't going to take chances.

Stoke at the King Power were up next. Ranieri's instincts about the Villa game were proved right: the wobble really was over. Leicester won 3–0, Kanté turning in another monster performance. And there was even better news from elsewhere. Arsenal contrived to lose at home to Chelsea, while Manchester City were held at West Ham. The lead was back to three points as Leicester faced an absolutely critical run of three fixtures. First up was the visit of Liverpool, one of only two teams to have beaten Leicester in the league in the past nine months. Then was a trip to the Etihad to take on Manchester City. And finally an away game at the Emirates against Arsenal, the other team to have beaten Leicester since last April.

Ranieri maintained his media stance, refusing to talk about the title or even a place in the Champions League. 'This season is not normal, it's crazy,' he said. 'This league is crazy. The table says there is no gap, but everybody who knows football knows there is a big gap between Leicester and the other teams.' But privately he knew what mattered was the league table position, not the gap in resources between his team and the others. And looking at the table, the title was undoubtedly a possibility, however remote, however improbable. One oft-repeated Ranieri saying was, 'We have to give everything and accept the outcome.' This time the outcome could be historic.

Being out of the FA Cup meant Leicester would have a full thirteen days between fixtures following the Arsenal match on Valentine's Day – the last of the 'terrible trio' – and their game in Norwich on 27 February. In situations such as these Premier League clubs often opt to go abroad for some warm-weather training or, if they're doing well, give players time off. 'You can have time off . . . if you get nine points from the next games,' Ranieri told the assembled players.

To some it may have sounded a bit like telling your eight-year-old son or daughter, 'Sure, I'll buy you a new bike . . . if you learn Chinese in the next two months.'

Promise the world in exchange for reaching a hugely difficult and highly improbable goal, but Ranieri felt the players took it a bit differently. They saw it as a sign that he believed in them. This group, most of whom had never tasted the thrill of being in contention for a top-flight title, was being told by a manager who, for all his foibles, had been around the block and had spent three decades coaching football, that the goal was not unattainable. He believed in them. He wanted them to get that holiday. And he thought it was within reach.

Meanwhile, other than finalising the Amartey deal, the transfer window closed without any further signings. It wasn't for lack of effort. The club knew that a situation like this might never arise again and they had to give it their best shot. Shifting Kramarić had left space for another striker and they were aggressive in their twin pursuits of CSKA Moscow's Ahmed Musa and Sampdoria's Eder.

They offered different skill sets, but Ranieri felt both could be a good match. Musa was a speedster who had notched up ten goals by the halfway point of the Russian league season. LCFC had tracked him the previous summer, and the thinking was that he could be both an alternative to Vardy and an additional option on the wing. At twenty-three, he was a player who was growing into his prime, and three and a half successful years in Russia proved he was a tough-minded character with the work ethic to adapt anywhere. Eder was a Brazilian-born Italian international who had scored twelve goals by the midway point of Serie A. He was very much the sort of player coaches love: humble, hard-working, disciplined and with a knack for understanding what is asked of them. And he was versatile too, capable of playing anywhere on the attacking front or as a second striker. He was a jack of all trades, who could be called on to replace anyone, from Vardy to Okazaki and from Albrighton to Mahrez. Most of all, both were blue-collar types with plenty of character and a strong work ethic. Ranieri was confident they could easily fit into the squad with minimal disruption.

According to several sources close to the situation, Leicester were even prepared to push the boat out and land both. After all, Musa was a long-time target and Eder was the guy who, Ranieri felt, could pull them over the top. Whichever way the season ended, even if they slipped down the table, Leicester were going to receive far more prize money than the club had budgeted for. It was a windfall and they were prepared to spend it.

As it happened, they signed neither. CSKA were in a title race of their own. They were unwilling to sell, quoting a price close to £25 million, which was beyond what Leicester were willing to consider. They would be proved right. As happened with Gray the previous summer, they went on to sign Musa the following June for £16.6 million, roughly two thirds the asking price a year earlier. Sampdoria did accept Leicester's £10 million bid for Eder, but the player opted to join Inter instead. It was a bigger club in a familiar league and, with the Euros coming up in the summer, it was a chance to remain well within sight of Italy boss Antonio Conte. As it happened, that decision was vindicated too: Eder ended up starting for Italy at the European Championships.

Leicester's fall-back option was a loan deal for Chelsea's French striker Loïc Rémy. This was a distinct possibility until the Londoners pulled the plug a few hours before the transfer deadline. They had signed the Brazilian Pato from São Paulo only to note that there were serious issues with his fitness. With Radamel Falcao also struggling for fitness – he hadn't played since Halloween – they couldn't afford to be left with only Diego Costa as an able-bodied striker.

Ranieri was disappointed, but there was still reason to feel encouraged. His team had surpassed his expectations thus far and proved so many naysayers wrong. Would he be kicking himself if the absence of a Musa or an Eder meant Leicester would end up missing out on their seasonal goals? Probably. But then again, this season had been such a rush, such a strange and wonderful trip, who even knew what their objectives were at this stage? Winning the Premier League? Qualifying for the Champions League? The Europa League? The most basic aim – avoiding relegation – had been reached and left far behind some time ago. Now, it was no longer about aims; it was about possibilities. And these men he led had already strayed into the impossible enough times, he wasn't even sure what the word meant. Or as that noted sportswear manufacturer tried to convince us: 'Impossible is Nothing.'

And yet the next match was all about the impossible, at least in terms of the goal that broke the ice against Liverpool and sent the Foxes on their way. It came at the hour mark. It was Vardy on the counter, but that was all that was typical. Danny Drinkwater won the ball in his own box and quickly passed to Mahrez, who received the ball a few yards outside his own penalty area towards the right touchline. The Algerian looked up and hit a long pass for Vardy, who had run into space, tracked by Dejan Lovren in front and Mamadou Sakho behind.

Familiarity, logic and expectation suggested a replay of a scene we'd seen before. It was Leicester's patented north–south quick counter. Vardy, well outside the penalty area and sprinting in from the right touchline, would surely collect the ball and then either take on Lovren or look for a teammate running from midfield. What he did next confounded everyone, even Ranieri. He let the ball bounce once and then unleashed a screaming angled volley that sailed over goalkeeper Simon Mignolet and into the far top corner. *What did I just see?!?* It was a special finish because it combined athleticism (Vardy sprinting into space to receive the ball), technique (hitting a volley at pace across your body from a distance of twenty-five-plus yards in such a way that it rises and then falls to hit a target smaller than a microwave oven) and presence of mind (he had the intelligence to note that Mignolet was off his line and process that information in a split second). Plus, of course, the audacity to attempt it.

Ranieri was stunned. So much so that he would compare the goal to Marco van Basten's famous volley for Holland against the Soviet Union back at the 1988 European Championships. That was a bit of stretch, if only because that had come at a sharper angle and because it was a true volley – Van Basten did not let it bounce – but the reaction in the stands and among the media was comparable. It was simply not the sort of goal that Vardy scores. It was his first-ever goal from outside the box. It involved a skill that most would have thought was not in his locker.

Thus was the umpteenth expectation defied in Leicester's season. And, because of the superstition that lives – to varying degrees – in all of us, you felt that, maybe, it was a sign. Certainly, Ranieri's conviction that anything – even the impossible – was possible only grew after seeing that remarkable strike. Vardy notched another twenty minutes before the end, and Leicester sailed to a 2–0 victory. Of the chasing pack, Manchester City and Tottenham won, but Arsenal were held at home by Southampton. Tremendous news all round and a real lift heading to the Etihad the following week.

There was another factor that played to Leicester's favour ahead of the Manchester City game. Bayern Munich coach Pep Guardiola had long been a target for City, going back to when he left Barcelona in 2012. The club had brought in former Barca executive Ferran Soriano and Director of Football Txitxi Beguiristain and had openly modelled themselves on the Catalans, which made sense since they were the global footballing gold standard. All that was missing was Guardiola himself, and by Christmas, when it was revealed that he had not extended his contract – set to end in June 2016 – with Bayern, rumours were rife that he would be coming to the Etihad.

Manuel Pellegrini was in his third season, and had delivered the Premier League title two years earlier, in 2013–14, and finished second the following year. To some this wasn't enough, particularly in light of the spending and disappointing results in the Champions League. To others Pellegrini was a fine human being, but simply not as good a coach as Guardiola, and if you can upgrade, you owe it to yourself to take the opportunity. Whatever the case, Pellegrini opted to put an end to the rumours shortly after Guardiola confirmed he would not be returning to Bayern.

At the end of his press conference before Manchester City's trip to Sunderland – the game before they hosted Leicester – he looked as if he was about to get up out of his chair but then sat back down. 'Before I finish, I'll tell you that I talked with the club and I'll finish my contract on the original date, June,' he said, adding that he was not going to take up the one-year extension offered the previous summer, thereby paving the way for Guardiola. He said the club had been honest and open with him at all times in their pursuit of the former Barcelona boss, but he didn't feel rumours and speculation were helpful, so he was making this announcement.

It was one of those strange situations you get in football sometimes. He was saying in public what most people knew but nobody admitted. Standard procedure for managers in these circumstances was for the club and the manager to maintain the pretence that nothing would change and it was all just speculation and tabloid talk.

Pellegrini clearly thought it would help the team. In fact, it may have had the opposite effect. It's one thing to be seen as a lame duck, quite another to admit that this is what you are. It may have been a coincidence, but Pellegrini amassed 296 points in 144 games in all competitions before his announcement. That's 2.06 points per game and a win percentage of 63.9 per cent. After his candid admission, City's points per game dropped to 1.39 and their win percentage to 34.8 per cent.

So Ranieri knew that an away trip to Manchester City was always going to be tough. But he also knew that this was the best possible time to visit.

Three minutes in and the visitors had already taken the lead, as Robert Huth held off Martín Demichelis and stuck out a big boot, which deflected Mahrez's free kick past Joe Hart. In truth, the early goal didn't change the pattern of the match. Leicester were always going to look to hit on the break, and Manchester City would always have the bulk of possession. But what it may have done is make the home side even more listless. Yaya Touré was a shadow of himself; David Silva, carrying a knock, looked like a child and Raheem Sterling continually ran into cul-de-sacs. N'Golo Kanté and Danny Drinkwater positioned themselves in the passing lanes and simply cut everything out. Mahrez tortured Demichelis again early in the second half to make it 0–2, and on the hour mark the home side contrived to leave Huth open – all six feet four inches of him – allowing him a free header that made it 0–3, before Sergio Agüero's late goal, which was no consolation at all.

Ranieri beamed. This was a textbook away performance in every area of the pitch, and Vardy was unlucky not to bag a couple of goals himself. The visiting Leicester fans turned the Etihad into a King Power annex. The home supporters actually applauded the Foxes as they walked off the pitch, perhaps consoling themselves with the prospect of better times ahead under Guardiola. Ranieri would later admit that this was the game during which it really hit him: they had what it took to win the title. He shared his views with his assistants on the way back and came to one conclusion: 'Yes, we can do it, we can do something here . . .'

In public it was a different story. He peddled the line that Leicester were like a gambler in a casino who had already won so much that they kept playing at the Blackjack table with 'house money'.

'We play without pressure because we don't have to win the league,' he said. 'The pressure was on us at the beginning, because we had to stay in the Premier League. But now the pressure is on the other teams who spent a lot of money to win the Premier League and the Champions League. Now, we just enjoy.' Pressed about Leicester's chances, he still wouldn't bite. 'No, I want to wait until the end of April because I know the last matches are very tough,' he said. 'This is a fantastic moment for the Premier League. Nobody knows who can win it.'

That last part was a bare-faced lie. Ranieri didn't know that Leicester would win it, of course. But this was the game that told him, in no uncertain terms, that they *could*.

Going into the Arsenal game, many bookmakers reluctantly now made Leicester favourites for the title. They really couldn't do otherwise. A five-point lead with thirteen games to go, better-resourced opponents who seemed to stumble just as they were about to pull alongside and the sense that the likes of Mahrez, Kanté and Vardy were on another planet. You had to make Leicester favourites if only because there was no clear alternative; just a bunch of more talented sides who really ought to be doing better. In many ways Arsenal were the epitome of this: their last league title was a full twelve years earlier and since then they had come close on multiple occasions. But now, with Chelsea mid-table, Liverpool rebuilding under Jürgen Klopp, Manchester United suffering under Louis van Gaal and Pellegrini treading water at Manchester City, Arsenal were in a three-horse race with Leicester and Tottenham, and were the big boys out of the three.

Twelve years without a title might be a long time, but it was a lot less than Tottenham's fifty-five, let alone Leicester's one hundred and thirty-one. Ranieri was right to say the pressure was on Arsenal. They had taken just one point in their previous two home games against beatable Chelsea and Southampton.

That's what made preparation for this game somewhat different to the Manchester City match. Yes, Leicester were on the road against a title rival packed with more talented players and keen to have the bulk of possession. But at the Etihad Huth's early goal had let the air out of the tyres of opponents who had started the match already somewhat deflated and probably thinking ahead to next season. Most of the City players had been in the side that won the Premier League in 2010–11 and again in 2013–14. They weren't necessarily sated, but one successful cycle had closed and they were ready to start a new one. Arsenal had been waiting twelve years. They would not give up without a fight.

Ranieri knew he might not have the luxury of an early goal to dampen the crowd and unsettle Arsenal. Leicester were unchanged, but the emphasis, even more than in previous games, was on the quick counter. The team had been depicted as an archetypal old-school Italian defend-and-counter-attack side although the truth was somewhat more complex. Counter-attacking was something they did well, but they also felt confident in their ability to pass their way to chances, with the front two running to create space, the invention of Mahrez and the decision-making out wide from Fuchs. But this was not a game in which to try to out-possess Arsenal. This was a match about disciplined aggression, defending and going north–south once in possession, testing an Arsenal defence that many felt had a soft centre.

Watching the game, some were reminded of an article Ranieri had written for *Corriere dello Sport* in which he laid out his idea of football. There was no single blueprint, he said. Arrigo Sacchi's AC Milan – still the last team to defend the European champions title back in the late 1980s – was his favourite team. But, he added, 'I'm not Sacchi. I can't try to ape him.' The traits he admired in teams were compactness, fight and organisation. 'Seeing a compact, tight side win the ball and attack in transition is exciting and beautiful to me,' he wrote. 'I think back to Helenio Herrera's Inter. I was born into that sort of football.' In more ways than one. It had been Herrera, at that point manager of Roma, who had given him his first professional contract. What you could achieve with spirit and aggression coupled with organisation and unity had stuck with him.

Kanté and Drinkwater set the tone and when they weren't enough to break up Arsenal's rhythm, Leicester turned to a more physical game plan. The first half was comfortable for the visitors, and they were rewarded just before the break. Kanté collided with Laurent Koscielny and the ball broke for Vardy, who slipped into the box and took on Nacho Monreal. The Spanish fullback defended uncomfortably, half-turning away and sticking out a leg. Vardy, in full flight, went over it and referee Martin Atkinson pointed to the spot. Vardy converted the penalty for his nineteenth goal of the season.

Arsenal weren't happy, as you'd imagine. They felt Vardy had conned Atkinson. You can go on YouTube and make up your own mind. What is obvious though is that in the modern game, turning away from an opponent and sticking out a leg is inviting trouble. And, however annoyed Gunners boss Arsène Wenger might have been at half-time, he was bound to know that soft penalties are given when defenders play that way. Not to mention that if the boot had been on the other foot – if it had been Alexis Sánchez or Theo Walcott running at a Leicester fullback who stuck out a leg – there would have been no complaints from the Arsenal dugout.

Ranieri knew that Arsenal were going to try to step it up several notches after the break. Against different opponents he might have considered a half-time change to counter what was to come and to give Wenger something different to consider, but Arsenal tended not to vary their tactics based on the scoreline. And, hand on heart, his players were doing so well, they were executing the game plan so proficiently in such tricky circumstances, he didn't feel right changing things.

Arsenal turned the screws, and Leicester responded. Predictably, that meant conceding more fouls. Two soft yellows in the space of seven minutes led to fullback Danny Simpson being sent off with just over half an hour to go. Ranieri was furious, and the dismissal would dominate much of the post-match discussion. Neither foul in isolation was a cast-iron yellow card, but within the context of what the referee felt Leicester were doing – disrupting the flow with niggly fouls – he opted to put an end to it. Simpson was sent to the dressing room.

It's fair to say the red card took Ranieri by surprise. Managers prepare for every contingency, but the fact is you only have seven substitutes at your disposal and one is a keeper. Amartey had not played a competitive match since 6 December. He had been training with the side but over two months without football for a twenty-one-year-old moving to the Premier League is a long time. And so Ranieri went into the game without a reserve right back, meaning he had to send on Marcin Wasilewski, a centre back by trade, and a rarely used one at that. Mahrez made way for him. It would now be all about defensive work rate. It would prove to be a momentous decision.

Without Simpson and a man short, Leicester hunkered down in their penalty area. Or, perhaps more accurately, were pushed all the way back by a rejuvenated Arsenal. With ten minutes to go, Theo Walcott equalised. It lifted the stadium like only a late equalising goal in a high-stakes game can, and the Emirates roared into life. The rest of the match was a siege. The Leicester centre backs, led by captain Wes Morgan, put their bodies on the line time and time again. Kanté and Drinkwater ran themselves into the ground. Kasper Schmeichel made a string of top-drawer saves, none better than the one from Olivier Giroud's close-range shot.

Arsenal were desperate. In the dying minutes Wenger sent on Danny Welbeck, who had been injured for a full nine and a half months. It was kitchen-sink time, the clock ticking on as Ranieri paced the touchline. As the teams battled deep into injury time the realisation started to wash over Leicester: *We're going to do this, aren't we?*

Nope.

In the fifth minute of time added on for stoppages Leicester cleared the umpteenth Arsenal attack with a long, looping boot. Arsenal's Monreal stepped up to collect the ball as it dropped. Out of nowhere Wasilewski stormed out of the Leicester penalty area, perhaps believing he could challenge for the ball, but there was no way he was getting there in time. While he appeared to realise this as he drew closer, it was physically impossible for him to stop or even slow down his fourteen-stone-plus body, not when it was at full sprint. His knee caught Monreal – who comfortably headed the ball first – in the mid-section, his flailing arm possibly struck the head. Atkinson had no choice but to award a free kick. Mesut Özil sent a flighted ball into the penalty area which Welbeck flicked past Schmeichel to give Arsenal the most dramatic of last-gasp victories.

Had it not been for his cult hero status, Wasileweski would have been the villain of the piece, but the big taciturn centre half from Poland was a popular figure among teammates and fans. With his tattoos, a beard somewhere between lumberjack and hipster and circus-strongman build, he didn't look like a footballer. And yet, here he was, a few months shy of his thirty-sixth birthday, still a part of a table-topping side.

There is almost something biblical in this story. Seven years earlier, while playing for Anderlecht, Wasilewski had been on the receiving end of one of the most horrific fouls in recent football history. Standard Liege's Axel Witsel caught him just below the knee with such force that the lower part of Wasilewski's leg appeared to crumple up. If you have the stomach for it, go ahead and check it out on YouTube. Odds are, you won't see something more gruesome on a football pitch. Go ahead. I'll still be here when you get back. Early suggestions were that Wasilewski's career was over. He was heavyset, and this was a severe compound fracture of both tibia and fibula. His recovery defied medical science, with one Anderlecht official saying that Wasilewski's mind and willpower made the impossible possible. He was playing again just over eight months later.

If his return to football was a minor miracle, his arrival at Leicester was almost as improbable. His contract with Anderlecht expired after the 2012–13 season and, for one long summer, nobody was interested in taking him, even on a free transfer. It's rare for clubs to grant trials during the season and rarer still for former internationals like Wasilewski to agree to them, but that's exactly what happened. Leicester gave him a shot; he stuck around and now he was part of the title run. Now the fairy tale had taken a dramatic turn as his mistake not only cost Leicester a draw but also gifted three valuable points to their closest rivals. He was mortified, but he also knew that every time you suffer a knock you have to pull yourself back up, something he had done time and again in his career. He turned to social media and wrote, 'Self-criticism is the best way to motivate yourself.'

Ranieri was stunned by what had unfolded before him. For an hour or so Leicester had shown strength, maturity and were tactically savvy enough to nullify Arsenal away from home in what was a do-or-die game for the Gunners. And yet they were going home empty-handed. Avoiding criticism of match officials, repeating his mantra ('We have to accept whatever outcome') and keeping his cool in controversial moments have been Ranieri hallmarks, but, as he himself admits, he hates to lose. Especially in this way.

Managers generally know better than to pick out isolated incidents. Football matches are fluid events: change one detail and everything can change, so A doesn't always follow B. Making connections between events early in a game and what happens later is illogical and irrational in the cold light of day. Yet this wasn't the cold light of day. You could work backwards and track a direct line back to what happened earlier, particularly if you were as caught up in the moment as Leicester were at the time. Yes, Wasilewski had made a mistake, because without the crazy lunge at Monreal there's no Arsenal free kick for Özil to put in the box and no ball for Welbeck to guide past Schmeichel. And Leicester get a point and remain five points clear of the Gunners. But, equally, had it not been for Atkinson's decision to send off Simpson for two soft yellow cards Wasilewski would not have been on the pitch. Which means that free kick to Arsenal in the final seconds of stoppage time would never have been given. And the game would have finished 1–1.

Fans sometimes think that way. Managers don't or aren't supposed to. But Ranieri is human after all and post-match he wasn't shy about sharing his thoughts on Atkinson's performance. 'If I think about the match, I am very angry,' he said. 'I think maybe I made some mistakes. But an international referee gave two yellow cards for normal fouls in a match that was full of fouls.' He then added that perhaps Atkinson allowed the crowd at the Emirates to influence his decisions, which is exactly the kind of criticism referees cannot abide. They'd rather be called incompetent and maybe even corrupt before being accused of being vulnerable to crowd pressure.

It was uncharacteristic for Ranieri, but it was also more than post-match venting. There was a design to it. He felt his team had played well – at least when it was eleven v. eleven – and wanted to make sure the players went away with a message: you beat Manchester City, you deserved to beat

Arsenal, you have nothing to fear. You will win the title. That last part was unspoken, but it was part of it. Indeed, Ranieri would say after the season that it was this game that gave him the conviction that the title was theirs to lose. It's a common coaching ploy. Expressing total confidence after a defeat is far more powerful than after a victory. The latter can lead to complacency; the former pushes players to live up to the manager's words. Provided, of course, they buy into them.

And Ranieri went further. Remember the promise he had made, that if the players returned with nine points from the Liverpool, Manchester City and Arsenal games, he'd give them a full week off? Defeat meant they hadn't made it three wins in three, but they were still getting a holiday. 'I gave them the week off because they deserve it,' Ranieri said. 'They produced a magnificent performance, and I am very proud of them, so they get a week off.' He added, 'I have never done something like this before in my career.'

It was a masterstroke and again showed how far Ranieri had come in his understanding of football and people. Some get more set in their ways as they get older, and others approach the world with an incessant curiosity, a hunger to learn and an openness to new ideas. Ranieri was in the latter camp. The advice of the conventional Italian coaching school – of the men who had trained and inspired him – would have been straightforward. Thirteen days without games? Great! What an opportunity to buckle down and work the life out of them for a whole week! Let's have a mini-preseason in February, with plenty of double training sessions to top up our fitness so that we can be stronger in April and May!

Ranieri could see the benefits of this, but he could also see the advantages of a week off. First of all it reinforced the notion that they had deserved to beat Arsenal: it made his post-game comments believable. In his mind they *had* beaten the Gunners; failing to get the three points was not down to them, so it was only right that they got the break. The British press presented it as a way of allowing the players to clear their minds and let off some steam. There may have been some truth in that, though at least one Leicester player would later say he felt lost during the break. How could he clear his mind, he said, when he spent every waking minute thinking about what Leicester were on the verge of achieving? And, to make matters worse, he was on his own, away from his teammates, surrounded by people who could not possibly feel the way he did.

Different people respond in different ways and without question most benefited from the break. The one fear that stalks English clubs – that players will go off, drink and party themselves silly – was not a concern for Ranieri. This was not a squad of hard drinkers, and the vast majority had never been involved in any trouble. Vardy of course was the exception. In addition to the old assault charge, he had been videotaped drunk in a casino the previous summer and filmed uttering a racial slur, for which he later apologised. Ranieri knew what players could be like, but he also knew that most of his squad had never won anything of note in their careers and for many this could well be their only chance to do it. In fact, with the exception of Mahrez and Kanté (and possibly Vardy), none of his starters were likely to ever have a chance at silverware again. He was confident that they would not let him down.

And they did not.

18. We Do Not Dream

Ranieri had finally conceded that, yes, Leicester were in a title race.

'The next five matches will determine whether we are there to fight for the title come April and May,' he said. 'If we get through these five battles, we will be there. This is a key moment.'

The run-in featured fixtures against mid-table sides and those fighting to avoid relegation. On paper you'd rather be facing teams like that than other title contenders, but each match had its potential pitfalls. Mid-table sides towards the end of the season have no pressure on them; they can take risks. And relegation-threatened teams are desperate, hugely motivated and often happy with a single point. The latter were the ones most likely to park the bus and defend in numbers. For a team that had performed as well on the counter-attack as Leicester had, this could be a problem.

This was the case against Norwich. The Canaries defended deep and defended stoutly. Leicester had very little room in which to play and were often second to the ball. Ranieri's solution, since he couldn't find a route around the Norwich defence, was to go through it or over it. He sent on his powerhouse centre forward, Leo Ulloa, late in the second half, bringing off fullback Daniel Amartey, who was playing in place of the suspended Danny Simpson. It was Ulloa who popped up at the far post to steer Marc Albrighton's cross into the back of the net. A share of the spoils may have been a fairer result, but the way in which Leicester kept attacking and believing meant they were rewarded.

So too was Ranieri's risk-taking. The striker-for-defender swap is the sort of thing managers normally do when they're losing or when they're desperate to win. Three points were important, of course, but a draw would not have been the end of the world. Leicester went into the weekend with a two-point lead over Arsenal and Spurs, who both played the following day. With a draw, at worst Tottenham and Arsenal would win and join the Foxes at the top of the league. Many managers would have thought that way and perhaps Ranieri too, back in the day. But not now. 'One point is not enough; you have to win,' he said after the match. 'You can lose, but it is one point less. But if you win, it's two points more.'

There was a bit of psychology at work here. Defeat would have been a blow, but the way Norwich were set up to defend – and seemed happy with a draw – made it feel like a remote possibility. This game was going to be a draw or a win. But with Ulloa on for Amartey, not only were Leicester increasing the chances of a win, they were also sending a message that they believed. And if it ended in a draw, Ranieri would have psychological leverage over his players after the week off: *I give you a week off and this is how you repay me?* As it happened, with the three points came more good fortune the following day. Tottenham won to stay two points behind, but Arsenal fell at Old Trafford against Manchester United, 3–2, with two dramatic goals by Marcus Rashford on his Premiership debut, and were five points adrift.

Next up was the visit by West Bromwich Albion. In many ways this was Norwich in reverse. Leicester, despite the absence of injured N'Golo Kanté, brilliantly replaced by Andy King, dominated the match but had to settle for a point. They conceded an early goal on the counter-attack, scored twice to regain the lead and then were punished by a brilliant free kick from Craig Gardner. Along the way Leicester created plenty of chances and hit the woodwork twice. Ranieri is savvy enough to know that good fortune comes and goes. Unfortunate this match, fortunate the one before. But if you play well, over time you'll come out ahead. To play this well against an opponent set up to defend and to do it without Kanté was important and encouraging.

'We are alive and we fight to the end,' he said. 'Everybody is ready to fight, to play well, to create chances. All we lacked today was the victory.'

Leicester also got a boost from the opposing manager. 'It would be absolutely fantastic for everyone in football if Leicester could [win the title],' said West Brom manager Tony Pulis. 'I am supporting Leicester City between now and the end of the season.'

Pulis was among the first major footballing figures to publicly pick a side in the Premier League race. His stance was not surprising – everybody loves an underdog, particularly other underdogs – but it's not often you hear such views aired in public. Neutrals voicing their support for Leicester would become a theme during the run-in, much to the annoyance of some of Leicester's competitors. Pulis gave Ranieri's crew a lift, compounded further by what happened the following day, when both Tottenham (away to West Ham) and Arsenal (at home against struggling Swansea) were defeated. You draw at home and still you extend your lead in the table. A superstitious man might take it for a sign.

The following weekend's early kick-off was the North London Derby. It finished 2–2, which gave Ranieri and his men a further boost when they faced Watford away a few hours later. Watford were a newly promoted side that some had tipped for relegation at the start of the season, but they were in mid-table, thirteen points clear of the drop zone and with an FA Cup quarter-final against Arsenal coming up the following weekend. Perhaps hoping that Watford might take their foot off the gas a little, Ranieri again did something the old Ranieri might not have done: he played his best eleven, with Kanté back from injury in place of King. It meant that nine of the starting eleven were playing their third game in seven days.

It was not what you'd expect from an Italian manager, often so stereotypically preoccupied with fatigue and squad rotation, and particularly given that Leicester simply weren't used to playing so many big games in such a short space of time. But the fitness team had given the green light, and whatever else he might be, Ranieri is not the stereotypical Italian manager. Not at this stage of his career anyway.

At half-time it was 0–0 and becoming clear to Ranieri that perhaps fatigue was starting to make itself felt. Watford were crowding the midfield, but Ranieri had King on the bench, who had put in a superlative performance the previous week. He made a double substitution: King and the speedy Jeffrey Schlupp for Shinji Okazaki and Marc Albrighton, two of his most tireless workers. Leicester moved to a 4-5-1. It worked. They were able to outgun Watford's midfield and ratchet up the pressure. The winner came from Riyad Mahrez, who latched on to a poor clearance and rifled the ball home from the edge of the box.

This was one match in which the manager had earned his bacon with his shrewd substitutions, but also a game where the players saw the opportunity presented by the earlier result and seized it. The gap over Spurs was now five points, while Arsenal were eight back and Manchester City ten away with just nine games to go.

Ranieri described the Watford match as a battle. The visit of Newcastle United was too, not least because it was scheduled for Monday night, and the previous day Tottenham had won at Aston Villa, temporarily cutting the lead to two points. The Magpies, threatened with relegation, had hired a new manager, and not just any new manager, but Rafa Benítez, a Champions League winner who had been coaching an obscure club called Real Madrid just a few months earlier. Newcastle's game plan was simple. Grab a point and steady the ship after a run of three straight defeats. Ranieri knew it would be a war of attrition, one that was not going to be won on the counter. Teams, especially smaller ones, simply weren't going to offer space behind, especially not away to Leicester.

In these situations managers rely on either a piece of individual magic or a set-piece. In Leicester's case it was both. Mahrez's free kick into the box was half-cleared by the Newcastle defence. Albrighton sent it back in. Both Wes Morgan and Jamie Vardy headed it on, and it came to Okazaki, with his back to goal. He launched himself into the air and delivered a spectacular overhead kick from the edge of the six-yard box.

It was inventive, it was spontaneous and it was brilliant

from a player who until that point had mostly contributed through his ceaseless work rate and tactical nous. Okazaki was the man who in Ranieri's eyes allowed Vardy to be Vardy and Mahrez to be Mahrez. He continually adjusted his movement and positioning based on what the other two were doing. If others opened up space, he was the one who relentlessly closed it and always made himself available as a passing option. It seemed fitting that he'd be rewarded with a crucial goal that would live on in Leicester's highlights reel for ever.

Okazaki's strike came after twenty-five minutes and played right into Leicester's hands. Benítez could no longer sit back and rely on the counter. Newcastle had to come at Leicester, and that suited Ranieri just fine. 'It wasn't nervy at all. We were close and compact and we defended well,' he said. 'We were in control.'

This was part of Leicester's evolution. If they had freewheeled on the counter earlier in the season, now they were minimalist and tough-minded. They were absorbing pressure and using it to their advantage. They reached levels of concentration few would have anticipated. With eight games left to go, their next tie, Crystal Palace away, further reinforced this. Palace were in free fall, having taken just two of a possible thirty points from their previous ten matches. They had not won a Premier League game in four months. Yet their impressive start to the season meant they were still mid-table and their FA Cup run meant Alan Pardew wasn't under pressure.

In other words they could simply go out and play freely, which is exactly what Ranieri was concerned about. But he needn't have worried. A Mahrez goal just after the half-hour mark broke the ice and, from there the objective once again was defending their lead, which Leicester were becoming incredibly adept at doing. Crystal Palace, like Leicester, were a side more suited to the counter-attack. With that option taken away, they simply pumped crosses into the box – something Ranieri was happy to let them do as his side defended tightly – and the twin towers of Morgan and Robert Huth dealt with everything comfortably.

With Tottenham playing the following day (they would beat Bournemouth 3–0) the lead was, at least overnight, a full eight points. It's not surprising then that the visiting Leicester contingent stayed behind at Selhurst Park and sang, 'We're gonna win the league! We're gonna win the league! And now you're gonna believe us, and now you're gonna believe us, and now you're gonna BELIEVE US!! We're gonna win the league!' Ranieri had believed it for some time, though he wasn't going to let on. Instead he talked about the Europa League and maybe a chance of qualifying for the Champions League. After all, they were 'only' sixteen points clear of fourth-place side, West Ham. They were applauded off the pitch by the Palace fans as well. By this stage they were everybody's second team, and other than Tottenham supporters and perhaps those Arsenal fans with enough blind faith to think they could still win the title, everybody wanted Leicester to be crowned champions.

The game also marked a third straight clean sheet for Kasper Schmeichel and his defence. Pizzas in exchange for not conceding seemed a long time ago. At the rate Leicester were going, if Ranieri had kept up the pizza-for-clean sheets deal, they'd be making weekly trips to Peter Pizzeria and shedding the lean, mean foxes image.

The question of whether there is such a thing as momentum in sports performance has been hotly debated for decades and not just in football. Is there any reason to believe that if you're on a good run it will continue? Academics say no. People don't get 'hot' or 'in the zone'; they achieve the success they are meant to achieve, and when good – or bad – streaks persist it's purely random variance. There's a famous academic text paper called 'The Hot Hand in Basketball: On the Misperceptions of Random Sequences' by Robert Vallone and Amos Tversky of Stanford University and Thomas Gilovich of Cornell University that pretty much trashes the idea of momentum in results. It's a bit like flipping a coin. You can get heads five times in a row, but the odds of you getting heads on the next flip remain fifty-fifty. There is no such thing as a lucky streak.

That may apply to coins, but humans aren't little pieces of copper and zinc. And almost everyone involved in sport – even those who just play sports recreationally – believes that when things are going well, they will continue to go well. And vice versa, of course. That's why we hear athletes talk about confidence or lack thereof. Of 'snapping out of' poor runs. Of how when you feel strong, you are strong. They can't all be deluded, can they?

The answer to this is a moot point, but the impression is that momentum in sport is a self-fulfilling prophecy. And since so much of sport – especially football – seems tied into confidence, perception does matter. A manager on a good run will be listened to that bit more attentively. A player might make a run that bit more sharply because he's doing well and believes that bit more that he'll get to the ball first.

That was where Leicester found themselves: filled with momentum. The test – the sequence of five games that Ranieri had highlighted – had been passed with flying colours. Four wins and one draw, thirteen of a possible fifteen points in the bag. And their lead had increased from two to five points, while the number of games left had shrunk from twelve to seven.

Confidence may have had a lot to do with how they went on to beat Southampton at home. Tottenham, playing the day before, had been held to a draw at Liverpool. This was a chance to go seven points clear, and they took it with the most improbable goal – Captain Morgan from open play in the first half. The centre half stayed up the pitch after a set-piece broke down; Christian Fuchs delivered a delightful cross from the left, and the ball was thumped past Fraser Forster. For the rest of the match Morgan led the defence as Leicester repelled Southampton's assaults, aerial or otherwise. It was their fourth consecutive 1–0 victory, their fifth in six games, the twelfth clean sheet in twenty-two league games since the 'pizza challenge' back in autumn.

This was beginning to feel like destiny. Like they were untouchable, a notion reinforced when a Huth handball went unpunished by the referee, drawing the anger of Ronald Koeman. But after the match even he conceded that if Leicester won the title, it wouldn't be because of referees' mistakes. And, he added, 'They deserve to win the title. I hope they do win it.' Another Premier League boss had jumped on to the Leicester bandwagon. With the team seven points clear, it was looking as if Koeman was going to get his wish.

Plenty of people had done the maths. A seven-point gap with six games to go meant twelve points would guarantee the title, come what may. That was four wins. Looking at Leicester's remaining fixtures – home games against West Ham, Swansea and Everton, away trips to Sunderland, Manchester United and Chelsea – many felt confident that it would happen.

Ranieri too felt he could no longer hide or spin tales of European qualification. It was time to come out in the open. He chose an unusual platform, albeit one with plenty of potential to be noticed. The Players' Tribune is a website founded by baseball player Derek Jeter of the New York Yankees. His idea was simple and clever: to afford athletes and coaches the opportunity to provide quality long-form content, unfiltered. Ranieri could have opted for a sit-down TV interview or a national newspaper, but then he would not have been entirely in control of the message. The Leicester website? He'd be in control, but it's a club website, smacking too much of officialdom.

The Players' Tribune was the perfect medium for what he wanted to say and, what's more, being a primarily US-oriented platform, he could capitalise on the growing global fascination with the Leicester story. Entitled 'We do not dream', his piece neatly summed up his mantra.

'The Leicester fans I meet in the street tell me they are dreaming,' he wrote. 'But I say to them, "OK, you dream for us. We do not dream. We simply work hard."' He didn't pass up the opportunity to push the Leicester brand overseas either, which no doubt pleased King Power. He talked about 'hearing noise from all over the world' and how fans were drawn to the Leicester story. 'To you, I say: "Welcome to the club. We are happy to have you. I want you to love the way we play football, and I want you to love my players, because their journey is unbelievable."'

He ended the piece with a line that may have been trite but was no less true for that: 'No matter what happens to end this season, I think our story is important for all football fans around the world. It gives hope to all the young players out there who have been told they are not good enough.'

It was compelling stuff, and ahead of the trip to Sunderland it dominated the headlines, taking heat off the players. Yet that match could easily have taken a turn for the worse, as Jack Rodwell missed an early sitter for the home side. Younès Kaboul later wasted another opportunity. Leicester held their nerve, focused on keeping the opposition out, and waited to break on the counter. The goal came twenty minutes into the second half and was reassuringly familiar. With Sunderland pushing forward, Danny Drinkwater grabbed a loose ball, looked up and went route one with a simple but direct ball over the top. Vardy burned Kaboul in the foot race, glided into the area and slipped it past the keeper. He added a second, again on the counter, deep in injury time.

His goal tally now stood at twenty-one, making him the first Leicester City striker to reach twenty top-flight goals in a season since a certain Gary Lineker more than thirty years earlier. It was Leicester's fifth straight clean sheet. And it was now three wins in five games to secure the title. Again, just as they did at Selhurst Park after the victory against Crystal Palace the Leicester fans stayed behind, wanting to squeeze every drop of emotion out of the moment and singing, 'We're gonna win the league!' They weren't the only ones feeling emotional. Ranieri wandered the pitch with a strange expression. Those used to seeing him either focused or smiling saw something different. There were tears in his eyes. There was a look of confusion, but delighted confusion, as if something unbelievable was about to come to pass and he simply did not quite comprehend it. He would later reveal that he was overcome with emotion remembering something he'd seen before the match.

'It was an elderly lady, dressed in a Leicester shirt, getting off the bus and making her way to the Stadium of Light,' he said. 'I looked at these people and it hit me. They come so far to support us. This means so much. We could not let them down. We owed it not just to ourselves, but to them as well.'

It had taken a septuagenarian to make Ranieri crack. But it had happened. And it was wonderful.

19. Rhapsody in Blue

Claudio Ranieri compared Leicester's remaining fixtures with those of Tottenham. He would not say it in public, but Leicester had a decent run-in. Three of their five opponents – Everton, Chelsea and Swansea – had little to play for. The other two – Manchester United and West Ham – were still chasing a top-four finish. Some speculated about winning the title at Old Trafford, but first they had to worry about West Ham visiting the King Power.

Ranieri knew this was a classic 'trap' game. The run of victories would come to an end at some point, and West Ham were spiky opponents with individual match-winners like Dimitri Payet, who also provided a worrying threat from set-pieces. He stuck to his familiar line-up and looked for the counter. He was rewarded early on. A free kick from Payet was gathered up by Kasper Schmeichel, who immediately spotted Riyad Mahrez breaking down the right. The keeper's long, powerful throw found him at the halfway line. Mahrez paused for a beat or two and released to N'Golo Kanté, motoring up the middle of the pitch. He carried the ball to the edge of the box and then, as the West Ham defence converged upon him, laid it off for Vardy, who had tracked his run. Leicester's top scorer slotted it home and the King Power erupted. The whole sequence had taken thirteen seconds, proving once again that the quickest way between two points is to travel in a straight line.

While others celebrated, Ranieri was relieved. Leicester could play their own game now. And they did, except eleven minutes into the second half it blew up in their faces. Vardy was again released on the counter-attack, except this time he went down in the box under the challenge of Angelo Ogbonna. Replays suggested there was contact, though it was minimal. Many watching expected referee Jonathan Moss to either point to the spot for a Leicester penalty or simply wave play on. Instead he booked Vardy for simulation – perhaps swayed by the fact that he clearly accentuated the contact – and then showed him a red card, as he'd already received a yellow in the first half. Incredulous, Vardy gave him an earful as he went off the pitch.

Ranieri sent on Leo Ulloa for Shinji Okazaki. With Jeffrey Schlupp replacing Marc Albrighton a few minutes earlier, he felt he still had enough pace to counter-attack if necessary, but the key would be hunkering down and protecting the lead while down a man. The game turned physical, particularly at set-pieces. There was shirt-pulling, grappling and shoving at seemingly every corner and free kick. It was coming from both sides, and Moss let it all slide until he suddenly decided to tighten up. Six minutes from time he awarded the visitors a penalty after Wes Morgan appeared to hold back Winston Reid. By the letter of the law it was clearly a penalty, but then so were at least three other incidents, for both sides, earlier in the match. Above all else, players need consistency from the match officials. Moss's actions implied that either he had not seen any of the previous incidents or he had suddenly changed his mind about what he would – and would not – allow. Andy Carroll buried it from the spot to make it 1–1.

There was barely time for Ranieri to register what had happened when Leicester went a goal down. Just two minutes after Carroll's equaliser – with the Foxes' defence still shell-shocked – West Ham left back Aaron Cresswell latched on to a clearance and delivered a stunning shot which tucked in just under Schmeichel's crossbar. Ranieri looked calm on the sideline, urging his players on, although some watching thought back to that fateful game nearly six years earlier at the Stadio Olimpico, when Ranieri's Roma gave up a 1–0 lead to lose 2–1, handing the top of the table back to Inter and paving the way for José Mourinho's historic treble.

Maybe Ranieri's thoughts would have turned to that memory too if not for what happened in the fifth minute of injury time. Another controversial penalty, this one in Leicester's favour. With literally seconds left, Schlupp accelerated towards the corner of the penalty box. Carroll came over to meet him and collided with the pacy winger. Again Moss pointed to the spot, this time angering the West Ham fans. It was a soft penalty and, more frustratingly for the visitors, entirely unnecessary. Schlupp was going nowhere; there was no need for Carroll to challenge him in the way he did. With Mahrez and Vardy both off the pitch, it was Ulloa, with all the pressure in the world on his shoulders, who stepped up to take it.

The man known as El Ciclon (the Cyclone) in his native Argentina sent Adrián the wrong way, and Leicester grabbed a share of the spoils. Even as the King Power exploded with joy, Ranieri remained impassive. There are things for which you can't legislate in football and one of them is a referee having a stinker. Both sets of fans vented their anger at Moss. You could say his decisions ultimately cancelled themselves out; the difference was that Vardy was now facing an automatic ban for one game, maybe two if his reaction to the red card was deemed serious enough.

Ranieri knew he had to be cautious because so much would depend on how players, fans and media reacted to the draw. Post-match he studiously avoided discussing the officiating while making sure those who listened knew he was intentionally avoiding talk of the decisions. The situation became even more delicate after Spurs played on Monday night and hammered Stoke City 4–0, cutting Leicester's lead to five points. Ranieri knew he had to act and so provided a spectacle at the press conference ahead of the next game, Swansea at home. He interrupted a journalist asking him about pressure and how he was coping by blurting, 'We are in the Champions League, man! Dilly-ding, dilly-dong! Come on, man!'

This was not something he had planned would feature in Leicester's 2015–16 title run, at least not in public. Dilly-ding, dilly-dong was an expression he used when he wanted to get his players' attention or when he noticed somebody was distracted. Its origins date back to a bell he used to ring for the same purposes in preseason training in the 1990s. Danny Drinkwater had brought it up in an interview a few months earlier; the media had latched on to it and naturally Ranieri had played along.

'It's fantastic, terrific, well done to everybody!' he went on, noting what many had overlooked in all the title talk: that Leicester had mathematically qualified for the Champions

League. 'It's a great achievement! Unbelievable! Now we go straightaway to try to win the title. Only this remains ... Mauricio, keep calm!' The reference was to the Tottenham manager. Mauricio Pochettino had a young side and was in an equally unfamiliar position. In fact, were it not for Leicester, Tottenham would easily have been the story of the season. This was Ranieri's way of shifting the attention and pressure on to Spurs.

'I don't need to win all the remaining matches; they need to win all their matches . . . We don't. We have everything in our hands.' As for the suspended Vardy, sure he had lost his Caesar as he called him, 'But I have twenty-three other Caesars ready to step in!'

It was theatre, and the media loved it. It also showed that those who imagined a meltdown from Ranieri like Kevin Keegan had suffered at Newcastle back in the mid-90s were well wide of the mark. Ranieri had been through this before, albeit on the losing side, and he had learned from it. Without Vardy, he gave the green light to Ulloa, and El Ciclon did not let him down, although Swansea did not put up much resistance and an early mistake from skipper Ashley Williams allowed Mahrez to score his seventeenth goal of the season. Two goals from Ulloa and one from Albrighton rounded out a very straightforward 4–0 victory.

After the game Swansea manager Francesco Guidolin joined the ranks of those openly cheering for Leicester. 'Now I can say it. I hope Leicester go on and win the title because they deserve it,' he said like Koeman and Pulis before him. This only underscored what a strange season this was. Leicester weren't just doing it for themselves and their fans; they had become some kind of symbol for every club outside the big-spending elite.

The Swansea match took place on a Sunday, and the Professional Footballers' Association (essentially the players' union) was holding its annual awards function that night. The club were keen to capitalise on the moment and arranged helicopter travel down to London, not least because Leicester were up for a clutch of awards. Wes Morgan, Kanté, Vardy and Mahrez had been selected – in a vote of PFA members – for the Team of the Season. In addition, Kanté, Vardy and Mahrez were all shortlisted for Player of the Year.

The trip was another example of how Ranieri had changed over the years. Disrupting the players' post-game recovery when a massive game at Old Trafford was just a week away? And with the title potentially on the line? Defeat at Old Trafford, coupled with a Tottenham victory the same week could have left Leicester just two points clear with two games to go. Why would you possibly risk screwing things up so close to the finish line?

There may have been a time when Ranieri thought that way. No more. His players had shown themselves to be responsible and professional throughout the season. The benefits of a night in the sun, an evening when their achievements could be celebrated by their peers, outweighed the post-game recovery cycle. There was no need to wind them up any tighter.

The fact that three of his men had been shortlisted for Player of the Year filled him with pride. He was also glad *he* didn't have to choose between them. Not just because of the old cliché in which a parent is asked to pick one child ahead of another, but because it was objectively difficult to decide who was the best. Vardy's goals and incredible work rate enabled Leicester to play in a way that suited them down to the ground. Kanté had been a model of consistency, and his ubiquity on the pitch was disconcerting even for Ranieri, who watched him every day in training. One of his staff had said, 'We play a midfield three: Danny Drinkwater in the middle and Kanté either side of him,' and while it was a joke it was also true. What's more, while everyone had highs and lows during the season, even Mahrez and Vardy, Kanté's output never seemed to drop, even during the run-in. Mahrez would finish the season among the league leaders for goals and assists. On top of that, all three had their own underdog story, which only made them more compelling.

The PFA voters chose Mahrez.

Ranieri's own appraisal of the Algerian leaves no room for doubt about what he thinks. 'When he's fit, he changes games on his own,' he said. 'Last year he played in the hole. I moved him to the right wing because I thought, as a left-footed player, he could cut back inside, find space more easily and hurt opponents. He beats opponents and he has plenty of vision. Every time he's on the move and receives the ball, you feel like something really important could happen.'

His success was at once a tribute to Leicester's recruitment team and Steve Walsh and an indictment of the French academy system. A bit like Vardy, who had also slipped through the cracks, his potential was clearly under-appreciated, which is why Leicester were able to sign him for just £400,000 from Le Havre, making him one of the bargains of the decade.

Growing up in Sarcelles, a suburb of Paris, and playing for his neighbourhood club, plenty of youth scouts would have seen him play from a very young age, yet none of the French academies thought of offering him a contract. The knock on him from those who saw him play from the age of twelve onwards was that, while he was technically gifted, he lacked two basic ingredients. He was extremely slender and physically weak, lacking strength and stamina; and though he had quick feet, he lacked pace. That combination is a huge black mark for any young player. Football will tolerate players who are slow if they make up for it with work rate and strength. And it will cope with those who are small and weak and maybe even a bit lazy if they have the speed to get away from opponents. Mahrez had intelligence and talent, but his physical deficiencies at the time meant plenty overlooked him.

Sarcelles were in the ninth tier of the French football system, and while Mahrez could easily have played in their first team, he knew he wanted to be challenged at a higher level. To do this, he had to move across the country at the age of eighteen, some 400 miles to a town called Quimper in the region of Finisterre, which, appropriately, means end of the earth. Quimper were in the second division of the French Amateur league (CFA), the fourth tier of the French pyramid. Strictly speaking, he was now a semi-professional and earned the first pay cheque of his career, around £125 a week. Quimper were relegated in his one season there and he only managed fourteen starts, but he showed enough quality to attract the attention of many clubs, among them the likes of Olympique Marseille and Paris Saint-Germain.

Both offered him a contract, but he opted instead for Le Havre, a smaller club but one known for its academy. The likes of Lassana Diarra, Vikash Dhorasoo, Jean-Alain Boumsong, Steve Mandanda and most notably Paul Pogba, all French internationals, had been through the academy there. He spent the majority of his first two seasons in the B-side, which again played in the fourth tier of the French system, before becoming a regular first-teamer in the second division. He was attracting attention for his quality and first caught Steve Walsh's eye in the summer of 2012, though the Leicester scout had originally travelled to watch another player. There were still doubts about his slender build, particularly in the French second flight, renowned for its physicality. Much to his frustration, he was in and out of the side as a result. Mahrez felt he needed a change of scenery, perhaps to a league – or at least a club – less bent on seeking out physical players, and so refused all offers of a contract extension. When Leicester swooped for him in January 2014 he was six months away from becoming a free agent and being able to move for nothing.

A bit like Kanté, the narrative of Walsh and his team, in which they plucked Mahrez out of nowhere and saw potential where others saw nothing, is not quite accurate. Plenty saw Mahrez's potential and had done for a long time. The difference though is that Leicester had the courage and intuition to get the deal done. A scout at another English club, speaking on condition of anonymity, told me his team had reports on Mahrez going back to his time at Quimper and that they continued to track him through Le Havre's B-side and on to the first team.

'Where it fell apart though is that some of us doubted whether he could handle the physicality in England,' he said. 'After all, if Le Havre weren't sure he could handle it in Ligue 2, what chance would he have across the Channel? That was the perception, although, perhaps, I think the idea that the English game is all about hyper-intensity and physicality is a bit of a myth. Other leagues are as physical, if not more. And England does have room for talented players who may not be super-athletic, as Mahrez's success points out.'

Walsh and his men thought Mahrez was worth a gamble,

not least because, despite his build, he was mentally tough and resilient. They pushed Le Havre to sell and, when it became clear Mahrez wasn't going to renew his contract, rather than lose him for nothing, they agreed to a sharply reduced fee. That too is a skill when it comes to delivering players.

Ranieri was proud of his players and the recognition they were getting. He was happy to have been a part of it. And he was happier still the following night when Tottenham were held at home by West Brom, 1–1. Pulis, who had openly expressed his support for Leicester, seemed to do them a huge favour. It's hard not to read it that way. West Brom were safe in mid-table, capping another successful year of avoiding the drop. From the outside it looked as if many of the players were 'on the beach', already thinking ahead to their summer plans since the season had nothing left to offer. They had lost three games in a row and went a goal down in the first half, while Tottenham also hit the woodwork on three separate occasions.

But after the break they came out a different team in terms of spirit and fight. They notched up an equaliser and refused to relent, even after an increasingly desperate Pochettino threw everything he had at them. In the end it was Tottenham who folded. Dele Alli, their outstanding young attacking midfielder, landed an unseen punch on West Brom's Claudio Yacob. As the minutes ticked away, Spurs looked like a young side devoid of leadership, crumbling in the face of the knowledge that what they had worked so hard to achieve was slipping away.

After the match Pochettino said, 'I am still very proud of my players. We still need to believe, though we know it will be difficult.' But his face said the opposite. He was hurt and angry.

The mathematics were known to all. Leicester needed three points from their final three fixtures – Manchester United away, Everton at home, Chelsea away – to be sure of the title. Tottenham effectively needed to win all three of theirs: away to Chelsea, home to Southampton and away to Newcastle.

It wasn't going to happen.

The day after the Tottenham result, Leicester received the news that Vardy would be banned for an additional game for his reaction to the red card against West Ham. That meant he'd be unavailable for the weekend trip to Old Trafford to take on Manchester United. But the news was mitigated somewhat when it emerged that Tottenham's Dele Alli had been given a three-match ban for the punch on Yacob. As a result, Alli would end up missing the rest of the season.

United still had something to play for. They were fifth in the table, five points from a Champions League spot but with a game in hand. Away from home at the Theatre of Dreams against a highly motivated opponent . . . Ranieri knew they could win the title with a victory there, but he also knew it was a tall order. While it had been a turbulent season for United under Dutch boss Louis van Gaal – and after his departure (as always occurs) plenty of acrimonious comments were made by certain senior players – this was still a team stacked with talent. Many of them knew Van Gaal was likely to be sacked in a month's time, but that didn't mean they were any less hungry to be in the Champions League the following season, playing for whoever replaced the Dutchman.

Leo Ulloa once again replaced Vardy up front. United took an early lead through Anthony Martial, and soon after Jesse Lingard had an outstanding chance kept out by an exceptional save from Kasper Schmeichel, playing for the first time on the stage where his father, Peter, had made history. Ranieri never lacked faith in his players, but he knew full well that going two goals down inside fifteen minutes at Old Trafford would have been a very steep mountain to climb.

But then Leicester City equalised. From a free kick some ten yards outside the box and off to the left, Danny Drinkwater floated the ball over the top of the defence to the far post, where Ranieri had sent Robert Huth and Wes Morgan, his heavy artillery. Both were marked, but Morgan simply bulldozed Marcos Rojo and nudged the ball down and past goalkeeper David de Gea. Ranieri gleefully clapped his hands on the sideline as Morgan raced to the visiting fans, blowing kisses, and United lost whatever impetus they had. The only blot was Drinkwater getting sent off for two bookable offences. It finished 1–1, and once again the Leicester fans stayed behind for as long as Old Trafford security would let them. Every second was to be savoured.

Now they really were on the brink. Many presumed they would win it at home against Everton the following weekend. But that game would only be relevant if Tottenham managed to win at Chelsea on Monday night. And there were plenty of reasons to think that might not happen. For a start, many Chelsea supporters see Tottenham as their biggest rivals. Chelsea had endured their worst campaign in twenty years and were going to finish mid-table, but denying Tottenham the title would provide extremely satisfying consolation. And then there was the fact that the beneficiary would be Ranieri. His four years at Stamford Bridge had not been forgotten. How could they be? It was during his reign that Chelsea reached the Champions League semi-final for the first time; it was Ranieri who had delivered the top-four finish which – it later emerged – was instrumental in persuading Roman Abramovich to buy the club, and it was he who had made John Terry a starter. Not to mention that his tenure at the club was the longest of any Chelsea boss since John Neal in the early 1980s, and that was in the lower divisions.

The fact that the likes of Cesc Fàbregas and Eden Hazard had both publicly backed Leicester, much to the delight of Chelsea fans, only served to ratchet up the intensity. And the annoyance of Pochettino. Leicester travelled to face Chelsea on the final day of the season. If – and it was a big if – the title came down to that game, could everyone be sure that the home side would be professional and give their all?

As for Ranieri, he chose to remove himself from the equation. He announced after the draw at Old Trafford that he would be flying to Rome on the day of the Spurs and Chelsea showdown to have lunch with his ninety-six-year-old mother, Renata. What's more, given the flight times, he'd be airborne when the match at Stamford Bridge ended and would only find out the result after landing back in England.

It was another media flourish, another unexpected turn. Here was a manager who had chased a top-flight league title for three decades and, on what could turn out to be the biggest day of his career, wasn't going to be around to witness a decisive match. Instead of watching and suffering along with the Leicester faithful, he'd be staring at the back of an airline seat. And all because he wanted to have lunch with his mum. How refreshingly unusual. How wonderfully sweet. How very Italian, putting 'La Mamma' above all else.

The media seemed fascinated. Ranieri simply explained that he'd promised his mother, and in any case there was nothing he could do to influence the result at Stamford Bridge. Of course there was more to it than that. Yes, he valued time spent with his mother and, yes, spending all day in Leicester waiting for the game to kick off would have been nerve-wracking. But it was also a way to keep things in perspective. Leicester had come further than anyone imagined. Remember the two Claudios? The calm one who accepts any result knew already that the season was a victory. The angry one who hates to lose was intelligent enough to know that there were things beyond his control. Both agreed it was the right thing to do.

Ranieri did go to Rome to see his mother, but he was back in time for the match thanks to the intervention of the Srivaddhanaprabhas. The club owners, hearing of his plans, offered him the use of their private plane, allowing him to be back home in Leicester by the time the game kicked off. (Ranieri won't admit it, but several who know him well suspect he was rather hoping they would offer to fly him to Rome and back.) He ended up watching the match at home in Leicester with his wife Rosanna, Paolo Benetti and Andrea Azzalin. Meanwhile, most of his players gathered at Vardy's house, which seemed appropriate given that for most of the season the fans had sung about how 'Jamie Vardy's having a party!'

The party seemed ruined at half-time. Harry Kane and Son Heung-min had given Tottenham a 2–0 lead. It's not that Chelsea weren't putting up a fight, it's just that Spurs were on autopilot, clinical and hungry, frustrating both the home side and their supporters. And the game became niggly. And nasty. There were several melees before half-time. The situation grew worse in the second half. Tottenham were getting rattled. Those who had questioned whether a Leicester side filled with players who were unused to winning silverware had perhaps forgotten that this Spurs side were also largely young and inexperienced.

Chelsea boss Guus Hiddink sent on Eden Hazard, and the

little Belgian played as if he was turning back the clock to 2014–15, when he was the Premier League Player of the Year. Spurs, perhaps more intent on the physical battle, lost track of Gary Cahill on a corner, and he pulled one back for the home side. Then, as the game continued amid a baying crowd demanding an equaliser, events spun out of control. There were horror tackles and a loss of discipline all over the pitch. Seven minutes from the end Hazard popped up at the edge of the box and delivered a glorious curling shot that beat Hugo Loris and made it 2–2.

Six-hundred and thirty seconds, plus stoppage time, and Leicester would complete the greatest achievement in the history of team sport.

There were more fisticuffs, more elbows, more posturing, more nastiness. Tottenham's frustration grew into violence, and Chelsea, with whom there is no love lost, were only too happy to provoke, egged on by their supporters. The post-match bulletin would record twelve yellow cards – nine of them for Tottenham players – countless melees, Érik Lamela treading on Chelsea's Cesc Fàbregas, Moussa Dembélé gouging Diego Costa's eyes, and Guus Hiddink ending up on his backside in yet another scuffle. A total of £600,000 was handed out in fines by the Football Association, as well as a six-game ban for Dembélé.

At the final whistle celebrations erupted at Vardy's house, all over Leicester, and in every corner of the Foxes' diaspora. Actually, it went beyond that. As Kane would later relate, Chelsea fans and players were celebrating too, as if they 'had won the title'. So too were the vast majority of neutrals. Ranieri's name rang out in the Stamford Bridge air. Twelve years and a few days after the meltdown in Monaco it felt to some that he had delivered the silverware which had eluded the club during his tenure.

The world's media were already in Leicester, anticipating the title would be won the next weekend, at home to Everton, so they were present to chronicle one of the most joyous and wild weeks in the city's nearly-two-thousand-year history. Ranieri did not reschedule training but, as you'd expect, it wasn't the toughest of sessions. A celebratory lunch followed in town, and when word of where the players were toasting the title got around, the restaurant was mobbed by thousands of supporters, causing havoc in the city centre.

All that remained were two more matches: the King Power Stadium celebration, with Andrea Bocelli serenading Ranieri, and the final trip to Stamford Bridge, where Ranieri received an ovation from his former supporters and applause from the side that helped him win the title. *This is what leading a team to the league title feels like*, he thought. Though, by his own admission, he still had not fully realised what had transpired in the previous nine months or, rather, the previous fourteen months, going back to the turnaround that began under Pearson.

The weeks after that title-winning Monday night at Stamford Bridge would see Ranieri in a daze. In assorted interviews he said fundamentally the same things in more or less the same way, if occasionally in a different order. They were all true. They were all honest. But they were all part of a defensive mechanism too.

To really get his head around what had happened would require time and maybe distance too.

20. Understanding the Impossible

There are two popular myths about Leicester City's title win that bear further examination.

Those 5000–1 odds that the bookmakers put Leicester at to win the title before the season started made for a great tale. They implied there was a 0.02 per cent chance of Leicester winning the title. Or that they'd win it once in 5000 years. Put another way, if the Premier League had begun at the time the Egyptians built the Great Pyramid at Giza in 2560 BC, and Leicester had competed in every single season there was still a chance they might not have won it.

The media had a field day with explaining what 5000–1 means. The easiest way was to compare it to other improbable events for which the bookmakers were offering similar odds. Like the discovery of the Loch Ness monster. Or proof that Elvis Presley – who many of us are pretty sure has been dead for nearly four decades – is actually alive and well. Not to rain on anyone's parade, and with apologies for being so blunt, but Elvis is dead and there is no monster in Loch Ness. Most of us know these two things to be true. So, by juxtaposing

Leicester winning the title with something we know cannot happen – unless you believe in monsters or raising the dead – the bookmakers (and the media who lapped up their numbers) were saying it was well-nigh impossible.

Was it though?

For a start, those 5000–1 odds were designed to attract attention rather than serious money. If you wanted to put a few pounds on Leicester at 5000–1, your bet would be gladly accepted. If, on the other hand, you showed up with, say, a thousand-pound wager, the bookies would politely turn you down or offer significantly lower odds.

Why? Because they weren't going to risk losing £5 million on a single bet. Not when they knew the real odds of Leicester winning were far lower than 5000–1. In all the research for this book, the biggest bet found placed on Leicester came from an 'unnamed punter' who wagered fifty pounds. He stood to win a quarter of a million pounds but settled early for just over £72,000. The biggest bet placed by a real, identifiable person – a Mr John Pryke of Leicester – was twenty pounds, and he too cashed out early, for £29,000.

Those stories about bookmakers losing millions because they priced Leicester at 5000–1? Take them with a whole bucketful of salt.

Another factor in play is purely psychological and has to do with how we think about long shots. Danny Finkelstein, writing in *The Times*, offered a wonderful summation of this. Basically, it was extremely unlikely that Leicester would win the title, but we would have been equally shocked by Bournemouth or Sunderland or Norwich or any other outsider doing the same. Any long shot crossing the finish line first is hugely unlikely but nowhere near as unlikely as a specific long shot. Put another way, let's say – hypothetically – that Leicester's chances of winning the title were 0.2 per cent or 1 in 500. If another nine clubs also each had a 0.2 per cent chance, then the chances that any one of those small clubs would win it becomes 2 per cent. Or one in fifty. Which is still a tremendous feat, but not quite as extreme. The reality is that weird and unusual things do happen, and while the chances of a single, specific weird and unusual occurrence are very remote, the chances that some kind of weird and unusual thing will take place aren't quite as slight.

The other myth relates to the extent of Leicester's turnaround from 2014–15 to 2015–16. More precisely, bottom in late March 2015 to winning it all fourteen months later. Clearly, in terms of points, it was a dramatic reversal. Between April Fool's Day 2015 and May 2016 Leicester lost just four league matches: one under Nigel Pearson, three under Ranieri. That's as many as they'd lost in the two months prior to the run beginning. But results are one thing and performance another. Were they really *that* bad before? One man who doesn't think so is the economist Dan Altman. He runs a football consultancy called North Yard Analytics and in an article in *The Economist* and a subsequent presentation at the Sloan Sports Analytics Conference, hosted each year by the Sloan Business School at the Massachusetts Institute of Technology (MIT), Altman pointed out that Leicester's starting point was nowhere near as low as had been suggested. True, in the first half of the 2014–15 season, they gained just 13 points from 19 matches, which works out to 0.7 points per game, but in the second half they tallied 28 points, which is 1.47 per match. Altman suggested the signing of Robert Huth to bolster the defence had a lot to do with the massive improvement. Whatever the case, if we think in terms of half-seasons (and when you get down to it, a whole season is almost just as arbitrary a measurement), Leicester were proceeding at a clip that would have been good enough for eighth place that year.

Altman goes even further. Using data from Opta, a company which provides statistical information on each Premier League game, including shots and shot locations, he assembled a model to strip out luck and probability – unforeseen events that can favour or hurt you – and concluded that Leicester played well enough to expect to gain 1.7 points per match in the second half of 2014–15. Project that over a full season and it works out to 65 points, which would have placed the Foxes fifth the year before Ranieri arrived.

As the saying goes, you can use statistics to prove just about anything, but models like those used by Altman – and also Rob McKenzie, Leicester's analytics guru at the time – played a key part in the club's approach and transfer strategy. And professional gamblers have used them for years to try and beat the system.

And then there are Ranieri's own words. When he arrived at Leicester and watched the first training sessions and friendlies in Austria, he was surprised by how good the players were and how he'd need to tweak the team rather than give it a complete overhaul. And remember we're talking about what Ranieri said in early August 2015, when he was essentially working with the previous year's squad with the exception of Shinji Okazaki. Christian Fuchs only made his first league start in October, N'Golo Kanté on 29 August.

It's significant to point this out because it shows just what Ranieri had inherited and how he was surprised at how they had finished the year before. So maybe the feat was not quite as improbable as everyone thought. Still, what contributed to it?

You can of course turn to the supernatural. Here the favoured theory has to do with Richard III, and was the perfect companion story to Leicester's resurgence. If you know your Shakespeare (and the fact that Ranieri had an assistant coach named Craig Shakespeare simply added to the deliciousness) you'll know he was a member of the Plantagenet family and king of England until he was overthrown by a distant relative, Henry Tudor (who went on to become king as Henry VII).

At his death in 1485 Richard III was buried in an unmarked tomb then possibly exhumed at some point and laid to rest elsewhere. In 2012 his remains were found beneath a car park owned by the city of Leicester, oddly enough under asphalt marked with the letter R. (For Richard? For Ranieri? For Riyad? Who knows?) After DNA testing and carbon dating proved his identity, plus a huge campaign from the people of Leicester, he was reburied in the city on 26 March 2015. A few days later Leicester's remarkable comeback began under Pearson, and the team rose from twentieth to fourteenth place.

Common sense suggests that we can discount this theory, fascinating as it may be, not least because there is no evidence that Richard III had supernatural powers or that he is sitting there in the afterlife amusing himself by watching Leicester shock the world. But that doesn't mean there weren't significant factors beyond Leicester's – and certainly Ranieri's – control.

For a start all the title favourites disappointed. Leicester won the title with eighty-one points, which represents the second-lowest points total of the previous fifteen years. Only Manchester United won the title with fewer points – when the

Class of '92 took it in 1996 with just 75 points. The average Premier League champion in that time span collected around eighty-seven points. In eight of those seasons the runners-up gained more points than Leicester's eighty-one in 2015–16. This suggests that in most years there is a dominant heavyweight or two that simply crushes most of the opposition. In 2015–16 that did not happen, and it was to Leicester's advantage.

Manchester United, despite spending massively for the second season in a row, were still in rebuilding mode under Louis van Gaal. The Dutchman proved unpopular with players and supporters, and the side were in turmoil for much of the campaign. He was sacked at the end of the season. United were beacons of stability relative to Chelsea, the defending champions. The reasons for Chelsea's dramatic drop from first to tenth are manifold. Whatever the truth, they severely underachieved, and halfway through the campaign dismissed manager José Mourinho.

Manchester City had finished first or second in each of the previous four years. They were second in the table as late as February, but they too fell away badly as the team went limp towards the end of the season. The announcement that Manuel Pellegrini would leave at the end of the campaign was meant to bring stability and lessen speculation. Maybe it did, maybe it didn't. (If it did, you shudder to think where City would have finished had it not been made.) Whatever the case, Manchester City's season ended with a whimper.

Liverpool weren't expected to challenge but were still seen as candidates for the top four – several rungs above Leicester. They also endured a tricky campaign and ended up dismissing their manager, Brendan Rodgers, mid-season. Arsenal did not change managers – if you're under the age of twenty, you'd be excused for thinking they never do – but again the season felt like a lost opportunity following a summer transfer window in which they added just one player, goalkeeper Petr Čech. Many felt a little bit of extra spending would have gone a long way, and maybe they're right.

That leaves Tottenham who, in the end, were Leicester's only real title rivals and in a 'normal' season would have been the story of the year. They had a young and hungry side and played some of the best football in the Premier League for long stretches. But when it came to crunch time, they folded, perhaps as a result of inexperience, perhaps because of lack of leadership.

Four of England's traditional 'big six' clubs changing managers either during or immediately after the campaign is a rare occurrence. It happened to coincide with Leicester's breakthrough. So too did the fact that Mauricio Pochettino, in his second season at White Hart Lane, was still in transition. You could not have predicted those events. (If you were unkind, you could have predicted what befell Arsenal: that Arsène Wenger would again sit on his hands, rather than push on and gamble to secure the title.) There's also luck, and though it might seem churlish to bring it up, it's safe to say that while there were times when Leicester reaped less than they sowed, overall the balance of luck and probability swung in their favour.

Using Altman's proprietary model, which aims to strip out factors of luck and runs 10,000 simulations, based on Leicester's 2015–16 season the Foxes' most likely finish was fourth. In case you're wondering, Arsenal, Tottenham and Manchester City would have finished as the top three – they finished second, third and fourth respectively. Liverpool would have been fifth, Chelsea seventh and Manchester United eighth. Again, it's key to stress that we're dealing with models and probability here. This is not an exact science. This isn't about Leicester fluking their way to the title or not being deserving champions. What it does suggest though is that more individual external events and incidents went Leicester's way than went against them in 2015–16.

These factors, by definition beyond Ranieri's control, had an impact on the title race, but there are two others which fall into a slightly different category, the make-your-own-luck variety. The first is injuries and suspensions. Simply put, Leicester had very few of either relative to other clubs and easily had the most settled line-up in the Premier League, perhaps retiring, once and for all, the Tinkerman label. The eleven most used Leicester players were on the pitch for 32,336 of 37,620 league minutes, that's 86 per cent. Tottenham were the only side that came close to this level of stability, weighing in at 82.6 per cent. The other big sides? Arsenal scored 75.4 per cent, Chelsea 71, Manchester United 70.5, Manchester City 69.5 and Liverpool 67.2. Leicester's top eleven regulars started 33.9 matches, well ahead of Tottenham (32) and Arsenal (29.1), then Chelsea (27.8), Manchester United (27.4), Manchester City (27) and Liverpool (26).

This needs to be taken with a pinch of salt. Teams who do well tend to make fewer changes because the manager tends to be happy with his line-up, so in some ways it's a self-fulfilling prophecy. Equally though, some managers like to alternate players in a certain position. Some need to rotate because they play a lot of matches: Liverpool had sixty-three competitive fixtures in 2015–16, Leicester just forty-three. And some managers are just tinkerers – though not Ranieri, not any more anyway.

All those caveats aside, a club will play its best players when they are available – when they're match fit, uninjured and not suspended. And the numbers suggest Leicester managed to stay remarkably injury-free throughout the season, to a degree not seen in recent Premier League champions. Part of that was down to Leicester's lack of European football and their early elimination from the domestic cups. Less midweek football means more time to recover from knocks between games. The media made a big deal of Leicester's cryotherapy unit, where players first enter a chamber cooled to minus 65 degrees Celsius and then go even further, shifting down to minus 135. No doubt it played a part, but then they weren't the only team using one during the season.

Leicester's exceptionally low level of injuries was due, at least in part, to luck. And, conversely, there was the misfortune of their opponents. Manchester City's record signing, Kevin De Bruyne, missed seven league games between 23 January and 2 April. Between those dates they managed two wins, a draw and four defeats. Now it's true that this was a particularly tough run of games – their four losses came against Liverpool, Manchester United, Tottenham and Leicester – but three of those matches were at home. It's not unreasonable to imagine a City side with De Bruyne getting perhaps two wins and two draws. And, because football isn't linear, maybe, when the last three games of the season roll around, they actually realise they're in a title race and end up doing better than they actually did: two points in three games.

That said, Leicester also made their own luck in this department, and not just because of the cryotherapy. The fitness, sports science and medical teams did their jobs well and made the right calls at the right time. Vardy's surgery is an excellent example of this. What's more, Ranieri's decision not to pursue the FA Cup with his starters meant fewer cup games and rearranged fixtures.

Another key factor – highlighted in Altman's research – was penalties. Leicester were awarded thirteen in 2015–16. That wasn't just the most in the Premier League that year, it was the most of any team since 2002. They converted ten of them. Only two teams, Crystal Palace in 2003–04 and Chelsea in 2009–10, scored more from the spot in a single season. Since the start of the Premier League the average number of penalties awarded per club per season is 3.76; Leicester's total was more than three times that.

Penalties aren't entirely random events. Teams that attack more tend to get awarded more, but it's not a great correlation. Arsenal and Liverpool, two of the more attacking sides in the Premier League, were awarded just two each in 2015–16. Leicester were near the bottom in possession statistics, and when you don't have the ball you generally don't get awarded penalties. What they did do was run at opponents, run at them quickly and run at them with Vardy. Altman's research, using data from Opta, shows that seven of the thirteen penalties were given for fouls on the Leicester centre forward. And six of those seven came after quick possession, which he defines as ten seconds or less from the time Leicester won the ball. In other words, the typical penalty came when Leicester won the ball back and launched Vardy to run at a defender and force a foul.

So luck may help with getting penalties, but there is little question that Leicester did everything they could – by attacking quickly, directly and with Vardy – to put themselves in that position. And he wasn't the only one. Vardy won a penalty every 447 minutes (or roughly every five games); Jeffrey Schlupp, equally direct and fast, if not faster, won a penalty every 693 minutes.

Altman dug deeper into Vardy's numbers and counted the number of times that he received the ball in the final third outside the box and then had a pass, shot, dribble, dispossession or foul in the penalty area. Essentially, it's a way of counting how many times he ran with the ball into the box. Vardy did it on sixty-two occasions, more than any other striker in the Premier League and marginally more than Sergio Agüero and Olivier Giroud, who did it sixty times each. The difference? Vardy received the ball in the final third but outside the box 258 times, meaning that 24 per cent of the time he was able to get into the area and make something happen. Agüero did it 17.6 per cent of the time, and Giroud clocked in at 19.6 per cent. In relative terms that's a major difference and it highlights Vardy's efficiency under Ranieri, who moved him central from a wide position and unleashed him to run at defenders as often and as quickly as possible.

There's another element in which Leicester truly stood out. Analysts like Altman use a metric called expected goals (xG) to measure a club's output. A very basic xG model looks at shot locations and assigns a value to each, based on where it was taken. So a central shot from the edge of the six-yard box (a sitter) might be worth 0.8 of a goal whereas one from outside the area and all the way to the right (or left) might be worth 0.02 of a goal.

But how do they know what value to assign to each shot and how do they know this is anything other than meaningless mumbo-jumbo? On the first question, they look at a decade or so of historical data, looking at what percentage of shots from an actual location resulted in a goal. Obviously there are caveats. An outstanding finisher like Sergio Agüero might score 50 per cent of the time from a certain position whereas a burly defender might convert only one in five chances from the same spot. And what the data doesn't tell you is whether there were defenders in the way. Shooting from near the penalty spot for example might have an xG value of 0.7, but xG models don't generally make a distinction between a shot taken from there with nobody but the keeper to beat (say, after a counter-attack) and one taken with a mass of defenders shielding the goal in a crowded penalty area.

Yet with a very large set of data these distinctions tend to become less relevant. Players don't generally shoot unless they have a clear sight of goal. And the shooting accuracy of players – especially over time – is remarkably similar across all abilities, possibly because worse players tend to pass up difficult shots.

Models – with a few further tweaks and modifications – based on expected goals have been very successful over the years at predicting outcomes, certainly more so than results. Why? Because they measure the quality and number of chances created versus chances conceded. And that is one way of boiling down the essence of a game and stripping out elements of luck. We know these models work – not all the time and not all equally well (there are differences between those used by different analysts) – because they are used by professional gamblers. And those guys tend to make money over time.

We saw before that, based on Altman's model, Leicester's most likely finish would have been fourth, and this is where things get interesting. Altman's expected number of goals scored – excluding penalties and opposition own goals – was spot on at fifty-seven. But based on the location and number of shots they conceded Leicester over-performed defensively. Altman's model said they should have given away forty-three goals, whereas they actually conceded a miserly thirty-two. Indeed, his simulations suggest there was only a 4 per cent chance of Leicester conceding thirty-two or fewer goals.

It's important to put this in context. This means that in a typical season, with a typical range of Premier League players taking shots from those locations against typical defenders and a typical goalkeeper, it was most likely that Leicester would concede forty-three goals, while there was only a one in twenty-five chance that they'd give away thirty-two or fewer.

It's not an exact science, as we said, but it does suggest that Leicester's defensive performance was far from typical. The question is why. Luck may well have played a part, but there are other explanations. One is Kasper Schmeichel. He clearly exceeded expectations and had a very good season. The same, by extension, applies to the defenders. Not just the centre backs, Robert Huth and Wes Morgan, but the central midfielders, Danny Drinkwater and N'Golo Kanté, and the fullbacks, Danny Simpson and Christian Fuchs. Of course, sometimes players play better from one season to the next because they simply improve for no specific reason. But in Leicester's case Altman identified key metrics which suggest that a lot of this was by design. And credit there must go to the manager.

Defensively, the impact of Kanté can't be overstated. But other numbers suggest a collective effort as well. In 2014–15 Leicester conceded a shot from a set-piece or direct free kick after 57 per cent of fouls in the final third (58 of 102) and 43 per cent of corners (102 of 239). Under Ranieri those numbers fell to 42 per cent (44 of 106) and 38 per cent (91 of 241). Those are fairly steep declines; they suggest more effective defending (doing a better job at preventing a shot from a set-piece) and better-organised defending (fouls conceded in less dangerous areas).

Furthermore, in 2014–15 Leicester's opponents had a 9.2 per cent chance of scoring when shooting from open play. The following season this fell to 7.8 per cent, which is a 15 per cent drop. This fall can be directly attributed to a decline in conceding through balls – which tend to lead to better chances – and also shots from rebounds, which tend to be at close range. Again the former is generally associated with better defensive organisation and the latter with more alert and composed defending.

There were several reasons behind Ranieri's shift from Pearson's back three to a back four. What's not in question is that the latter worked better for Leicester in 2015–16, partly because of the personnel available and partly because of Ranieri's tactical instructions and organisation.

At the attacking end the biggest, most obvious change was the use of Vardy. Ranieri made him the main striker and attacking terminus, whereas Pearson had often used him to cut inside from wide areas. That's a big part of the reason why Vardy's goal return rose from five in 2014–15 to a whopping twenty-four under Ranieri. Altman's numbers bear this out. Vardy took forty-three shots from open play in 2014–15 and more than twice as many, ninety-seven, the following season. Just as importantly, Vardy was receiving the ball closer to the goal in 2015–16 as well as moving it further (nearly 50 per cent further in fact) compared to the year before.

Vardy wasn't just getting more shots, he was getting better shots, according to Altman. The closer you are to goal when you shoot – broadly speaking – the more likely you are to score. Under Pearson Leicester moved the ball very quickly when they attacked (4.5 metres per second, according to Altman's elaboration of Opta data), and that did not change under Ranieri. The difference was that they ended up closer to goal when they pulled the trigger: under Pearson they ranked tenth in the Premier League; under Ranieri they were second only to Arsenal. The result of this? Overall, Leicester's shots in 2014–15 – taking location and other elements in the xG formula into account – had an 8 per cent chance of scoring. The following season that shot up to 12 per cent. For all the focus on Ranieri's personality and charm, this was evidence that he made Leicester – who were already better than many thought – into a more efficient, more tactically sound team, both defensively and at the attacking end.

Those are the numbers, but success is about more than the physical game. A manager's job also involves finding the right mix in his starting eleven, motivating his players and fostering the kind of unity and harmony that can see a side through periods of turmoil and extreme pressure. Even his critics would concede that man-management has been one of his strong suits, and his experiences over the years have enriched him professionally. He treated every job as an opportunity to learn and in fact he often grew further after a setback.

Managers love to say that whatever the pressure on them from external factors – media, club, players, fans – this is dwarfed by the pressure they put on themselves to succeed. This may be true to a point, but it also feels a little clichéd. The issue isn't so much the pressure itself, it's the time and energy spent dealing with it. Whether it's angry fans disrupting a training session, an owner asking for an explanation for a defeat or the media grilling you with pedantic questions or trying to catch you out, it's simply gruelling and time-intensive.

Ranieri had dealt with all this at his previous clubs. He landed at Napoli in the immediate post-Maradona era. He moved to Valencia and handled mega-egos like Romário and Ariel Ortega. He dealt with Jesús Gil at Atlético Madrid in the year which saw him arrested. He guided Chelsea through both near-bankruptcy and Roman Abramovich's first season in what was at the time the biggest spending spree in history. He took over at Juventus a year after relegation and the Calciopoli scandal. He managed Roma as a native-born Roman, possibly the most high-pressure goldfish-bowl situation in football short of being reincarnated as Francesco Totti. He worked with a seemingly limitless budget on a newly promoted Monaco team with another Russian oligarch, Dmitry Rybolovlev, at the helm. And he got to experience the chaos masquerading as a football club we otherwise know as Inter Milan. It's difficult to come up with another manager who has dealt with such a range of high-pressure, high-visibility jobs and lived to tell the tale.

Compared to that, Leicester was a holiday camp. The club actually worked and worked well. The staff were competent. There was no in-fighting behind the scenes. The owners may have been foreign billionaires but they were respectful and committed and not the types to get on the phone an hour after the final whistle to demand an exact account of everything that had happened during a football match.

And yet Ranieri lacked the 'winner' tag after his four

second-place finishes. To the knee-jerk media he was a lovable loser, too nice, too gentlemanly, too wimpy to whip a team into shape.

Football folk like to believe in intangibles when they can't explain something. Heck, not just them, some might say that's why we have organised religion. One sporting mantra is that there is such a thing as a winning mentality, that there's a special skill in getting teams over the line, but there is scant evidence that this exists. Instead, what you have are managers who make a team greater than the sum of their parts. For Ranieri to have taken that Roma side into second place behind José Mourinho's treble-winners was as much of a win as leading a club to their fifth Scudetto in a row. So too was taking over Parma deep in the relegation zone and steering them to mid-table. Or taking a newly promoted side, however well resourced, into the Champions League, as he did with Monaco and Juventus.

Ranieri has long believed this. The question to many at Leicester was how his players would cope with being in a title race. After all, other than Shinji Okazaki, who was a key part of the Japan team who won the Asian Cup, and Huth, who had two Premier League winners' medals from his time as a youngster at Chelsea, where he was the fourth-choice centre back, starting just thirteen league games over two seasons, nobody at Leicester had won any major silverware. Some said they were not winners simply because they had never won.

But if you believe there actually is such a thing as a winning mentality, Leicester had plenty of it. Of Ranieri's preferred starting eleven, Schmeichel, Morgan, Drinkwater, Mahrez and Vardy had all been part of the Pearson side that had not only won promotion but the Championship itself two years earlier.

Schmeichel had also won the League 2 title with Notts County, while Vardy had won other league titles further down the food chain: the Conference Premier at Fleetwood Town and the Northern Premier League Premier Division at Halifax. Danny Simpson had won not one but two Championship titles, at Newcastle and Sunderland. The only players with a bare silverware cupboard at home were Albrighton, Kanté and Fuchs.

Sure, the Northern Premier League Premier Division isn't the English Premier League – the competition isn't as good, there is less media attention, you get paid a whole lot less – but to any player involved in getting across the finish line, the process is the same. You still need to insulate yourself from pressure. You still need to have belief and trust in yourself and your teammates. You still need to work as a unit. And that was what Ranieri fostered.

The other factor which set this group of players apart and proved to be a huge resource, as Ranieri would later explain, was that most of them had overcome major disappointments and hardship to get where they were. And, for all of them – bar Mahrez, Kanté and maybe Vardy – realistically this run at the title was as good as it was going to get. Most would not be moving on to a Manchester United or a Real Madrid. Most had accepted that this was their level: a mid-table Premier League club which had somehow defied the odds. There was a humility to his squad which Ranieri appreciated from day one. So many had clawed their way up the ladder or bounced back from failure, misfortune, rejection and in one case even tragedy. They were grateful to be where they were, and this gave them common ground with their manager.

Kanté, Mahrez and Vardy weren't the only Leicester

players to have followed circuitous routes to the top. Kasper Schmeichel grew up in the shadow of one of the greatest keepers of the modern era. Lots of children of top athletes deal with the 'son of' syndrome, but in his case there was the added wrinkle that there was a striking physical resemblance and a similarity in goalkeeping style. He came through the ranks at Manchester City and went on loan to five different clubs before he turned twenty-two. City released him, and he dropped all the way to League 2, the fourth tier of the English game, before working his way back up.

Robert Huth went from being the 'next big thing' at Chelsea and a member of Germany's 2006 World Cup squad aged twenty-one to never again appearing in a competitive game for his country and playing for mid-table sides. When Stoke loaned him out to the Foxes in January 2015 he had played a grand total of four minutes of league football in the previous thirteen months.

Wes Morgan, LCFC captain, was told by Notts County at the age of fifteen that he wasn't good enough. He then spent a year not playing any organised football at all, before joining an amateur side and crawling back up the ladder and making his top-flight debut at the ripe old age of thirty: a year later his fellow professionals would vote him into the PFA Team of the Year.

Christian Fuchs didn't even go through a youth academy in his native Austria, attending a mainstream school instead. He got his shot at a Champions League club when he joined Schalke in Germany, but injuries eventually persuaded the club to give up on him. He let his contract run down and left as a free agent for a new life at Leicester.

The two Dannys, Simpson and Drinkwater, had the

footballing equivalent of an Eton or Harrow education at Manchester United, remaining on their books for seven and thirteen years respectively, but managed just one first-team league start between them and both were let go. What's more, Simpson, who subsequently established himself as a solid Championship-calibre player, was let go by Queens Park Rangers after having helped them earn promotion to the top flight, while Drinkwater had made just sixteen starts the previous season under Pearson and was deemed by some to be surplus to requirements at Leicester.

Marc Albrighton, who would appear in every single league game, had been released by Aston Villa, the club he first joined as an eight-year-old, back in 2014. He only started ten league matches under Pearson and arrived at preseason camp just a few days after learning that his long-time girlfriend's mother had been killed in a terrorist attack at a Tunisian holiday resort. Finally there was Shinji Okazaki. His career was on a steady upward arc in Germany at Stuttgart until he seemingly lost his mojo. He went nearly a year and a half without scoring a league goal from open play. He's not an out-and-out striker, and his game is more about unselfishness than finishing, but eighteen months without a goal for any type of forward is bound to lead to introspection and self-doubt.

That's the entire starting eleven, right there.

Contrast them with some of the coddled superstars and privileged players that Ranieri worked with at other clubs, and it's not surprising he could tune into their wavelength so readily. They had all built character – lots of it – by overcoming adversity. The man who was rejected by his home-town club as a player and who started his coaching career in a non-league club in Calabria could relate to them. And they related to him.

At the start of the season Ranieri had the sense and humility to arrive at his new club with neither the entitlement of a man who had coached the world's biggest clubs, nor the zeal of the revolutionary who was going to rebuild from the ground up. And during the season Ranieri ramped things up or down as needed. He dispensed quips in public but kept just enough of a lid on the dressing room to maintain the right level of tension. The title celebrations that followed the final game at the King Power stadium, the parade through Leicester, the standing ovation at Stamford Bridge on the last day of the season . . . all of it put him in a daze.

What had they done?

They had pulled off the greatest upset in the history of sport.

Whether you buy the 5000–1 odds or not, nothing is comparable. And certainly not over a thirty-eight-game season. In 2011 a fan in Las Vegas bet that the St Louis Cardinals – at the time dead and buried in the Major League Baseball National League wild-card race – would make the World Series, and they did. That bet was made just over two months before the end of the season. Not only did it require a shorter spell of excellence from the team, there were also play-offs involved and a head-to-head series, which is an entirely different proposition. Most other upsets have occurred in one-off games or knockout competitions, whether Mike Tyson losing to Buster Douglas in Tokyo, Goran Ivanišević winning Wimbledon or indeed Greece winning the 2004 European Championships.

In league football such feats are even rarer. Blackburn Rovers won the Premier League in their third season back in the top flight, but they spent massively to do it, including breaking the English transfer record. Stuttgart were shock

Bundesliga champions in 2006–07, but they had finished fifth and ninth in the previous two campaigns and were in the Champions League the year before that. Montpellier leaped from fourteenth to first in 2011–12 to become French champions, perhaps the closest parallel, but then again they had finished fifth the year before that. In Italy many drew a parallel with Verona, a provincial side who won the 1984–85 Serie A title. Yet they had been sixth and fourth the previous two seasons.

Leicester – just to remind ourselves – were rock bottom of the Premier League less than fourteen months earlier, and, as Ranieri pointed out in a November 2015 interview with *Corriere dello Sport*, the gap in resources by any metric – experience, spending, wages – between the half-dozen traditional title contenders and the rest was enormous and unprecedented. The truth is, nothing like this had ever happened. Ever.

Maybe that's why, when reflecting on what had happened, more than once Claudio Ranieri went back to that out-of-body experience in May when he and Rosanna sat in his living room late at night and watched news of Leicester's title triumph.

We did it, thought Ranieri. He'd say later that it felt as if he was watching a movie about somebody else, some other club that had pulled off the greatest upset in the history of team sport.

Nope. He did it. He and Rosanna and his staff and the players and the club and the Srivaddhanaprabhas and the tens of thousands of Leicester supporters who had been there from day one. And the tens of millions of neutral football fans who projected their own aspirations on to the Foxes and the thousands of coaches and players throughout the world who knew they would never be at a 'top club' with a chance to win the title and the millions of people who a few months before had never even heard of Leicester – the club or the city – and who probably did not even like football but who couldn't help be moved by a true-life fairy tale.

It was all of them.

They did it.

We did it.

Epilogue

If you had told Claudio Ranieri in May 2016 that his reign as manager of the Premier League champions would last 304 days, he would not have believed you.

Or perhaps he would.

After all, getting the sack the year after winning the league was a far more plausible proposition than Leicester City winning it in the first place.

By late February 2017 – when Ranieri received his marching orders – Leicester had been knocked out of the FA Cup by lowly Millwall and had exited the League Cup even earlier, back in September. A run of bad results had seen the side sink from mid-table in November down to 17th, one point above the relegation zone. The only real positives had come from the unlikeliest source, the Champions League. In their first ever European appearances, they had sailed through their group, winning it outright. And they still had every chance of advancing to the quarterfinals, having returned from their Round of 16 first-leg clash with Sevilla with a manageable 2–1 deficit.

Ranieri truly believed he had the backing of the owners and the players. It's a belief he holds to this day.

The Srivaddhanaprabhas had assured him privately that his job was not in jeopardy. And they went so far as to issue a public statement to that regard, stating unequivocally that his job was safe.

Half a century in football had taught him to be sceptical. Or, rather, to be fully aware of the way the game works. If you don't deliver, if the owners don't see a clear path forward or, worse, if they fear a sudden step back, particularly one that will cost money, like, say, relegation, all promises go out of the window.

But this was different. Ranieri had been a part of history. The owners were honourable men. The dressing room – or, at least, the vast bulk of it – was with him.

All of this was turned on its head on 23 February 2017. He was stunned. And it hurt.

He knew the side weren't performing. Theories abounded.

Most likely it was a combination of factors. He knew that the title run had sapped his team mentally and, for some, reaching comparable levels of performance was always going to be tough. The likes of Danny Drinkwater, Riyad Mahrez and Jamie Vardy – pillars of the team the year before – were shadows of themselves.

He didn't blame them. He always knew it was going to be difficult. As one long-time Leicester-watcher put it: 'A few years ago Vardy was stacking shelves and playing football on the side. He scrapped, scratched and clawed his way up the ladder. Now he's playing for England and they want to make a biopic about him. That's bound to affect you.'

Ranieri had budgeted for a drop in performance and for a toll to be paid as the team adjusted to playing European football along with the domestic fixture list. And he knew that N'Golo Kanté, who would go on to win the PFA Player of the

Year at Chelsea, would be sorely missed. The plan was to address this over the summer, expanding the size of the squad so there would be more competition for places and more rotation. But things didn't quite go according to plan.

Steve Walsh, the architect behind the signings of Kanté and Mahrez, left for Everton halfway through the summer. Bigger job, more money, more opportunity. He did make a number of signings before he left, but his golden touch evidently deserted him. Ahmed Musa, whom they had chased for years, turned out to be a bust. So too did Nampalys Mendy, a midfielder who had been tracked for years (and had played for Ranieri back in Monaco) and Luis Hernández, a versatile defender who was tapped to take pressure off Robert Huth, Wes Morgan and Danny Simpson.

Ranieri realised early on the newcomers weren't going to work out. Musa played ninety minutes in the opener – a defeat at Hull City – and then became a fringe player. Hernández played little and would be sold on in January. Even before he suffered a nasty injury, it was obvious to him that Mendy was not going to be replacement for Kanté.

Late in the transfer window Ranieri felt Leicester still needed another centreback and an experienced target man. With Walsh gone, however, the club's transfer activity was stunted. Ranieri was left short-handed at the back and, up front, he only landed Islam Slimani, the club's record signing, in late August. And he promptly picked up a series of knocks.

Leicester attempted to address this in the January transfer window, bringing in a centreback, Molla Wague, from Udinese on loan and, finally, a genuine Kanté replacement, Wilfred Ndidi from Anderlecht. Except Wague got injured and Ndidi was too little, too late, at least for Ranieri.

The losses mounted. He repeated his mantra about working hard, about togetherness, about belief. The media, still enamoured with him, blamed the players. Some went so far as to say they had 'downed tools'. The spin machine went into effect. The laid-back, cuddly Ranieri of 2015–16 was gone, in his place was the guy who tinkered with everything from the menu in the training ground to tactics on the pitch. At least that was the counterargument.

Ranieri knew some on board might be rowing against him, though the real negativity only emerged once he had been sacked and replaced by Craig Shakespeare.

Was he the traitor, the Iago of the piece?

Shakespeare vehemently denied the charge. Ranieri kept his counsel. When an assistant rises to number one, folks draw their own conclusions.

Ranieri said he had hoped to finish his career at Leicester. Getting sacked had 'killed that dream' he added.

Maybe so. But his departure was met with near-universal incredulity. The owners were seen by many as ogres, the sort of people who would tell a child that Father Christmas wasn't real. The players were slated as backstabbers, particularly after league results picked up following his sacking.

Ranieri, however, never blamed them. He had rarely done so in the past and he wasn't about to now.

He had brought about the impossible and been a victim of the incredible: a sacking which, to him, was entirely unexpected. One day he would come to terms with all of it. And realise that even the pain of a sacking – and perhaps a betrayal – wasn't going to wipe out what he had achieved.

He had crossed over into the land of fairy tales a year earlier. And he did not want to leave. And even being sacked wasn't going to get him out of there.

Acknowledgements

The accounts and quotations in this book are all either from contemporary media reports or direct interviews with the protagonists. Where appropriate, we have credited the source in the text.

Two books in particular helped inform the chapters relating to Chelsea and Leicester City. They are Claudio Ranieri's *Proud Man Walking* and Rob Tanner's *5000-1: The Leicester City Story: How We Beat the Odds to Become Premier League Champions*. The data used in Dan Altman's analysis was provided by Opta.

Our thanks have to start with David Luxton, without him this book would never have come to light. Despite an impossibly tight turn-around and a jam-packed summer with the European Championships in the way, he persuaded us it could be done and it was.

Credit also to Frances Jessop, Tim Broughton, Anna Redman and Rachel Cugnoni at Penguin Random House, as well as the unseen typesetters, copy editors and everyone who works behind the scenes to turn ideas and words into a coherent narrative and a physical book, including Josh Ireland, Hugh Davis and Phil Brown. Frances, in particular, was a pleasure to work with: professional, insightful and understanding at every turn.

This book would not have been possible without the assistance of the more than one hundred men and women who generously donated their time to share their experiences of working and playing with Claudio.

We need to offer the biggest thanks to the two men who accompanied him for the biggest chunk of his career. Giorgio Pellizzaro was at his side for nearly forty years going back to their playing days as 'foreigners' in Catanzaro and later became his goalkeeping coach. Angelo Antenucci was his right-hand man for seventeen years. They helped us tell the story of the man who managed Leicester to the greatest miracle in sport.

Giorgio Perinetti was there to witness the birth of both Ranieri the footballer at Roma and Ranieri the top-flight coach years later at Cagliari. *Grazie* also to his former teammates who shared their memories with us: Paolo Conti, Angelo Domenghini, Francesco Rocca, Sergio Santarini, Pierino Braglia, Leonardo Menichini and Gianni De Biasi. Plus, of course, the incomparable Gianni Di Marzio and his wife Concetta ('Tucci') who played such a big role in his development.

Then, there are those who played for him and we are so grateful to them as well: Francesco Totti, Daniel Fonseca, Ciro Ferrara, Stefano Pioli, Simone Perrotta, Hernan Crespo, Javier Zanetti, Mario Melchiot, Amedeo Carboni, Sokratis Papasthatopoulos, Gianfranco Zola and Carlo Cudicini. We can't forget the insight learned from club executives like Luciano Tarantino, Oreste Cinquini and Tor-Kristian Karlsen.

Plenty of journalists were also immensely helpful with their recollections, among them Neil Barnett, Andrea Palombarini, Eduardo Esteve, Antonio Ruiz and Ian Stringer. Ed Malyon and Alessandro Mita provided invaluable research.

A special mention must go to Dan Altman of North Yard Analytics who was instrumental in providing original work on Leicester's 2015-16 season from a football analytics perspective. It seemed primarily apt given the role football analytics played in the Foxes' season and the increasing role they are playing in the modern game. Also, many thanks to Richard Ewing and the team at Opta for providing the data that made Dan's work possible.

A big thank you to those who spoke to us on background and helped tell Claudio's story without being identified. You know who you are.

Even though we've never met Rob Tanner from the *Leicester Mercury* his book *5000-1: The Leicester City Story: How We Beat the Odds to Become Premier League Champions* was a hugely valuable guide to the campaign and an excellent first-hand account.

Thank you also to our employers, *Corriere dello Sport* and ESPN, for their support in allowing us to work on this project.

And a huge *grazie* too to the man who we've known for nearly a combined half-century and, without whose contribution to Leicester City's season this book would not have been commissioned. (Of this, we're pretty sure.)

Finally, our gratitude goes out to our families who put up with the hours of research, writing and travel and continue to be our biggest supporters.

List of illustrations

8. Ranieri at a press conference as AS Roma's manager (Getty Images/ AFP Photo/Filippo Monteforte); Francesco Totti and Ranieri during a training session for AS Roma (Getty Images/AFP /Filippo Monteforte); Ranieri in Athens as Greece's new national manager (Reuters/Alkis Konstantinidis)

9. Ranieri poses as the new Leicester City manager with Leicester's Director of Football Jon Rudkin and Vice Chairman Aiyawatt Srivaddhanaprabha (Getty Images/Plumb Images); Ranieri's first game as Leicester City manager, against Sunderland at the King Power Stadium (Getty Images/Matthew Lewis)

10. Jamie Vardy scores against Manchester United (Plumb Images/ Leicester City FC via Getty Images); Vardy breaks the Premier League record, scoring in eleven consecutive games, (Getty Images/Michael Regan); Christian Fuchs and Shinji Okazaki tuck into pizza (Plumb Images/Leicester City FC via Getty Images)

11. Robert Huth celebrating scoring with Danny Drinkwater against Tottenham (Getty Images/Dan Mullan); Wes Morgan and Danny Simpson celebrate beating Manchester City 3–1 (Plumb Images/ Leicester City FC via Getty Images); Riyad Mahrez scores Leicester's second goal against Manchester City (Getty Images/Michael Regan)

12. Ranieri gesturing from the sidelines against West Ham United (AP Photo/Rui Vieira); Leo Ulloa celebrates after equalising 2–2 against West Ham United (Getty Images/AFP/Adrian Dennis); Roman Abramovich welcomes Ranieri to Stamford Bridge ahead of the Premier League match between Chelsea and Leicester (Getty Images/ Plumb Images)

13. Ranieri mobbed by fans outside a restaurant (Justin Tallis/AFP/ Getty Images); Ranieri celebrates after winning the league (Adrian Dennis/AFP/Getty Images); Fuchs showers Ranieri with champagne during Leicester's post-league win press conference (Plumb Images/ Leicester City FC via Getty Images)

14. & 15. Leicester celebrate their winning season (Plumb Images/ Leicester City FC via Getty Images)

16. Leicester's two open top buses make their way through Leicester city centre (Paul Ellis/AFP/Getty Images); Young Ranieri-masked fans wait for the bus parade on 16 May 2016 (Getty Images/Michael Regan)

Index

CR indicates Claudio Ranieri.

PLANET FOOTBALL

CROATIA

GREATEST FANS

CONTENTS

First published in Great Britain
in 2016 by Wayland
Copyright © Wayland, 2016
All rights reserved

Editor: Victoria Brooker
Produced for Wayland by
Tall Tree Ltd
Designer: Gary Hyde
Editor: Jon Richards

Dewey number: 796.3'34-dc23

ISBN 978 0 7502 9573 4

Wayland, an imprint of
Hachette Children's Group
Part of Hodder and Stoughton
Carmelite House
50 Victoria Embankment
London EC4Y 0DZ
An Hachette UK Company
www.hachette.co.uk
www.hachettechildrens.co.uk

FSC

Printed and bound in China
10 9 8 7 6 5 4 3 2 1

The website addresses (URLs) included in this book were valid at the
time of going to press. However, because of the nature of the Internet,
it is possible that some addresses may have changed, or sites may
have changed or closed down, since publication. While the author and
Publisher regret any inconvenience this may cause the readers, no
responsibility for any such changes can be accepted by either the
author or the Publisher.

FANATICS!

Football is the most played and enjoyed team sport in the world. FIFA – the organisation that runs world football – estimates that as many as 220 million people regularly play the sport. Even more are football fans who watch games live, on TV or via the Internet.

More than 10 million people went to games in Spain's La Liga in the 2014–15 season, while over 5.25 million fans turned up to watch the 18 teams take part in Japan's J-League matches in 2014. Millions more support their local clubs in the lower leagues, experiencing the highs and lows of wins and defeats and the excitement and drama of the game.

GUANGZHOU FANS

ARGENTINA FANS

Argentina fans watch sadly as their team loses the final of the 2014 World Cup against Germany. Fans get upset at a bad defeat, but quickly look forward to the next game as there is always hope of a memorable victory in the future.

EVERG

Football has an incredible grip over many supporters. They attend as many games as they can and spend much of their spare time debating team news, who their side should buy and play and other football matters. Some name their pets or children after their favourite players. These people really are football crazy!

As well as following their favourite club, many people, such as these Polish fans, watch their country's team as it takes part in international competitions, such as the FIFA World Cup.

POLISH FANS

Fans of Chinese club Guangzhou Evergrande celebrate as their club wins its first-ever AFC Champions League competition in 2013 – the biggest prize in Asian club football. More than 42,000 fans came to each one of their games in the 2014 Chinese league season.

"THE SUPPORTERS ARE THE LIFEBLOOD OF PROFESSIONAL FOOTBALL – THEY ARE THE IDENTITY OF THE CLUBS. OWNERS, COACHES AND PLAYERS CHANGE BUT SUPPORTERS ALWAYS REMAIN."
UEFA PRESIDENT, MICHEL PLATINI

KITTED OUT

Most fans like to say it loud and proud by wearing their football team's shirts and other items – from wigs to gloves – in their team colours. Fans are passionate about these colours. It is part of the identity of the club or national team they support.

Many famous clubs today play in different coloured kits to those of the past. Liverpool, famous for playing in red today, used to play in blue and white, while the black and white stripes of Juventus came after the Italian club's original bright pink shirts.

EURO 2012

Ireland fans in green mix with Croatia fans wearing their distinctive red and white squared shirts at Euro 2012. The Irish fans were awarded the best fans of the tournament by UEFA.

NUMBERS GAME

1,580,000

The number of replica shirts, Spanish club Real Madrid sold in the 2013–14 season.

SPAIN

A collection of Barcelona shirts are on display at the Spanish club's giant megastore at their Camp Nou stadium. In 2014, more than 2 million people visited the store, many buying replica shirts.

Club shops sell thousands of replica shirts each year. Turkish club, Fenerbahce sold 325,000 shirts in 2014, while Italian league champions, Juventus sold 375,000 and Bayern Munich a staggering 945,000. Most top clubs change their kit design each season and some fans insist on buying the latest kit each year.

SWEDISH FANS

Lively fans of the Swedish national team wear yellow and blue shirts, wigs and facepaint at the 2012 European Championships. Swedish fans are well known for their passion and good humour.

HOME AND AWAY

Football clubs in a league play half of their matches at their home stadium and the rest at other team's grounds. Some fans travel long distances to offer their support when their team plays away.

Many club fans buy a season ticket which gives them access to all their team's home games. These vary wildly in price even among the top leagues of the world. In Germany, an adult season ticket at Bayern Munich can cost less than £150, while at Arsenal, season tickets can cost more than £2,000.

PORTUGAL

For fans of major Portuguese teams, Benfica and Sporting Lisbon, an away game at their rivals doesn't involve a great deal of travel as their two grounds are just 3 km apart.

Club Deportivo Guadalajara fans wait patiently in a long queue for tickets at the Omnilife Stadium in Mexico. Demand for tickets for a crucial big match can be huge and priority is often given to season ticket holders first.

MEXICO

Going to away games can be an exciting experience for fans, but also an expensive and time-consuming one. It can involve hours on the road, on trains or in the air. Once they have arrived at the ground, away fans are often directed to a dedicated area of the stadium to sit, separated from the home fans.

BELGIUM

These Belgian fans dressed as devils have travelled more than 9,000 km to attend the 2014 World Cup in Brazil. At major tournaments, like the World Cup, foreign fans tend to be given a very warm welcome with stewards employed by the hosts who speak their language.

"THE SAMPDORIA FANS APPLAUDED ME AFTER WE SCORED... THE STEWARDS OFFERED ME COFFEE... COMPLIMENTING ME ON MY PASSION."

UDINESE FAN, ARRIGO BROVEDANI WHO ARRIVED FOR AN ITALIAN SERIE A GAME IN 2012 TO DISCOVER HE WAS THE ONLY AWAY FAN IN THE GROUND!

THE MATCH DAY

Every fan's matchday experience may be slightly different. However, they all start with the trip to the ground, perhaps meeting friends outside, and then heading into the stadium as the atmosphere builds before kick-off.

Fans may buy drink, food or matchday programmes at the ground. But if they visited Swiss club FC Sion in 2014, they were served a free dish of raclette – a hot meal of cheese and potatoes! Some clubs also put on pre-match entertainment, such as bands, before an explosion of noise greets the two teams coming out of the players' tunnel onto the pitch.

EURO 2012 FANZONE

Fans enjoy the big game atmosphere at a Euro 2012 fanzone. These are built at major tournaments and contain food and drink stalls, entertainment stages and giant screens, which display match action for fans without tickets.

During the match, a stadium can be transformed into a noisy riot of colour as scarves and banners are waved. Fans of Uruguayan team, Penarol, unveiled the world's biggest football banner in 2011. It measured over 48 m high and needed 300 fans just to carry it to the ground!

SOUTH AFRICA

In South African football, noise can be ear-splitting due to the vuvuzela – a plastic trumpet-like horn which became very popular with fans of all teams at the 2010 World Cup.

NUMBERS GAME

80,423

The average number of fans who went to every 2014–15 league game of German club, Borussia Dortmund.

ATHLETIC BILBAO

Bilbao fans congregate outside Barcelona's Nou Camp before the final of the 2015 Copa del Rey. Stewards inside the ground direct fans to their seats and prevent crowd problems such as pitch invasions.

"WHEN YOU START SUPPORTING A FOOTBALL CLUB, YOU DON'T SUPPORT IT BECAUSE OF THE TROPHIES, OR A PLAYER, OR HISTORY, YOU SUPPORT IT BECAUSE YOU... FOUND A PLACE WHERE YOU BELONG."
DUTCH FOOTBALLER, DENNIS BERGKAMP

SUPERSTITIONS & TRADITIONS

Some fans have unusual superstitions, such as wearing an item of lucky clothing to the match. Here are some fun fan traditions and actions performed at matches.

The first Mexican waves weren't Mexican but American, performed by American Football crowds at the start of the 1980s. The move got its name and worldwide popularity, though, when it was performed by football fans at the 1986 World Cup held in Mexico.

Spain's superfan bangs his drum and urges the crowd on. Known as 'Manolo el del bombo', Manuel Cáceres Artesero is found among Spain fans at every national team game, and has only missed one match since 1982.

 MANOLO EL DEL BOMBO

Two unusual traditions occur in football stadiums after games have finished. Japanese fans have a tradition of picking up litter after a match, leaving their part of a football stadium clean. Around 20,000 fans of German club, FC Union Berlin, come to their ground every Christmas Eve to sing carols.

Legia Warsaw fans throw hundreds of paper streamers during their Polish league match against Jagiellonia Bialystok. Fans of some clubs, particularly in South America, throw torn up paper to create a ticker tape welcome for their team.

POLISH FANS

LECH POZNAN FANS

Another crowd move is named after Polish football club, Lech Poznan and is thought to have begun in the 1960s. When a goal is scored, the fans turn their back on the pitch, link arms and jump up and down.

"WE TRY TO DO A LITTLE BIT OF A CLEAN-UP TO SHOW RESPECT TO THE HOST COUNTRY AND SHOW OFF HOW CLEAN THINGS ARE IN JAPAN."
KEI KAWAI, JAPANESE FOOTBALL FAN AT THE 2014 WORLD CUP

MAD MASCOTS

Many clubs have some form of mascot that often parades around a football ground before the game. The mascot poses for photos, urges the crowd to encourage their team and, away from the match, is used in promoting the club and to support local charities.

The first mascots were real animals. These included a St Bernard dog for Newton Heath in the 1900s (before the club changed its name to Manchester United) and Cologne's Hennes the goat who appeared in team photos alongside the footballers from 1950 onwards. Most mascots today are cuddly animals or fantasy characters with a person inside who meets and greets the fans.

FERENCVÁROS EAGLE

The person inside the Fradi Eagle – mascot of Hungarian club, Ferencváros – takes a rest before a match. At some clubs, people inside the mascot are volunteers. At others, they are paid employees of the club.

14

Milanello became Italian club AC Milan's new mascot in 2006. The mascot was designed to look like a little devil by famous cartoon film makers, Warner Brothers, and is named after the club's training ground.

AC MILAN'S DEVIL

WILSA KRAKOW DRAGON

The Wawel Dragon is the official mascot of Polish club, Wisla Krakow. They play in Poland's top division, the Ekstraklasa, and have won the league title 14 times.

15

COMPETITION MASCOTS

Many major football competitions have their own mascot or mascots. These are unveiled several years before the tournament and are used to publicise the event in advance.

GOLEO

The first FIFA World Cup was held in 1930, but it wasn't until the 1966 World Cup in England that a tournament had a mascot – a lion wearing the national flag as a shirt called World Cup Willie. Since then, mascots have included a chilli pepper called Pique at Mexico in 1986 and Footix the cockerel at France 1998.

Goleo – a lion wearing an old-style German football shirt – was the mascot of the 2006 World Cup held in Germany. He was built by the company who made the Muppets and Sesame Street puppet characters.

SLAVEK AND SLAVKO

Euro 2012 was jointly held in Poland and the Ukraine, so the tournament had two mascots, Slavek in Polish colours (on the left) and Slavko in Ukraine's (on the right).

Other competitions, beside the World Cup, have got in on the action with their own mascots. The 2015 African Cup of Nations, for example, had a porcupine named Chuku Chuku. The 2015 Copa Libertadores in Chile had a red fox whose name, Zincha, was chosen by the public following an internet vote. Zincha even had its own Twitter account.

ZAKUMI

Styled on a leopard, an animal found in South Africa, with a shock of green hair, Zakumi was the mascot for the 2010 World Cup. Its name comes from ZA, the letters for South Africa, and the word 'kumi', meaning 'ten', for the year of the tournament.

FULECO

NUMBERS GAME

47

The number of different designs from which Fuleco was chosen by the organisers of the 2014 FIFA World Cup.

Fuleco was the mascot of the 2014 World Cup in Brazil. Fuleco was designed as a three-banded armadillo, a creature found in Brazil.

DERBY GAMES

Derby matches are passionate games between two rival clubs. Some have a long history such as Penarol and Nacional contesting derby games in Uruguay since 1900. For many fans, these are the most eagerly anticipated matches of the season.

Most club rivalries come from the two sides being neighbours. Many cities around the world have two leading teams which compete for supremacy. These include Roma and Lazio in the Italian city of Rome, Celtic and Rangers in Glasgow, Fenerbahce and Galatasaray in Istanbul, Flamengo and Fluminense in Rio de Janeiro and Al-Ahly and Zamalek in the Cairo derby in Egypt.

MILAN VS INTER

Devoted AC Milan fans put on a colourful display before the Milan derby match against Internazionale. Inter have won 76 of the 213 official derbies between the two teams, just two wins ahead of AC Milan.

One of the biggest derbies in South America pits Boca Juniors and River Plate against each other. The Boca fans call their opponents 'gallinas' (meaning 'chickens'), while the River Plate fans call their rivals 'los puercos' (meaning 'pigs'). Charming!

BOCA JUNIORS

Sometimes, the rivalry extends well beyond city limits. Teams like Paris Saint-Germain and Marseilles in France and the Mexican sides of Chivas and Clube America are each based in separate cities. The Barcelona v Real Madrid derby in Spain, known as 'El Clásico', is watched with interest by the entire country.

BARCA V REAL

Barca and Real Madrid fans mingle before a derby match hoping for plenty of goals, as 988 have been scored in El Clásico derbies up until August 2015.

"I DON'T WANT ANY CUPS, I DON'T WANT TO BE A CHAMPION EITHER, I'VE GOT TWO WISHES, TWO WISHES TO BEAT FENER."

A POPULAR CHANT OF GALATASARAY FANS WHEN THEY PLAY FENERBAHCE

SPORTING SOUVENIRS

For many fans, owning a replica shirt of the team they support is not enough. To show their allegiance and loyalty, they want lots of items branded in their team's colours. Clubs and national teams are happy to sell them all sorts of merchandise to make a profit.

ITALY

Merchandise bought by fans ranges from pens, aprons, bags and bathroom rubber ducks in team colours to slippers which make a crowd noise every time a fan takes a step. These and hundreds of other items are sold at a club's shop or online over the Internet.

An official shop in Milan sells football shirts and other merchandise. In 2014, rivals AC Milan and Internazionale sold approximately 775,000 shirts between them – a staggering number.

NUMBERS GAME

105.2

The number of millions of Euros, German club Bayern Munich, made in 2014 from sales of merchandise including scarfs and clothing.

SOLDADO

SILVA

KUN AGUERO

DZEKO

WILSHERE

S.CAZORLA

WALCOTT

HAZARD

OSCAR

MATA

ETO'O

CAVANI

IBRAHIMOVIĆ

MESSI

A.INIESTA

ISCO

BALE

RONALDO

BENZEMA

HIGUAIN

Fans of Ukrainian club, Shakhtar Donetsk turn a stand black and orange with their club scarves during a 2013 league match. The fans had a great season as Shakhtar won the league championship and the Ukrainian Cup.

SHAKHTAR-DONETSK

Some merchandise can be very strange. Hull City sold a toilet seat in their black and gold colours when the club reached the 2014 FA Cup final. MLS club, San Jose Earthquakes, sell clay heads of their striker, Steven Lenhart, in which fans can plant seeds that grow to form the player's long hair. Italian club, Fiorentina, even sold cans of air taken from their stadium.

THAILAND

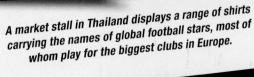

A market stall in Thailand displays a range of shirts carrying the names of global football stars, most of whom play for the biggest clubs in Europe.

CRAZY FANS

Football fans care about their team, but some fans are absolutely football crazy. These fanatical fans go further than most. One example is Jan van Kook, a fan of Dutch club, Feyenoord. He bought two tickets for all the home games one season – one for him and one for his dog!

Fans' passion can get the better of them. In 2005, after a seven-year battle in the courts, a Colombian football fan was allowed to change his name to the club he supports, calling himself, Deportivo Independiente Medellin Giraldo Zuluaga! In 2015, a Norwegian-Liverpool couple named their baby daughter YNWA – short for 'You'll Never Walk Alone', the song sung by Liverpool fans.

SWEDISH FANS

Swedish fans have fun in skintight suits coloured like their country's flag before a crucial Euro 2012 match in Kiev. The 'Blue-Yellows' are known for their good humour and turning up at major tournaments in large numbers.

Graffiti from Boca Juniors fans in Buenos Aires. When attacker, Carlos Tevez rejoined Boca, his childhood club, in July 2015, over 40,000 Boca fans turned out at the club's stadium to greet him.

BUENOS AIRES

This mad-keen Irish fan with a beard dyed to look like his country's flag was just one of over 20,000 Republic of Ireland supporters who travelled to Poznan in Poland for Ireland's Euro 2012 match versus Croatia.

IRISH FAN

"I'M A SOCCER SLAVE. I DRINK FOOTBALL, I EAT FOOTBALL, I TALK FOOTBALL. EVERYTHING IN MY LIFE REVOLVES AROUND SOCCER. IT IS MY PASSION."
SADAAM MAAKE, SOUTH AFRICAN FOOTBALL FAN

CHANTS AROUND THE WORLD

Fans love to sing together and every team's fans have a number of different songs and chants they sing. Here are a selection of commonly sung chants and songs from different countries of the world.

 HUP HOLLAND HUP

"Go Holland Go / Don't let yourself be stripped of your vest / Go Holland Go / Don't put slippers on the beast / Go Holland Go / Stay undaunted / Because a lion in football boots / Can beat the whole world."

 SLOVENIA

"Kdor ne ska e ni slovenec!"
"He who is not jumping is not Slovenian, hey hey hey!"

 SPAIN

"Andrés Iniesta, Vamonos de fiesta!"
"Andrés Iniesta, Let's go party."
After the Spanish midfielder, Andres Iniesta, scored the goal th[at] won Spain the 2010 World Cup.

NUMBERS GAME
114
The number of years that fans of Norwich City have chanted their song, 'On The Ball City'. It is believed to be the oldest football song still sung by fans.

CZECH REPUBLIC

"My Chceme Gol!"
"Give us a goal!"

BRAZIL

"Sou brasileiro, com muito orgulho, com muito amor."
"I'm Brazilian, with a lot of pride and a lot of love."

CHILE

"Vamos. Vamos Chilenos, esta noche, tenemos que ganar."
"Let's go Chileans, tonight, we have to win."

MALAYSIA

"Kami turun ke stadium sehati sejiwa."
"We went down to the stadium, One heart one soul."

CLUB CORNER

"Arise and sing for the tigers (players) of FC Liaoning"
FC Liaoning fans, China

"Carefree, wherever we maybe, We are the famous SKC."
Sporting Kansas City fans, USA

"Come on boys, make some noise, We're a team of class and poise, And our Adelaide is rolling along."
Adelaide United, Australia

"Ore no Tokyo, hokori o mochi! Tachi agatte minna de utaou!"
"We have pride in Tokyo! Everybody sing together!"
Fans of Japanese club, FC Tokyo

DUTCH FANS

Fans of the Netherlands football team are known as 'Oranje' for their bright orange colours. Here, they form a giant, noisy wall as they chant during a European Championship match. One of their most frequently sung songs is 'Hup Holland Hup' ('Go Holland Go').

FUNNY FOOTBALL CHANTS

Football fans often enjoy humorous jokes and chants aimed at themselves, the fans of the opposing team or, sometimes, the referee when he or she makes decisions they do not agree with.

SEONGNAM FANS

"Merciful Seongnam FC, How merciful they are! They could have scored 7 but scored only 3, How merciful they are!" Sung by Seongnam FC fans during K-League games in South Korea when they are winning well.

BARCELONA FANS

"Blaugrana al vent un crit valent tenim un nom el sap tothom: Barça, Barça, Baaarça!"
"Blue and claret blowing in the wind, One valiant cry, We've got a name that everyone knows: Barça, Barça, Baaarça!"

BOCA JUNIOR FANS

"River, tell me how it feels to have played in the second division? That stain will never be erased!" Boca Junior fans taunting their fierce rivals, River Plate, who were relegated to the Argentinean second division for the first time in 2011.

Some rival fans find it funny that Barcelona had a deadly serious hymn called 'Cant del Barça' composed for the club's 75th anniversary. It was first performed in 1974 by a 3,500 person choir and is now sung on the terraces by fans.

Some countries and clubs take chants very seriously. In 2015, MLS team New York City FC gave out chant sheets to all their fans so they could learn lots of new songs. Nine years earlier in the UK, the job of Chant Laureate was formed for a season with an amateur poet, Jonny Hurst, employed to tour English grounds and write new chants.

 HULK

"Green in a minute, he's going green in a minute!"
Arsenal fans singing about Porto's striker, Hulk, during a UEFA Champions League match.

 SCOTTISH FANS

 BRAZILIAN FANS

"He has the hands of a lettuce!"
Chant of fans of Brazilian clubs when a goalkeeper fumbles a ball or lets in an easy goal.

"Deep fry your pizzas, we're gonna deep fry your pizzas!"
Scotland fans, taking the mickey out of themselves and their love of fried food, sung as a jokey warning to Italy's supporters during a World Cup qualifying match.

27

GOOD FUN FANS

Fans can be bright, colourful and noisy. They can be passionate and loyal, following their team whatever the result. For all their rivalry with opposing supporters, almost all fans are fun, friendly and keen to help out others.

From giving directions to the ground to helping someone who doesn't speak the language, fans frequently aid others. In 2013, Irish fans raised money to buy tickets for two young Austrian fans who lost theirs in Dublin. In 2015, Spartak Moscow's oldest fan, Otto Fisher was robbed. Other Spartak fans started a collection online and thousands of pounds were donated to the 102 year old.

AMAZING COSTUMES

Some fans like to stand out in the crowd and wear outrageous costumes as this fan of the Spanish national team wearing a superhero outfit illustrates. Spain fans have had a lot to cheer about in recent years with their side becoming World Cup champions in 2010 as well as winning Euro 2012.

CROATIA FANS

A Croatia fan poses for a photo before an important World Cup game. Supporters of differing teams regularly mix with each other at major tournaments, comparing their football experiences and enjoying friendly arguments over players and teams.

Many football fans raise money for charity or lead charity schemes to help make other people's lives better. Founded by football fan Gordon Hartman, the San Antonio Scorpions football club's entire profits are given to special needs charities.

Fans of Ukrainian club, FC Volyn Lutsk, wrap up warm to withstand sub-zero temperatures on the open terraces of their snow-covered ground. Fans brave all weathers to turn up and support their team.

NUMBERS GAME

6,525,072

The number of pounds raised by Soccer Aid 2014, a charity football match held in Manchester featuring teams of celebrities and footballers including Alessandro Del Piero and Andriy Shevchenko.

"WE'RE TRYING TO HARNESS THE PASSION OF FOOTBALL FANS TO MAKE A DIFFERENCE."

JON BURNS, FOUNDER OF LIONSRAW, WHICH LEADS FOOTBALL FAN VOLUNTEERS TO BUILD COMMUNITY PROJECTS IN POOR COUNTRIES

QUIZ

1. Which club sold 945,000 replica football shirts in 2014: Kaizer Chiefs, Bayern Munich or AC Milan?

2. Which country's national team fans often clean up their litter after a match?

3. Which famous English club was previously known as Newton Heath?

4. To which Italian club did Benfica sell an eagle to be their mascot?

5. Who or what did Feyenoord fan Jan van Kook buy a second season ticket for to accompany him on his team's home matches?

6. Can you name either of the two teams that contest the Cairo derby?

7. Which Italian club sold cans of air taken from inside its stadium?

8. What sort of creature was Fuleco, the mascot of the 2014 World Cup?

WEBSITES AND BOOKS

http://www.stadiumguide.com/figures-and-statistics/lists/europes-highest-attendances/
This website lists the top 100 teams by how many fans attend each of their home games.

http://www.thebesteleven.com/2009/08/mls-and-usl-soccer-mascots.html
Check out photos of 25 of the best mascots in MLS and USL football in the United States.

http://www.bbc.co.uk/sport/0/football/29242557
Details and pictures of five of the world's greatest football derbies.

Truth or Busted: Football
by Adam Sutherland (Wayland, 2014)

Radar Top Jobs: Being a Professional Footballer
by Sarah Levete (Wayland, 2013)

Football Joke Book
by Clive Gifford (Wayland, 2013)

GLOSSARY

AFC Champions League
A competition for the leading clubs of each country in Asia held every year.

African Cup of Nations
The tournament for the best national teams in Africa.

A League
The top football league competition in Australia, contested each season by ten teams.

attendance
The number of people who watch a particular football match.

Bundesliga
The German league championship competition.

dugout
The covered bench and seats sat on by a coach, his or her staff and the team's substitutes during a game.

FIFA
Short for the Fédération Internationale de Football Association, the organisation that runs world football.

merchandise
All sorts of objects and clothing branded in the colours or logos of a football club or national football team.

MLS
Short for Major League Soccer, it is the top league competition for clubs in the USA and Canada.

professional
Someone who is paid for playing a sport.

relegated
To drop out of one league division and to play the next season in a lower division.

season ticket
A ticket which allows a fan to go to all of a team's home games throughout a season.

Serie A
The top division of the Italian football league.

UEFA
Short for the Union of European Football Associations, the organisation that runs football in Europe.

ANSWERS
1. Bayern Munich
2. Japan
3. Manchester United
4. Lazio
5. His dog
6. Zamalek, Al-Ahly
7. Fiorentina
8. An armadillo

31

INDEX

The publisher would like to thank the following for their kind permission to reproduce their photographs:
Key: (t) top; (c) centre; (b) bottom; (l) left; (r) right
All images **Dreamstime.com** unless otherwise indicated.
1 (b) iStock. com; 10 (bl) Graeme Maclean; 12 (bl) Benutzer:Elwedritsch.